THE MANAGER

THE MANAGER

The absurd ascent of the most
important man in football

Barney Ronay

sphere

First published in Great Britain as a paperback original in 2009 by Sphere

ISBN 978-1-84744-250-5

Typeset in Bembo by M Rules
Printed and bound in Great Britain by
Clays Ltd, St Ives plc

Papers used by Sphere are natural, renewable and
recyclable products sourced from well-managed forests and certified in
accordance with the rules of the Forest Stewardship Council.

Mixed Sources
Product group from well-managed
forests and other controlled sources
www.fsc.org Cert no. SGS-COC-004081
© 1996 Forest Stewardship Council

Sphere
An imprint of
Little, Brown Book Group
100 Victoria Embankment
London EC4Y 0DY

An Hachette UK Company
www.hachette.co.uk

www.littlebrown.co.uk

For Kate

Contents

The Ascent of the Manager

Something strange began to happen to football managers during the early Premier League years of the mid-1990s. Like Major Tom floating in his tin can, the football manager began to drift up into the celebrity firmament, leaving behind his old haunts and hang-outs and becoming instead a face behind the velvet rope of the A-list lounge.

The modern football manager adorns not just the front and back pages but the middle ones too. Before the 2005 general election the Manchester United manager Sir Alex Ferguson made a headline appearance at a government rally, taking time out to praise 'two brilliant barnstorming speeches from Tony and Gordon'; later the same year he had to be protected from excitable teenage girls on a club tour of the Far East. At the end of 2008 the former Chelsea manager Jose Mourinho was the subject of an official and an unofficial photo-calendar (both sold out). Even the reclusive Arsène Wenger was recently 'spotted' by the *Daily Mirror*'s '3am' gossip girls getting on a plane to Switzerland, fresh from hosting a public reception for the state visit of French President Nicolas Sarkozy.

The job itself has also changed fundamentally. Being a manager is now a kind of televised public performance. With his windmilling arms and spittle-flecking displays of emotion, the modern football manager is a magnetic figure. He reminds us of a stadium evangelist or a charismatic young leader of the opposition. Strutting and telegenic, his gestures are thrillingly decisive, his utterances destined for interminable reinterpretation.

Even with the benefit of hindsight, this still seems an extremely unlikely state of affairs. For the first forty years or so of professional football there was no concrete idea of what a manager actually did. Club directors picked the teams. In the background, buried within his understairs office, lurked the secretary-manager. His assistant, the trainer, did most of the shouting. And that was about it for the men on the touchline.

The story of how we got from there to here – from backroom boy to role model, pin-up and ace face – has for the most part been told only in instalments. So much so that at times it can seem as though the modern manager came surging fully formed out of his late-Victorian broom cupboard, peeling off his borrowed clothes, and assumed centre stage almost before anyone had noticed what was happening.

Attempting to fill some of the gaps in this ascent-of-man-style rise has been a meandering process involving many pungent diversions. From the early fashion for managers who died on trains; to the Marvellous Magyars and alien invasion paranoia; the role of the John Major government in getting an England manager sacked; and the final word on Gordon Banks's preference for both boiled and roast potatoes as a pre-match meal.

In any event this is a book about the manager we all know, because we see him every day. His shadow looms, fully evolved, now erect and miraculously walking on his hind legs: priest, messiah, hard-nut, patriarch and visible emblem of over a hundred years of confused and piecemeal progress.

This is not intended as a comprehensive history. Those with tribal associations will no doubt feel put out at any one of its terrible oversights and unforgivable omissions. It's also not an exercise in deciding who's the best. There is no extended discussion of the top trumps scores of Bob Paisley and Brian Clough, no exhaustive analysis of the merits of zonal marking or the genesis of the 4-3-2-1 system. Instead this is a popular history, the back-story to that strangely prominent figure in the overcoat who, until the last decade or so, might have been surprised even to find that he had such a thing.

From a personal point of view, I've always been fascinated by managers. Growing up in the 1980s, at the tail-end of the great boom in the cult of the managerial personality, there was still a baffling mystique about these men. In those days managers were largely mute. They tended to be ancient, wrinkled and unstyled. They smoked and frowned. But even through the filter of the oddly mannered TV coverage, you felt the force of their desperation and their charisma.

This is also a very English kind of story. In the leagues of mainland Europe club presidents tend to wield the real power, to hire and fire coaches vigorously, and to have the whip hand when it comes to grand gestures and moments of egomaniacal self-indulgence. In England football bears the imprint of a century of slow-baked, class-ridden evolution. The manager is the single most interesting figure in all this, English football's great reformer and its gift to the world beyond its boundaries.

This is a book about English football in its wider context. Above all it's intended as an entertainment, an argument, and an answer to the question of where exactly the manager – this most energetic of middle-aged celebrities – came from.

CHAPTER 1

The Birth of the Manager

Part One: The Sad Dead Men

The modern football manager has an air of being settled. We know what he's like. Managers are impetuous. Managers are cross. Managers are superstitious. Managers are tired. Managers are obsessed with football.

This identity has been accumulated rather than created. Nothing has been thrown away. Not even the lasting imprint of the football manager's very earliest days, when he barely existed at all. This is a story that starts right back at the beginning of organised football, when the world moved in black and white, men in hats presided over an empire where the sun never set, and when most of the things that have come to make up our daily infrastructure were being furiously smelted into existence.

The first managers appeared in the late years of the nineteenth century, during the great flowering of soon-to-be-professional football clubs. Recruiting from the ranks of ex-players was out. At this stage there was no such thing as an ex-player. So managers were sourced from other industries, usually the senior ranks of manual labour, the factory clerk and shop steward.

Often very little is known about these early men. They have above all an air of remoteness about them, forbiddingly moustachioed, entombed within the indifferent prehistory of their caste. Much of this is to do with the passing of time. The early days of football are only patchily documented. The game was conceived on the hoof. What survives of the people involved is a patchwork of potted biography and newspaper clippings.

Throughout all of this the manager is in shadow, a high-collared silhouette skulking on the fringes. We know that 'Little Dave' Ashworth, Oldham Athletic manager from 1906–14, wore a bowler hat and had a waxed moustache. He was five feet tall. And that's pretty much it for Little Dave. Like the most laconic Victorian fathers he remains no more than a moustache, a hat and a profession.

We have photographs: blank, stern, narrow-eyed men in waistcoats and watch-chains. The best surviving likeness of Harry Newbould, manager of Manchester City in the early years of the last century, shows a baby-faced man in a funereal hat with an unruly fan-shaped moustache that conceals his entire mouth. He looks like a vaguely defeated provincial accountant (which he was).

This is the face left to us by the early manager. It glowers in portrait. It looms from the back of those lounging, absurdly posed team photos. It isn't, it has to be said, a particularly happy face. This air of sadness has some basis in fact. The early managers lived on the edge of things. Like the heavy industrial economy to which it was tethered, football was a harsh environment. Managers often worked seven days a week. During the 1891–2 season Sunderland manager Tom Watson travelled over fourteen thousand miles on trains. Being an early football manager was a business of sleeper cars, boarding houses and the many mechanical perils of nineteenth-century domestic infrastructure.

Death on the job was common. In fact for many years death by way of transport mishap was a genuine hazard. John Nicholson, appointed Sheffield United secretary-manager in 1899, was run over and killed by a lorry at Sheffield Midland Station on the way to a match thirty-three years later. The list of fatalities also includes Sheffield Wednesday manager Robert Brown (collapsed while boarding a train in March 1935), Leicester trainer Thomas Bromilow (died on a train at Nuneaton in 1959), and Coventry City's Dick Bayliss (fell ill after drive back from Southend during 'the great freeze' of 1947).

Managers who died of the cold form a club of their own. The great Herbert Chapman succumbed to a chill a week after watching Arsenal's third team play at Guildford on a freezing night in January 1934; Norwich manager James Kerr did the same a month later. Some even managed to die on club premises. William 'The Doctor' Holmes, manager of Clapton Orient, collapsed on the job in 1922. Swansea's Harry Griffiths keeled over in the club's medical room. On a more positive note, Millwall manager Bill Voisey survived a direct hit on the Den during a Second World War air raid (he merely retired from his post with severe injuries).

So much for death, then. Misery and depression also form a regular motif. West Ham sacked Syd King in 1932 after he arrived drunk at a board meeting. King killed himself a month later. At his inquest it emerged that he had been suffering from delusions, which became chronic during West Ham's relegation the previous season. Tom Whittaker suffered a nervous breakdown while he was Arsenal manager and died in the job in 1956. Stan Cullis was sacked by Wolves two days after returning from a week's convalescence in Eastbourne. His behaviour had grown increasingly uneven: after a game on the club's American tour Cullis had been seen chasing the referee from the ground. Most poignant of all, John Hacking died of a heart attack on being told he was to be sacked as Barrow manager in May 1955.

Even now this seam of misfortune and unhappiness sits deep

in the gene pool. The modern manager still carries it around with him. It's a part of his peculiar power, derived from that umbilical connection to these early men. We see it in his face, we see it in his smile. We saw it in the grizzled and ravaged features of Joe Kinnear during his resurrection as Newcastle's caretaker manager in the 2008–9 season.

Kinnear was sixty-one and had been unemployed for four years when he got the call. And back he came, like some tracksuited monster from the deep. Beached on the padded armchairs of the Newcastle dugout, his square-cut face seemed chiselled with ancient misery, his heavy jowls carrying a great sadness, a sense of some deep ancestral wrong.

Kinnear's appearance brought to mind the transformation the same job had wreaked on his immediate predecessor, Kevin Keegan, during his first spell at St James' Park. Keegan took the Newcastle job, his first in management, in 1992. At the time he'd spent the previous eight years cocooned in a kind of golfing purgatory in La Manga. He still seemed a vaguely silly person, synonymous with KK-branded Shetland knitwear and that lingering perm.

Six years into the job Keegan was white-haired and fearful. His final match in charge was an FA Cup tie at Charlton. On the touchline in front of the TV cameras he had an air of the ancient mariner: frighteningly thin, watching the match but seeing something else, perhaps some trace of the vivid sorrows of Syd King, Stan Cullis and the rest.

At first the reasons for all this might seem straightforward enough. Football management is a famously exhausting job. It carries impossible strains and a crushing workload. Luck plays a ludicrously prominent role. Failure is inevitable. Success is simply a matter of delaying the inevitable jeering dismissal. It's just the job, we hear the manager mutter to himself, just the job.

But how did the job get like this? The constant sorrows of the football manager are more than an inexplicable affliction. This isn't something that just happened to him. Look far enough back and you see a founding instability in the very notion of being a football manager. For a start he has no job description. For all the manager's complex evolution, he is still a hybrid and an afterthought, a bastard fusion of hostile forces. This is the back-story to the gaunt club portrait. The manager was never meant to be. Called into being by forces beyond his control, he began life as little more than a pressed-man and a fall guy.

This is central to his rise too. In many ways the story of the football manager is a revenge story: the revenge of the stiff-collared clerk and the tweed-suited corpse in the railway carriage.

Part Two: A Useful Idiot

In these frontier times the role of the football manager was at least fairly straightforward: he had no role. The dugout was yet to be dug out. The musty third-floor office was yet to be grudgingly furnished. The contacts book was empty, the drinks cabinet unstocked. These early men were at least one hop up out of the malaria swamp short of the manager as we know him.

It takes a leap of the imagination to connect them to the current breed of swaggering polymaths. Something needed to happen to force the issue. And something did happen. Forces were at work: forces that would soon drag the manager, fists bunched, out into the foreground.

Football was an industry forged amid the emerging structures of Victorian capitalism. Looking back there's a yeasty historical certainty about its early gains. Positioned in the geographical heart of the new urban economy, clubs provided a nexus between the prosperous industrial shop-floor class and the boom in what we would now call 'leisure'. Football simply opened its gates and the crowds came rolling in.

In these early days the crowd came as a bit of a shock. No other form of public entertainment had gathered such vast swathes of people together. Attendances rose from just over half a million in the first Football League season in 1888–9 to nearly nine million by the start of the First World War.

Still giddily expanding, football became a volatile arena. The crowd contained much trapped energy and, at times, an unavoidable whiff of the picket and the mob. Pitch invasions were common. Barely twenty years after the formation of the Football League, the crowd had already acquired its reputation as something wild, close to hysteria, and above all dangerous.

During an FA Cup semi-final between West Bromwich Albion and Small Heath Alliance in 1886, the Small Heath goalkeeper was violently pelted with snowballs. Aston Villa fans smashed all the windows of a pub owned by their goalkeeper after defeat in the FA Cup final of 1892. In April 1909 the crowd at the Scottish Cup final rioted and were charged by mounted police as they set fire to fences, destroyed the pitch with a roller and generally hurled bits of wood around.

What, exactly, was football going to do about all this? The ruling elite responded with a general retreat from view. Many club directors – men who had other, less troublesome businesses to run – felt uneasy with their degree of exposure. There was a sense that a buffer was needed, a dispensable layer of ballast against the ire of the masses.

An obvious candidate presented himself. The crowd called for blood, and they got it: secretarial blood. Mute, office-bound – but also dressed in the directorial waistcoat and watch-chain – the sacrificial lamb was already on the premises. The secretary was about to get his big break. It seemed unlikely to be a very happy experience.

Here we come to a central dramatic irony in the manager's story. The fact is, his first real high-profile public act was to be sacked. Getting the boot was where it all started. The manager was born to be sacked, and sacked with some sense of cathartic public ceremony.

Early sackings came in a rush. Coventry City had eleven secretary-managers in the first twenty years of the twentieth century. Leyton Orient changed the name on the office door ten times between the wars. In 1930 Manchester United supporters passed a motion of no confidence in the club directors after a run of bad results. It didn't amount to much. But a few weeks later the manager, Herbert Bramlett, was duly sacked. This was the lot of the early secretary-manager: accountability without power. He stands alone as football's kamikaze general, the puppet dictator hurled from the balcony window.

The long-term effects of this are still with us. Being sacked – and the certainty at all times that he will be sacked – is central to the manager's existence. Perhaps the defining moment of Graham Taylor's thirty-year managerial career was his traumatic departure from the England job in 1993, not sacked but violently hounded out. Of his own career as a player Taylor told me: 'I had five managers in six years at my first club, Grimsby Town. The first manager who signed me from school, Tim Ward, had left by the time I started at the club from school.'

Being sacked is just what the manager does. Football managers are sacked and somehow this is oddly reassuring. To everything there is a season. And sometimes only half a season.

Andy Scott had been manager of Brentford for just two months when I visited him at the club's Osterley training ground. At the time Brentford had had thirteen managers in the last decade, a lingering background echo of taxi doors slamming, heads called for and briefcases packed. Does he feel that air of transience around him?

'This office,' Scott said gesturing around his large and dingy corner room. 'Martin Allen has been here, Leroy Rosenior, Terry Butcher. And that's just the last couple of years. You move things around, you clear the shelves, you try to make it your own room. So in the end it doesn't feel like you're sitting in someone else's seat.'

Currently Rosenior also holds the record for the shortest managerial reign. In May 2007, six months after leaving Brentford, he was unveiled in front of the press as Torquay's new manager. Ten minutes later he was sacked. The club had been sold and it was felt he had no future there. Like some secretarial throwback, Rosenior had been publicly elbowed from the stage, a patsy to directorial ambition.

He is at least in good company. The Valhalla of the fallen manager is a busy place, its benches packed with the released, the mutually dispensed with and the hounded out. Between 1899 and 1993 there were 1900 managerial changes in England. For a while in the 1960s this tally became a peculiar national obsession, continually updated, as though managerial sackings were just another barometer of human achievement, like the arms race or the 100-metres world record.

Excitingly, it's a problem that is becoming ever more chronic. In the 1920s a manager could expect to stay on average just under four years. In 1992–3 that had fallen to 2.72. Currently we're down to 1.72 years.

There is a peculiar sense of gravity to all these deaths in miniature. They leave their mark. We see the sacked manager in a different light. A common refrain among sacked football managers is that they are 'desperate to get back into football'. Quite right too. Between 2003 and 2008 there were 225 managerial dismissals; of those involved only twenty-eight were still in charge of League clubs at the end of that period. The rest continued to stalk the margins, restless spirits consigned to a nothing place.

Beyond this, we're still fascinated by the novelty sacking and the money-shot sacking. Everton manager Johnny Carey was sacked in a London taxi in April 1961. Cowdenbeath manager

Peter Cormack was sacked at a roadside burger van on the Forth Bridge in December 2000, ten days after taking on the job. In 1939 Charlton manager Jimmy Seed sacked himself. The club was bankrupt and twenty-four of his players had been called up by the military. 'He thought it was the best thing to do,' the *Daily Mirror* reported. Eight years earlier William 'Kitty' Cameron had resigned as Rochdale manager simply to 'save money'. The club's directors let it be known they wouldn't be bothering to seek a replacement.

In the decades that followed, the sacking would become an element of the manager's peculiar romance. We saw this in Graeme Souness's appearance at the 1992 FA Cup final, beached and grimacing on the Wembley bench just days after major heart surgery. Souness had risen from his hospital bed against doctors' orders to send his Liverpool team out to face Sunderland. It made for painful viewing, the manager grimacing on his touchline seat like a wounded cowboy in a Spaghetti Western clutching his blood-soaked shirt to his chest.

We also saw it in the strange light around Ruud Gullit in his final match as Newcastle manager, watching sodden and paralysed as his Newcastle team lost 1-0 to Sunderland in the pouring rain of St James' Park.

This lingering pathos is, in part, a gift from the silent ancestor with his accounts book and his pince-nez. Take away the manager's fine tailoring. Remove the telephone earpiece and oversized plastic microphone. Forget, for a moment, the elite media coaching and platitudinous post-match interview. Underneath it all we can still feel the icy touch of the long-dead secretary.

CHAPTER 2

The First Manager:
The Search for the Yeti

At this point it would be nice to be able to identify the pilgrim father: the first ever fully formed football manager. Unfortunately it's not that easy. The search for the first manager is like the search for the yeti. It's a never-ending story, a grail quest, and also largely a waste of time.

This is because the early history of the football manager is in fact the history of two people: the secretary and the trainer. Together, they represent the manager's half-formed antecedents. They're the embarrassing family secret, the blurred portraits at the back of the photo album. Today, who thinks of the secretary? Who mourns the trainer? They linger only as managerial ptero-dactyls, balsa-wood prototypes, outmoded and unlamented.

To the modern nostril it's the trainer who seems the more swamp-stinking. The trainer had a wide range of duties. These included basic shouting, medicine ball-hefting, goalpost renovation, diagnosis and treatment of all injuries, player punishment, player roughing up, player paternal guidance and provision of dubious dietary supplements.

Even as recently as the mid–1960s, it doesn't seem to have been that hard to become a trainer. Barry Fry got his first break in coaching as a trainer/physio, or what he still calls 'a sponge man'. Fry was a player at Leyton Orient under Dick Graham when the club trainer disappeared overnight. 'He never came back,' Fry told me. 'I think he might have run off with a woman but I can't be totally sure. Dick wanted a sponge man and I was injured at the time so he gave me the job for seven games.

'Seven games. He was superstitious like that. He'd phone in and say, "I'm caught in traffic, can you take training?" so I'd do it. And then I'd look over and see Dick's head sticking out watching me, making sure I was doing it right.'

But doing what right though? Mainly the trainer's role boiled down to shouting. In this he does at least touch on something important. The problem of what to shout, or how to shout right, has always been a sticking point. The football manager knows it's important. Something in his dormant trainer gene tells him this. But what to shout exactly?

Malcolm Allison, manager of Manchester City in the late 1960s and early 1970s, used to stand by the edge of the training pitch as his players completed a lap and shout 'How do you feel?' The rehearsed reply was: 'Sharp!'

Arsenal's manager Bertie Mee would make his players run up the concrete steps of Highbury while he shouted 'Explode! Explode!' at them. In 2003 QPR manager Ian Holloway hired an army fitness instructor who – besides introducing Rangers players to a pre-match meal of pasta and fresh fruit – would fill silences in his team talks by shouting 'Stand up, keep your legs moving and keep your brains lively . . . some sharp runs, turns and power jumping when you get outside, come on lads!' Which is enough to put anyone off their penne rigate.

Even more foolproof, Alec Stock of Orient employed a pro-fessional sign-writer to paint slogans which were then hung up around the dressing room and club premises. These were intended to 'establish good habits'. One sign read: 'Start quickly'. Another urged: 'If you don't think you can win, don't play'. Another sign read simply: 'Remember Watford'.

Besides the shouting, the trainer was considered a stand-up guy and a figure of some moral conscience, albeit a terribly menial one. Writing in 1955, Charles Buchan gave a good idea of the division of labour between the secretary and the trainer during his time as a player at Sunderland forty years earlier. Secretary Bob Kyle handed out pay packets, signed players and made stirring patrician speeches. Meanwhile the man repeatedly referred to as 'trainer Billy Williams' ferreted about the place keeping an ear to the ground and feeling collars like a hyperactively diligent army sergeant.

At one point Buchan pays him this stirring tribute:

> I owed a debt of gratitude to trainer Billy Williams that I never repaid nor ever could repay . . . After I had been a few weeks at Sunderland, he noticed that I smoked quite a number of cigarettes during the day. Cigarettes were his pet aversion. One day he handed me a new pipe, a pouch full of tobacco and a box of matches. 'I want you to promise me that you will give this a fair trial and leave cigarettes alone,' he said. Taken by surprise, I gave him my promise. I smoked nothing but a pipe from that day until just over three years ago when I parted company with my teeth.

Trainers generally had little knowledge of physical conditioning. Their hands were tied by the state of the art. In 1904 Tottenham's training schedule involved an hour and a half of running and skipping in the morning, two sessions a week where they actually touched a football, and a walk in the afternoon. The walk was optional.

When they won the FA Cup in 1889 Preston's training involved going for a walk and then driving twelve miles in an open bus to have tea at the Ship Inn in Lytham. Before their final game of the season at Aston Villa the players smoked and played cards on the train, changing into their kit as they passed Wolverhampton and being driven from the station to the ground just in time for kick-off.

Mainly the trainer was the straight man and the gimp. Herbert Chapman famously sacked his trainer George Hardy during a match for speaking out of turn. As George Hardwick said of Middlesbrough's trainer Charlie Cole during the 1930s, 'He had little or no authority . . . Poor Charlie, he had a hell of a time because everyone was taking the piss out of him.'

Clearly, we can forget about the trainer when it comes to finding our original yellow-jersey manager. He remains no more than a hardy prototype, like dial-up internet, the brick-like mobile phone or the horse-drawn train. Instead our attention turns to the secretary.

The secretary was at least a front-office man. He wore a suit and he made occasional decisions, albeit extremely minor ones. At the turn of the twentieth century most clubs were the play-thing of their directors. The secretary was the admin man, the temp and the office boy. His duties included match ticketing and sorting the post-bag. He sent telegrams to players letting them know which train to catch. Occasionally he appeared on the fringes of the team photo, crushed in at the edge of things.

But at least, here, we're not short of likely lads when it comes to potential first man status. Scrubbed up and made-over, assorted long-dead secretaries have been wheeled out of cold storage by club historians and fan websites during the boom times of the last fifteen years and presented as management's original Adam.

So we have lobbyists for George Ramsey of Aston Villa. Ramsey's case is bolstered by the fact he got the job by replying to an advert in the *Birmingham Daily Gazette* in 1884 that began: 'Wanted, Manager for Aston Villa Football Club'. But he still stinks overwhelmingly of secretary, as do J. G. Morgan, secretary of Coventry City in the 1880s, and Bob Blyth, a Portsmouth player who later became manager and then chairman.

We also find a subset of long-servers. These are the marathon men, the spindly long-distance merchants, for whom secretary-dom was a life sentence. Jack Addenbrooke of Wolves usually gets a mention. He got the job in 1885 and stayed there for thirty-seven years. This is the Reggie Perrin school of secretary-managership, the bowler-hatted depressive with his *Times* crossword, his same seat on the train for thirty years and his sense of quietly thwarted ambition. The other great elephantine presence was Fred Everiss of West Brom, who racked up forty-six years. This is technically a League record. But still something prevents us from embracing it as truly a managerial feat. In November 1934 the *Daily Mirror*'s football correspondent wrote, rather miserably: 'I spent half an hour or so on Wednesday in the company of Mr. Fred Everiss, West Bromwich's manager, and after I had left him I realised that he had not told me a word about his team . . . Most managers never tire of singing the praises of their team. Fred Everiss needs news to be dragged out of him.'

At the time Everiss had been in the job for thirty-two years. Somehow this very longevity makes us treat him with a little suspicion. As Malcolm Allison said, 'you're not really a manager until you've been sacked', and in truth the marathon secretaries were simply people who stayed in the same clerical job for a long time and then died. We may even disdain them, slightly unfairly, as bosses' men, time-servers, committee wonks.

Of all these distant figures, Tom Watson, secretary of Sunderland and then Liverpool, is probably the most vivid. Watson managed Sunderland from 1889–96 and became known for the unusual practice of 'managing' from the touchline, the former iron moulder in his three-piece, strolling the fringes like a general in the field. His great physical bulk – Watson weighed up to twenty stones – made him a visible emblem of authority and he was the first secretary to be mentioned consistently in the national press, becoming known as 'genial Tom Watson'.

Genial Tom was also the first secretary to be poached by another club, leaving for Liverpool in 1896. Liverpool duly won the League in 1901. Returning to Lime Street Station after the season's decisive victory, the team were greeted by a huge crowd, which briefly hoisted Watson into the air and tossed him about the concourse.

The search for the prototype circles around Genial Tom, without ever quite convincing us it stops here. In truth the dawning of the manager came slowly. It was a communal shuffling forward. There is no eureka moment, no first man on the moon. It may be a fruitless quest, but it's one that throws up a degree of collateral interest. Mainly because it gives us time to consider the rarely considered trainer, Caliban to the secretary's Prospero. And oddly enough, while the secretary has long since been made redundant, the trainer is still pretty much with us, if we look closely enough.

Unchanged from his original state – like some walking, yelping, swearing fossil – the trainer is a feature of the dugout even now. He has other names. He might be called assistant manager, or head coach, or technical skills consultant.

On match days you can look out for him, just a few seats down from the main man, gum-chewing, grim-faced, anonymous in club training kit. That's the trainer. That's your enduring relic from the game's long-distant past. That bloke. The one who just kicked over that bucket.

CHAPTER 3

The Manager's New Trousers

The First World War provided the manager's first really violent career jump start. It brought with it a sense of old bonds being cast aside. Here was a social hierarchy about to be ruthlessly overturned by brusque, pipe-smoking men who weren't afraid to say the word 'bloody', and who wouldn't rest until they'd been handed an exciting opportunity to travel the Thames Valley area selling rubberised surgical trusses. Suddenly everything seemed up for grabs. Social advancement. A new order in the workplace. Not to mention a small terraced house in East Acton and the opportunity to be repeatedly snubbed by the local golf club. These were the tantalising fruits of having 'a good war'.

After the armistice in 1918 there would be much talk of those who had had a good war. This tended to involve more than simply staying alive, or failing to contract an aggressive fungal disease of the toenail. A good war meant promotion and ascent. Winston Churchill had a good war. The capable lower-middle-class officer had a good war. And guess what? The football manager had a good war too. Fizzing with an entirely personal ambition, always ready to leapfrog and to elbow aside, the manager was never going to miss out on this one.

The second generation of managers – and the first to be plucked from the ranks of former pros – was always going to crave a bigger slice of the action. They did meet resistance along the way. The cult of the power-hungry manager has always rankled. In the gathering dawn of the secretary these prejudices were sharpened. The sport now had a visible face; albeit one with sad eyes and an immovable moustache.

In 1924 *Allsports Weekly* noted, with an audible smirk, that 'some secretaries sport big watch-chains, glittering rings and cigars the size of a policeman's truncheon'. Here we see the early bling of the burgeoning manager: check his ice, marvel at his fat gold chain, snigger at his clerical background and unaspirated consonants.

Snobbery towards the rising man wasn't restricted to football. This was the new world of the upwardly mobile prole, the era of the salesman and the middle manager characterised, with some horror, by Evelyn Waugh in *Brideshead Revisited* as 'the travelling salesman, with his polygonal pince-nez, his fat, wet handshake, his grinning dentures'.

The First World War broke the seal on all this. It gave us social flux. It gave us a newly mass media. It gave us the grinning dentures of the secretary-manager. And it gave us Major Frank Buckley of Blackpool, Wolves and Leeds, and his famous – his revolutionary – plus-fours.

Kitted out in matching tweeds and long socks, Major Buckley had the air of a gentleman farmer or some ne'er-do-well golfing partner of the Prince of Wales. He was known to players, directors, newspapers, even his wife, as simply 'the Major'. The Major was cheerful, raffish and dictatorial. He was the first 'personality' to become a daily presence in the football press; now he looks prescient and innovative, a direct antecedent of the modern complete manager.

Most of all, however, he looks like a man in a pair of plus-fours. A piece of golfing apparel popularised in the nineteenth century, the plus-four was an adapted knickerbocker that fell four inches lower on the shin (hence 'plus four'). Throughout his career the Major was rarely pictured outside of one of his many pairs. They became his leitmotif, and an abrasive statement of intent.

It's worth noting that, at this point in its history, the plus-four was an incendiary garment. For the upwardly mobile gentleman of the 1920s, these were violently provocative trousers. In February 1925 an undergraduate at St John's College, Cambridge, was convicted of assault of a policeman while being thrown out of a dance for wearing a pair. That same night, the *Daily Mirror* reported, 'Thirty young men in plus fours and flannels were turned away.'

In the years that followed there was even talk of a nationwide ban on wearing plus-fours at work. In June 1928 thirty men in plus-fours were sent home from a warehouse in Glasgow. A year later the president of the Commercial Travellers' Association called the wearing of plus-fours during office hours 'deeply inappropriate'.

At the same time the plus-four was being celebrated as an emblem of the youthful, the rakish and the thrillingly unconventional. These were pop cultural trousers, commemorated in the music hall songs 'Percy's Posh Plus Fours Are Priceless' and 'In Your Plus Fours: I Love You John'. Fashionable Prince Edward wowed the US by wearing them on a diplomatic trip in 1924. Tintin wore the same mud-brown pair matched with white socks until the 1970s, when he briefly adopted an unflattering groovy semi-flare.

More recently, the plus-four has threatened a comeback, once more from left-field. The American rapper André 3000's clothing line, launched in 2008, features a pair of tweed plus-fours, matched with Ivy League-style cardigans and sweaters with leather-patched elbows, confirming once again – Buckley-style – the potential of these dangling knickerbockers to provoke and shock.

'Prep style comes from mostly affluent families,' 3000 mused at the launch of his trousers. 'But when you come from a background that has more struggle, your take on it will be different. There's a certain kind of rebel to it.'

A certain kind of rebel indeed. At this point you can almost picture the respectful high-five between rapper and Major. Buckley might seem peculiarly middle-aged to the modern eye. But in his time he too was thrillingly gangster, white hot with his own galloping contemporaneity. The Major's plus-fours were the equivalent of Marlon Brando's biker jacket, the Beatle mop-top or the bondage chic of early punk. They spoke not just of a desire to play golf but of an outlaw sensibility, the manager's refusal to bend the knee to authority. These trousers said: I wear the trousers.

It was a heady blend. Buckley was box office. In fact he was almost pantomime. He took up his first managerial post at Norwich in 1919. From there – from Blackpool to Wolves, to Leeds – he bashed out a broad-sketched template for the manager: part impresario, part mad scientist, part quixotic commanding officer.

We can assume some of this came from Buckley's time in the military during the violent manoeuvres of the early twentieth century. Buckley had enlisted at the age of sixteen. He served in the Boer War and was injured in the shoulder and lung at the Battle of the Somme. On demobilisation he headed straight back into football. His obituary in *The Times* would later note his 'stern sense of discipline and an uncommon flair for public relations'.

This came across most clearly in his love of signing players, a big part of the Buckley repertoire. He was appointed Wolves manager in 1927, having replied to a newspaper advert that ended with the words 'A Spendthrift is Not Needed'. With the Major you didn't exactly get a spendthrift, just a man with a mania for commerce: one season he made the directors a profit of over £100,000 in transfers.

His legacy isn't best measured in cups and trophies, mainly because he didn't win many. Wolves finished second in the First Division in 1938 and 1939 and also reached the FA Cup final. Buckley's real success lay in the infrastructure he created, the groundwork of commercial success and player development that would be brilliantly exploited by Stan Cullis in the 1950s as Wolves became one of the most powerful clubs in Europe.

Buckley's broader legacy was in the person of the manager himself. He introduced the notion of the wheeler-dealer, in the process helping to mint a new language of transfer hokum. He was the first manager to feed rumour, gossip and half-truths directly to the press. So he was also the first manager to 'swoop' for a player, to 'plot a transfer raid' and to 'launch an audacious bid'. Many of the transfer gossip terms we still use have a military bent to them. There is no hard evidence of this – how could there be? – but it's difficult not to suspect the long-dead hand of martial Major Buckley in the ongoing daily cliché of the marketplace. And thrilling too to imagine his raffish snigger, lounging plus-foured at his celestial walnut desk, at such a wheeze surviving down the decades.

Buckley presented his signings to the press with much theatre, creating the template for the modern 'unveiling'. In the Major's time this involved him looming in threateningly patrician stance over his new charge. The unveiling is still an important ritual, a visible demonstration of the manager's hunter-gatherer prowess, the footballing equivalent of stalking through the palm huts dragging his betrothed by the hair. Buckley understood this. In staging the showpiece-signature he spoke to his public free from directorial interference, a propaganda victory that said: I am powerful. I summon. I sign. I manage.

And I do it while wearing baggy tweed trousers that expose a provocative length of sock. Somehow this is the image that endures. Armed with these combustible trousers the manager completed his first great shoulder barge into the forefront of popular tabloid celebrity, a forerunner not just of the lounging postmodern rap artist but of the strutting Premier League peacock in his culturally complex overcoat.

Of course Buckley was just the first manager to use clothing in this way. Clothes have always been significant. For many years the manager's camel-coloured overcoat said: I am serious. And not just serious, but also successful and a man of means. It first appeared regularly in the 1970s as part of the uniform of the showman, the flash-harry and the hustler. Malcolm Allison famously teamed the camel-coloured overcoat with a fedora hat, creating a Chicago bootlegger template, the manager as outlaw aristocracy.

More than twenty years later, on his first day in office as Stockport County manager, the novice Carlton Palmer would arrive at the club wearing a striking brand-new camel-coloured overcoat and carrying an empty briefcase. Palmer lasted two years and a single relegation. But he did definitely look like a manager.

Earlier generations of managers experimented with the tracksuit. The tracksuit says: I have ideas, I am rigorous. It's football's equivalent of the lab coat. The Sunderland manager Bob Stokoe's decision to wear a tracksuit at the 1973 FA Cup final was perhaps the most famous example, his training gear decisively outflanking Don Revie's sober single-breasted. Stokoe and Revie had a famously hostile relationship and Sunderland were underdogs on the day. Stokoe's response was to position himself emphatically as one of the boys. The team were encouraged to relax at the hotel. Drinks were taken. And on the big day Stokoe came barrelling off the bus in a tight blue tracksuit twinned with a brown overcoat and a pair of formal black leather shoes.

He looked scarecrow-like, but also compelling. Watching him march along opposite Revie for the pre-match pageantry, you sense there can be only one winner here. Stokoe's capering sprint across the Wembley turf at the final whistle is one of the great managerial moments. The grasping hands, the utter conviction, the naked egomania: those fifty yards expressed the managerial sensibility at the peak of its popular cult.

At the same time the classic sheepskin was also popular. The sheepskin said: I hustle, but I am also socially mobile. It was a compromise between the outdoor and the formal. It looked good with a tracksuit; it passed muster with a suit. There's a famous picture of Bobby Charlton during his unsuccessful stint as manager of Preston North End during the 1973–4 season. He's hunched in the dugout dressed in a pristine sheepskin. He knows this isn't going to work out. We know. Even the sheepskin knows.

Later, Sven-Goran Eriksson would prove influential as England manager with his sharp designer suits, a level of fine tailoring never before associated with the touchline. Perhaps because rather than in spite of the ongoing embarrassing revelations about his sex life – Eriksson dated the same '36DD glamour model' who would later provide a graphic kiss and tell story about the England captain, John Terry – he was unusually close to his players. They admired his fame. They dug his threads. Eriksson may not have actually been a player, but he looked the next best thing: a playa. Much of which was simply in the suit, the watch and the fine leather shoes.

Occasionally the manager can seem to be communicating with us through his clothes. At Newcastle Kevin Keegan did more than anyone else to propel the recent trend for padded nylon sportswear. During the denouement to his first spell at St James' Park it was as though the upward progress of the zip on his quilted training jacket acted as an informal barometer of his mental wellbeing. Zipped right up to the throat indicated no more than a standard level of inner turmoil. The covering of the Keegan mouth warned of stormy times ahead. Right up to eye level and it was anything goes time, the frenzied touchline dance, the immediate resignation.

The recent era of popular leisure wear points to another of the manager's sartorial functions. For men of a certain age the manager now acts as a role model and style guru. We've all seen the manager manqué strolling the shopping centre in his padded overcoat, or the Sunday-morning dog-walker in his gaffer-issue executive sportswear.

For Major Buckley the choice of managerial outfit signalled a zesty and uncompromising ambition. For the leisure-suited polymath of the Premier League it seems to signify something more. Looking behind him into the crowd he sees a healthy smattering of manager clones. He sees his influence spread. The manager doesn't follow fashion now. He sets it. He looks great and he knows it. He bestrides the high street. For this he owes much to his ancestor, the man in the short trousers.

CHAPTER 4

The Manager Gets Serious

Major Buckley was fun. He had a seductive air of the whisky-fuelled and the pipe-smoke-wreathed. But he was basically just the warm-up act. Where Buckley seemed vivid and cartoon-like, Herbert Chapman was deadly serious. Chapman was the real deal. Look at him, staring at you from beneath the brim of his large-brimmed hat. He's not smiling.

The big thing about Chapman is that he did everything first. Not just marginally ahead of everyone else, but ages, eras and epochs. A stocky, dapper man with the look of a prosperous northern green-grocer, he arrived at Arsenal in 1924 like a time traveller from the distant future, some managerial Marty McFly bent on teaching the world how to play the electric guitar thirty years ahead of schedule.

His methods were advanced, his success genre-defining. Among managers Chapman represents all-time top-three aris-tocracy. He's Citizen Kane, he's Ulysses. This is the managerial Elvis. He introduced the voice. He patented the moves. Even now his gyrating managerial hips are with us, present in every one of his many imitators. Chapman is the King.

In the interests of completeness, here's that list of things Herbert Chapman did first. He was the first manager to insist on picking the team himself. He came up with the idea of the white ball, numbers on shirts, rubber studs, European competition and proper tactics. He also rigged up the first-ever set of floodlights, staging an Arsenal practice game lit by lanterns dangling from trees after he'd seen a match in Austria lit by the headlights of forty cars.

Turning his reformer's eye towards public transport interchanges, Chapman lobbied the London Electric Railway to change the name of Gillespie Road tube station to Arsenal. Chapman promoted. He hustled. He borrowed the silk hat and neckerchief of the theatre impresario, transforming Arsenal into a 'brand' sixty years before the irresistible dawn of the marketing wonk with his mania for club-crested toothbrush holders. As Bernard Joy wrote in his book *Forward Arsenal*, 'He looked beyond the cloth-capped supporters and made big soccer games as fashionable as Wimbledon or a Test Match.'

Chapman was also the first de facto England manager: he went with the team to play in Italy in 1933. One of Chapman's players, Cliff Bastin, was in the room when Chapman was introduced to Benito Mussolini. Bastin later reported himself so impressed by the personal magnetism of Il Duce that he felt the dictator had even, on balance, managed to out-charisma Arsenal's title-winning manager.

This was Chapman's other great first: he was the archetype for the big personality merchant, the inspirationalist, the too-big-for-this-boardroom type. Suddenly the manager was staring out Il Duce, being interviewed by Peter Batten for *My Greatest Hour* on the BBC and receiving the French medal for physical culture.

How did this happen? Chapman was manager of Arsenal for just nine years. Before that he'd been an inside forward at Tottenham Hotspur, described variously as 'lacking in skill' and 'slow', although he did become well known for his splendid, innovative and pointless yellow boots.

He got his first break in management at Northampton Town, having been offered the job in the Spurs dressing room by a team-mate who'd decided he didn't fancy it. Then during the First World War he worked as chief storekeeper at the Number One National Shell Filling Factory near Leeds. This is a brilliant-sounding job. By the end of the war he had an even better one: labour manager at the Olympia Oil and Cake Works in Selby. Oddly, Chapman was lured back to management only when the cake works was sold and he lost his job.

Happily, oil and cake works labour-managing's loss was football's gain. Appointed at Huddersfield in 1921, his success was stark and instant. Over four seasons he won the FA Cup and the League twice. He then moved on to Highbury, where his progress was so phenomenal there's really not much point in describing it. Safe to say, before Chapman Arsenal had never won a major trophy; by the time he left they were the most famous club in the world.

And all the while Chapman was busy doing stuff. He invented the table with players chalked on it to demonstrate tactics (which he also, incidentally, invented). He conjured up the counter-attack, team meetings and the managerial bollocking. At the same time he was a finger-in-every-pie control freak. Members of the admin staff weren't allowed to leave work until they'd phoned his office at 5.30 p.m. and asked permission. He oversaw the opening of the new Highbury tearoom. He personally accompanied the Arsenal brass band on its Christmas visit to Pentonville prison where, according to newspapers, 'the prisoners joined in a vigorous rendering of "Onward Christian Soldiers"'. On one occasion he visited a local resident whose garden fence had been damaged by fans in order to offer his sympathies (and not very much else).

He was an early master of man-management ('Chapman

knew when to blow you up and when to blow you down,' Huddersfield winger Alec Jackson remarked). When the Scottish player Alex James dug his heels in over a salary increase he was told he was being sent on a cruise. James arrived at the dock to find himself being packed on to a primitive tramp steamer cargo ship.

The list goes on. You point at it, Chapman's already done it, and done it better than you. Finally, and with a sense of some inevitability, we get to his irreproachable death. Aged fifty-five, it was a classic death on the job. This was a textbook death. Not only was it firmly within the tradition of the early martyr-manager, it also preserved him whole, untainted and still rock-star pretty. Chapman lived fast, died middle-aged and left a title-winning corpse. He's football management's Jimmy Dean, its Marilyn, its Jim Morrison in a heavy tweed three-piece.

As a result we never saw Chapman grow old. We never saw him slowly lose the plot, fail to reinvent himself, fall out of fash-ion, grow a beard, become involved with an unsuitable younger woman or make unintelligible and confused remarks as a septu-agenarian TV pundit. He burned briefly but brightly. And then, crucially, popped off before anything else could happen.

On the face of it, there's nothing new to say. Chapman suc-ceeded. And then he died. The usual biographical response to this would be something along the lines of a revisionist Channel 4 documentary. The temptation is to dig under the fingernails for dirt. We might hear about Chapman's carefully concealed membership of the Ku Klux Klan; the fact that he secretly pre-ferred rugby; his debilitating addiction to hot malted milk drinks. Unfortunately none of this is true. Chapman is what he seems: irritatingly perfect, unassailable, the enduring head pre-fect.

But still. There is a problem here, albeit not one that impacts on the perfect world of Herbert Chapman. Instead it's the emerging figure of the craven, stooped, leeringly power-hungry manager who suffers in Chapman's shadow. The Elvis-type role model can be terribly damaging. The King has great power, perhaps too much.

For a start, becoming a manager in the Chapman era can't have been easy. It must have felt a bit like trying out for a Herbert Chapman lookalike agency dressed in your best rubberised Herbert Chapman body suit in a room decorated with Herbert Chapman wallpaper while a team of Herbert Chapman technicians inserted a feeding funnel into your gullet, force-fed you concentrated essence of Herbert Chapman and then diligently tattooed the words 'HERBERT CHAPMAN' on to the inside of your eyelids. Chapman became inescapable. He created the blueprint for management, but it was an impossibly over-arching one, an inimitable show-closer, an act you just couldn't follow.

He taught us that to be a good manager you had to be a showman, a pioneer and a visionary. After Chapman the manager was expected to be like Chapman: to transform fundamentally with his overwhelming personality, his magic dust. He taught us we could expect our managers to be Spiderman, Mao Zedong, Isambard Kingdom Brunel and Ian Botham at Headingley hitting Terry Alderman into the confectionery stall and right back out again.

And while this might come as a shock to his fellow managers – their bedroom walls festooned with glossy Chapman pull-outs from the centre pages of *Managerial Monthly* – or to connoisseurs of the Herbert Chapman collectible plate industry, Arsenal's great one-off manager might have even turned out to be something of a drag for everybody else.

Until now the early manager has been our anti-hero. He's been plucky, ingratiating, thwarted and quiveringly ambitious. He's been the little guy. We've cheered his progress. We've whistled and wee-ha'd and shouted 'Get in the hole!' at each incremental step forward. In Chapman, though, we reach a crisis point. Arsenal's great early pioneer is also the most visible early embodiment of something subtly damaging and retrogressive in the manager. Under the Chapman blueprint, the manager became a cure-all and a panacea. Suddenly English footballers expected to be told what to do. They expected a grand plan from the man in the corner with the frown and the waistcoat. Swearing blind allegiance to a charismatic leader, they had a get-out-of-jail-free card, a pass to helplessness. The cult of the magnetic personality had taken hold. We wanted a leader and for our sins we got one.

It's not Herbert Chapman's fault of course. The problem is more what we've done with him. Our post-Chapman mania was just too much for the burgeoning manager to handle. Suddenly everybody wanted to be like the King. And as ever there were misunderstandings, short cuts taken, presumptions made and a raft of deluded bedroom imitators with their hairbrush micro-phones. Just as Elvis gave us Cliff Richard and Shakin' Stevens, so Chapman spawned a lifetime of bogus Chapman clones.

Over the years this has shown itself in many ways. The most obvious is the ongoing fashion for bad science. The manager has always been hungry for innovation. This has tended to go hand in hand with an endearing naivety towards the details. The man-ager knows little of science, beyond the fact that it could be helping him in all sorts of mysterious ways. So he loves his boom stick, his flying machine and his iron horse.

Chapman had an engineering background. He thought empirically. He was familiar with the notion of technology and progress as problem-solver and deus ex machina. Hence his air of specialist scientific knowledge. His Arsenal team became known as 'the Machine'. On his hip and edgy blackboard he produced the manager's first set of winning formulae. He brought light and publicity and progressive thinking along the lines of maybe doing something about that brown, mud-soaked ball.

He also brought a mania for imitative gimmickry. Major

Buckley stepped up to the plate here. Influenced, perhaps, by his all-conquering contemporary, the Major's high-profile forays into bad science helped to ram home decisively the notion that the manager was now a pointy-head go-to guy. Buckley starred in a Pathé news film called *The Football Robot*. The Robot was a man-sized metal structure with a single huge piston capable of belting a ball 'up to one hundred yards'. This was the brilliant new mechanised future in action. 'Keeping the Wolves from the door, or rather the goal, is going to be even more difficult now they're using this Football Robot!' a cheerful voice announced, over shots of Buckley, in shirtsleeves, feeding balls into the Football Robot, while his players cowered in the distance under its huge marmalising robot punts.

Oddly perhaps, the Football Robot failed to catch on. It's probably even now gathering cobwebs in an allotment shed somewhere on the outskirts of Wolverhampton, a faint light still pulsing behind its eyes, the desire to exterminate long since-dulled into an older, wiser sense of robot appeasement.

The Major's other contribution was the diathermy machine, an electric shock generator, which he used to create 'therapeutic' tingling in the muscles of his players. An account of its use in *The Times* in September 1934 described its effects as 'like standing on a bucking horse – and a horse bucking at a rate that no horse ever bucked before'. The diathermy machine also slipped out of fashion quite quickly.

Together Chapman and Buckley gave licence to these instincts for groping innovation. It was a trend that flourished in particular during the late 1960s and early 1970s. Bill Lambton introduced trampolining sessions to training while he was manager of Scunthorpe in the 1950s and later lost his job at Leeds United shortly after hobbling in agony from the training pitch following a demonstration of his own bare-foot mastery of the heavy leather ball.

In the 1970s Freddie Goodwin of Birmingham City schooled

his players in yoga and conducted complex psychological tests. Gerry Summers of Oxford United devised a state-of-the-art dietary programme with the help of Dr Muckle, senior registrar at the Radcliffe Infirmary. This involved training the players to exhaustion on a Thursday and then insisting they gorge themselves on cornflakes, coffee, sugar, milk and bread on a Friday. In the first year of this they did come eighth in the Second Division. The following season they came eighteenth. Two years later Summers left the club and his team were relegated.

One embedded quirk remains the use of the sports psychologist. Often found lurking close to the manager, the psychologist remains a divisive figure. This despite the fact that the use of psychology goes right back to the 1930s when the managers of both Arsenal and Sheffield Wednesday employed the Reverend M. Caldwell, a chaplain at two large London mental hospitals, who gave lectures on 'psychotactics'.

The psychologist has often been something the manager associates with abroad. At the 1958 World Cup Tommy Docherty bumped into a man called Professor Carvalhaes in a café in Stockholm. They had a long chat about football, during which the professor said things like 'training must be done to the needs of the individual, depending on the right psychology'.

On the morning of a match Carvalhaes explained that he would 'blindfold players and ask them to do a series of drawings of horizontal and vertical lines, circles and steps . . . He could tell whether a player was in a state of anxiety, too tense or lacking confidence from the way the line had deviated to the right or left'. After the World Cup final, which Brazil won, Docherty noticed two of their players, Vava and Orlando, embracing Carvalhaes as they left the field.

A quarter of a century later, in the alternate dimension of the Premier League a strain of weird science still flourishes. This usually comes from left-field: snowboarding instruction, primal scream therapy and team-building exercises based around learning to restore a Victorian bentwood chair. It's an eclectic methodology, but one that still seems as vague and hopeful as the Major's diathermy machine.

For a while the former Watford manager Adrian Boothroyd built a reputation based around his fetish for number-crunching and stat overload, talking publicly about borrowing ideas from baseball, and taking his players on motivational log-chopping and forestry expeditions. As manager of Crystal Palace Iain Dowie attracted an early buzz with a genuine mad scientist routine based around swimming, boxing, psychology and inspirational slogans. 'You make a living by what you get, you make a life by what you give,' he told reporters in May 2004, shortly before Palace were promoted. They were relegated the following season. Dowie left 'by mutual consent' a year later. That same year he was sacked by Charlton. A year later he was sacked by Coventry City. Six months later he was sacked by QPR.

Before his public fall from grace the former England manager Steven McClaren established a position as informal high priest of Premier League technologies. This was based on his time at Derby County where, by all accounts, he did something with injured players and the kind of vibrating leather massage chairs you see on makeshift stands at deserted out-of-town shopping centres.

McClaren provides us with a salutary tale of post-Chapman scientific opportunism. Unfortunately for him, English football aggressively called his bluff, swallowed his baloney and appointed him to the most visible managerial job in the country. Here McClaren was characterised rather sadly as a gimmick merchant.

This is all too often the lot of the scientific English manager, destined to be exposed as a crank and a snake-oil vendor. His science is a temporary lab coat three sizes too big and with someone else's name in it. And as ever, beneath the veneer of his bad science, the manager is naked.

Elsewhere Chapman left perhaps an even more damaging imprint. He created the notion of the magnetic personality. The magnetic personality is a confusing thing. It's pure managerial absinthe. Those stirring words, the steely gaze, the thrill of his sweat-stinking charisma: just the thing to leave you stumbling around the next day with a terrible headache wondering what it was you were supposed to be doing and why you seem to have a toothpick stuck in your eyebrow.

After Chapman the notion of the guru and the rainmaker took root. An underbelly of small-time eccentric inspirationalists emerged. Bill Norman was a macho fitness fanatic with a waxed moustache and love of extreme Spartan training methods. Once, at Hartlepool, he ordered the players out to train on a bitterly cold day. When they hesitated Norman stripped naked and rolled around in the snow in front of them. Charles Hewitt of Millwall concocted a high-profile twenty-year reputation as a livewire, a man of moods and a tempestuous tactician. Without actually ever winning anything. But never mind. He was wreaking his own peculiar magic.

The English have shown themselves to be in thrall more than any other nation to this idea of the manager-magician. This is not a healthy fixation. Before Herbert Chapman tactics were a murky business. But the players did at least try to work things out for themselves. Nick Ross, captain of Preston North End, helped to fathom the fine points of the all-conquering Invincibles. The Newcastle back-line of the early years of the twentieth century between them devised the first real offside trap. Players talked things out. Wisdom was shared.

Post-Chapman thinking about how to win football matches became the manager's job. There is a paradox in this. One of Chapman's other firsts was to pioneer the mass team talk, at which the entire playing squad would be encouraged to speak up. But to the imitators Chapman was the man. As time passed his shadow loomed ever larger. And so the English player waited to be led. He slowly lost his forensic skills, his on-field intellect, his problem-solving instincts. Instead he waited for Professor Charles Xavier to come wheeling in through the door and tell him what to do.

The cult of the manager was born out of Herbert Chapman's supreme success. Perhaps it's unfair to blame him for any of this. Perhaps it was all inevitable and he simply sped up the process. And perhaps, as the Chapman heritage industry itself might point out, he was, once again, just the man who got there first.

CHAPTER 5

The Manager Goes Abroad

Abroad, and all matters relating to abroad, have remained a source of much furrowed unease for the manager. In general, though, the response to the whole problem of abroad has been fairly straightforward. Will it go away? And if not, can we ignore it?

Over time the overwhelming answer to both of these questions has turned out to be 'no'. But there have been exceptions along the way. Like some suburban teenager slumped within the blackened walls of its upstairs back-bedroom, some part of the manager has always dreamed of escape. Fortunately, an alternative has presented itself, a secret history of happy travellers that begins right back in the days when the manager was still young. In the tiniest of advance parties, the manager was about to make his first pilgrimage abroad.

There is something excitingly evangelical about these early travels. From the early days of empire Britain had sent guns, then trade and then religion. When these had begun to wear thin, it sent football. It's here that the figure of the manager first becomes entwined with that of the priest and the carrier of good news. Hallelujah. He is come. And he's brought a ball.

Following the trade winds, and the well-grooved path of imperial conquest, various hopeful, mutton-chopped types set sail in the early years of the twentieth century. Like the dog-collared missionaries of the nineteenth century, the manager was zealous and energetic. Freed from the feudal ties that bound him at home, he moved happily among the masses. Charles Miller left Southampton in 1894 carrying a ball and a set of rules, and became one of the founding fathers of football in Brazil. In 1907 Jock Hamilton followed him, becoming the first British 'trainer' at a Brazilian club, and returning home with the ominous comment that 'their combination is really clever'.

The likes of Miller and Hamilton were still battling against the tide. It would be another fifty years before abroad was taken seriously in the manager's founding homeland – a quality it did, at least, share with the manager himself. And so they came in a trickle, monk-like, elemental, weather-beaten, fleeing the old country in search of some managerial Eden. Most notably, in the form of Jimmy Hogan, who first left England for Holland in 1910.

Hogan is arguably the most influential single manager anywhere at any time, the man who first concocted the blueprint of the coach as footballing seer, teacher and guide. Not to mention performer, showman, demagogue and magician.

He grew up in Burnley, one of eight children in an Irish Catholic family. Pretty much from his birth in 1882 Hogan seems to have been a football obsessive, a perfectionist, a technician and a nutcase. As a teenager he was deeply religious, at one stage finding himself torn between a career in football and training as a priest.

This seems about right: in time Hogan would become a travelling missionary, albeit one chiefly concerned with the chest trap and the cushioned back-heel lay-off. The priest-like persona was a big part of his shtick. Among English players his nickname was 'the Parson' (explanation: he rarely swore). At Celtic Peter McParland recalled Hogan coming into the dressing room and 'putting the rosary beads close to me – he was almost holy in his ways'.

Hogan made his way as a professional player at Burnley, where he showed a taste for innovation. He bought his own ball, because at the time players were still ordered not to train with one. He rigged a pushbike up to a wooden stand, allowing him to cycle thirty kilometres a day inside his garden shed (when the club found out he was dropped from the team for 'over-exercising').

Aged twenty-eight, he accepted an offer to coach at Dordrecht in Holland. Although he smoked a pipe and was known to carry a secret hip flask, he was still vaguely appalled by the habits of his fun-loving, educated Dutch players: 'They drank like fishes and smoked like chimneys but they were a jolly lot of fellows, intelligent and able to pick up the science of the game.'

Hogan's big break came in 1912 when he was invited by Hugo Meisl of Austria to become trainer to the national team for the Olympic Games. Meisl was the de facto head man in Austrian football and son of a wealthy banker. In Hogan he found an amanuensis, an acolyte and a lifelong friend. Hogan became manager of Austria Vienna. Here, working feverishly late into the night, he founded with Meisl what became known as 'the Vienna School', a football sect based around short passing and tirelessly honed close control.

Hogan's instinct for the guru-ish and the preacherly began to flourish. When he returned to England he would sign his autographs 'Jimmy Hogan, the World's Number One Coach'. He carried a set of business cards describing himself as a 'Football Professor'. And everything in Austria went swimmingly until the first morning of the 1914–18 war, when Hogan was pulled out of bed, arrested and interned.

Bailed out of prison by two Viennese department store owners, he spent two years playing tennis in a stately home, before being shipped off to Budapest. Here he flourished again, building from scratch the all-powerful MTK Club (despite being followed everywhere by a policeman) and earning himself the title of 'father of Hungarian football'.

Returning home after the armistice the father of Hungarian football presented himself at the FA seeking financial help and perhaps a job offer and was given three pairs of khaki tights by Sir Frederick Wall. Duly belittled, he went abroad again and accepted a lucrative post lecturing on football for the German FA.

Here Hogan's appalling command of the language almost led to instant dismissal. His hesitant early efforts brought an ultimatum to give a lecture in German, unassisted, in front of five hundred students, including his fiercely critical rival coaches. Initially Hogan made such a hash of it that he was almost laughed off stage. In some desperation he called an intermission. Backstage he changed into his football gear and returned to give a demonstration of barefoot juggling and shooting so ferocious that he gashed one of his feet. He left the stage to thunderous applause.

Hogan went on to develop this into a successful travelling stage show. He toured German towns shooting a ball through a blackboard with a hole in it and booting a whole string bag-full into a bucket. One evening, by way of riposte to a local mayor who disapproved of his footballing crusade, he performed 350 successive headed keep-ups. 'The mayor was a football convert,' the *Daily Mirror* recorded triumphantly.

The travelling, ball-bashing, preacher-man demagogue: Hogan was a nationwide hit. He had also founded a routine – the show-off personal demonstration – that would become his chief coaching tool. In the process he'd also given the manager a decisive first nudge into the dizzy realm of showbusiness and performing celebrity. Already patriarch to Austrian and

Hungarian football, Hogan was well on his way to siring German football too.

Which really is a lot of fathering. Hogan, the swaggering paterfamilias of central Europe, certainly did put it about. Although somehow you feel this kind of father dom comes closer to the dog-collared instructor, the confessor. Father, forgive me: I have failed to perform the volleyed instep lay-off correctly. My effective domestic coaching structures are frankly non-existent. Say five Hail Marys, do two hundred keep-ups and catch the ball on the back of your neck. Amen.

Hogan's achievements are remarkable, and impossible to match outside of their pre-modern time. What lingers above all now is the priestly bearing, the white heat of his travelling faith. Like the church, we don't really like to think about him too much. In fact he even seems a little odd. The manager still pays his respects now and then, borrows his black-caped gravitas on occasion. Yeah, cheers Jimmy. Lovely job. You keep up the good work. We're off now. There's a fiver in there for the roof. The windows. Whatever.

This pious quality is confined almost entirely to the manager's earliest migrations. His later travels would prove more chaotic, louder and more disorderly. In the years that followed, abroad would prove a perplexing place for the manager, a netherworld, a funhouse even. Since the 1950s there have been periodic attempts to establish some kind of bridgehead there. The 1970s saw a new and exciting travelling phenomenon: the manager in exile.

For a period of several years being summarily banished was a common fate. Greece was the favoured destination, acting as a kind of managerial naughty step, the geographical embodiment of beyond the pale. Wilf McGuinness headed straight to Aris Salonika after being sacked by Manchester United in 1971. Alan Ashman was sacked by West Brom in 1971 while he was actually on holiday in Greece: he stayed on to become manager of Olympiakos.

If Greece had a bounty hunter-ish appeal, the main attraction being the large salaries paid by its ruling military junta, it could still be a fretful experience for the manager, unskilled as he is in the nuances of international diplomacy. John Barnwell, later head of the League Managers Association, managed AEK Athens, but was eventually banned from Greek football for suggesting it wasn't very good. Joe Mallet, who moved from Birmingham City to Panionios in 1970, was arrested for a while following the junta's overthrow in 1974.

Other parts of southern Europe were equally exile-friendly. In 1970 *The Times* carried a long interview with Jimmy Hagan during his banishment at the Portuguese club Benfica. 'If it's possible to be happy as manager of a football club, then I suppose I'm as close as maybe to it over here,' Hagan told Geoffrey Green, who noted that 'Mr Hagan, for all his calm temperament amid Latin emotion, the sun, sea and bougainvillea, seems even to have added a furrow or two to his chiselled features beneath the greying hair'. For decades this was the overriding effect of abroad. It stilled the managerial juices. It made you go grey. Of all the various punishments visited on the manager, abroad remained one of the most gruelling.

From the 1980s onwards abroad has begun to represent something else, mutating into a variation on the lads on tour smash and grab, the Italian Job. High drama is never far away. The English manager exposed to a southern European climate can be expected to involve himself in horseplay, dramatic misunderstanding and all kinds of high-profile culture clash.

Ron Atkinson took up an offer to manage Atletico Madrid in 1987. He was sacked after three months by the tyrannical president Jesus Gil. Atkinson was pictured coming back through customs suntanned, laden with duty-free, looking for all the world like a man returned from a jolly, his mojo restored by his brush with wild abroad.

At times the manager has followed the snog-sun-punch-up

template of annual sunbed break. Graeme Souness set an early 1990s benchmark with his famous Turkish cup final episode. Souness was manager of the Istanbul club Galatasaray. Prior to the second leg of the cup final against local rivals Fenerbahce, an opposition director had described him as 'a cripple', an unkind reference to Souness's recent heart surgery.

Galatasaray duly completed their cup victory at Fenerbahce's violently intimidating Sukru Saracoglu stadium. At which point Souness took revenge by marching to the centre circle and planting a huge Galatasaray flag in the turf, causing a near-riot in the process. He'd made his point. He was duly sacked at the end of the season.

In June 2007 Chris Coleman was appointed head coach of Real Sociedad. In November of that year he arrived ninety minutes late for a press conference, offering the explanation that his washing machine had exploded. At the same time the Spanish media were reporting that Coleman had been seen dancing until the early hours of the morning in what turned out to be a student disco. Contrite, holding his hands up and taking it on the chin, Coleman admitted, 'It was very late, I've had a lot of people over from England and Wales and I've showed them San Sebastian', expressing perfectly the new managerial school of abroad as stag do, or city-break knees-up. He resigned in January and came back to manage Coventry City.

The fact remains that managerial success abroad is still a source of lurking mistrust in England. It's almost better simply to make a terrible hash of the whole thing, exploding in a tantrum of cheap sangria in the arrivals lounge, and getting yourself deported by the military police with your suitcase still unpacked. Just look at what happened to Jimmy Hogan after the heady years of the German soccer circus.

Hogan returned to England intermittently after his early successes in the axis of central Europe. By now he was being described in the British press as a 'wonder coach' and a man 'whose name as a Soccer coach is a household word from one end of the Continent to the other'. His reward, having escaped Nazi Germany with his life savings sewn into the folds of his trademark plus-four trousers, was the manager's job at Fulham.

It was a disaster. He was sacked after thirty-one matches while lying ill in hospital. The reason given was that the players 'didn't need coaching'. His dismissal wasn't even mentioned in the club's next match programme.

It's not hard to see why English football didn't take kindly to Hogan. For one thing, he kept pointing out very cogently and methodically how useless it was. This didn't go down well. In an article in the *Daily Mirror* written shortly before his dismissal he noted: 'Since I returned to England and expressed my ideas about the game, it appears that I have stepped on somebody's toes. Certain people have laughed me to scorn. Others regard me as a foreigner.'

Sadly for Hogan, nobody wanted to know about his insubstantial, fancy-dan litany of unassailable triumphs. In post-war England there seemed to be some terrible unspoken stain attached to him, an erroneous whiff of the traitor and the cheat. This was of course totally baseless. But even now Jimmy Hogan looks like another semi-biblical character, the prophet without honour in his own land. He managed Aston Villa, with a little success, before being sacked again. He did some coaching for the FA, notably in a revolutionary series of mass outdoor classes organised by Sir Stanley Rous. He coached Austria at the 1936 Berlin Olympics. And finally the World's Number One Coach became a glorified odd-job man at Burnley, and then a Yoda-like skills coach at Celtic.

He did at least enjoy a peculiar public vindication in 1953, watching from the stands as the Marvellous Magyars of Hungary – who explicitly name-checked him after the match – demolished England at Wembley, still the most shocking moment in the national team's history. Hogan was invited to the

Hungarian team's post-match celebration as a guest of honour. After much consideration he declined, apparently in a funk of patriotic guilt.

Over this period Hogan was by no means the only one to flee the mother country in search of opportunity. In a defiant trickle they had come forth. Most notably, the former England players Fred Pentland and Steve Bloomer emerged from the same First World War concentration camp to manage successfully in Spain after the armistice. Pentland in particular became a kind of 'father of Spanish football', winning the league five times with Athletic Bilbao and introducing a revolutionary short-passing game, the same style with which the Spain national team would win Euro 2008. His birthday is still celebrated at Bilbao, where he's known as El Bombino, or the Bowler Hat. Returning to England, the father of Spanish football was grudgingly re-assimilated. He managed Barrow for a single season.

These, then, were the early missionaries, the managers who got on their bike, their twin-propeller aircraft and their passenger steamship to seek an ascetic overseas vindication. This lightness of foot has remained an element of the manager's mystique. We feel at all times his readiness to leave, to seek new frontiers, to sling dramatically his hook.

Also still there – even with the waters muddied by the recent Club 18–30 managerial generation – is that sense of smock-wearing evangelist and a whiff of the preacher teacher still lingers about the manager. This is something he owes to Hogan, Pentland, and all the other banished men. Thanks to them the manager has always carried a little bit of abroad – just enough, mind, and no more – around with him in his pockets.

CHAPTER 6

The Manager Has Fun

Being a football manager isn't just a calling. It's also a massively serious business. We know this by now. In fact you'd be hard-pressed to come up with too many other callings quite so bound up with a sense of their own bowel-tightening gravity. This is the football manager's default setting. It's a steeliness assumed out of necessity, a protective armour against the many dangers that stalk his revolving dugout. The lingering threat of the cull, the terrible private misfortunes, the death by winter chill. This is no laughing matter. This is above all deeply serious.

Still, the manager has had his moments. There lurks within him something more mercurial and romantic. Gathering dust beneath his managerial bed, if we look closely enough, buried but not forgotten, we might still find his velveteen smoking jacket, his ivory-tipped cane, his managerial disco flares.

It was in the years immediately after Herbert Chapman that the manager first began to stretch his wings, given confidence, most of all, by Chapman's qualities as an operator and a figurehead. For the first time in his miserable, stooped existence, the manager had found the confidence to strut, to dandify and to emit a braying snort of laughter from the stalls. This was the era of the gadfly and the good-time Charlie.

And not just in football. The 1930s was a period of progress and modernisation everywhere. It was the decade that brought the emergence of a professional managerio–clerical middle class. The travelling salesman bestrode the land, hawking his pills, powders, books, cars, clothes, toys, self-propelling pencils, shoelaces, sporting goods, plant pots, contraceptives, cigarettes, home furnishings, pet food and sixteen kinds of miracle tooth-paste. A new kind of man had sprung into the public imagination: socially gregarious, energetic, a practical man with a loud voice and a bag of samples. In among the alternative world of unemployment and depression a tentative kind of fun was being had, a plastic prosperity enjoyed.

The manager was about to get a slice of this. Chapman's influence had been selectively absorbed. For many it was above all the licence for showmanship that appealed. So we got the gadabouts. Jack Tinn of Portsmouth became famous for his signature 'lucky' spats, which a member of his team would polish theatrically in front of the crowd before each match of Pompey's FA Cup run of 1939. In fact the spats were pretty much all the players ever saw of Tinn, who was remote, dictatorial and quite scary. One of his players, Jimmy Dickinson, described him as 'the God in the office'. By then Tinn was already safely dead.

We think of Bill Tulip, the authoritarian businessman–manager-director figurehead of Gateshead Town, notorious for 'forgetting' to put his hearing aid in while grandstanding his way through board meetings. We think also of Johnny Cochrane, who made an enduring name for himself as an emblem of stylish managerial loucheness. Cochrane was manager of Reading for just thirteen days in April 1939, sacked by his directors for being too laid back. Years later one former Sunderland player painted a vivid portrait of Cochrane's applied methodology: 'Just before a game this man wearing a bowler hat, smoking a cigar and drinking a whisky would pop his head round the dressing room door and ask, "Who are we playing today?" We would chorus, "Arsenal boss." Johnny would just say, "Oh, we'll piss that lot", before shutting the door and leaving us to it.'

These were the fun-time Frankies, the humorists who strode into office emboldened by the Chapman template, and then put their elegantly shod feet up on the desk. A step up from this we get the more socially mobile man of the world. Not all managerial gadflies were attracted simply by the fat salary, the easy authority and the bunking-off potential. There were hustlers out there too. This was the era of the entertainment entrepreneur; and in football of the impresario manager.

Albert Prince-Cox, Bristol Rovers manager of the 1930s, also made a name for himself as a boxing promoter and a big noise in wrestling. Uniquely among football managers, he once had a job delivering the weather forecast to Buckingham Palace. Prince-Cox was symptomatic of the more dynamic strain of go-getting gentleman drawn into the managerial orbit. Suddenly the manager had outside interests. He was a broker of opportunity.

He was also an estate agent. In December 1930 the *Daily Mirror* carried a pictorial spread with the heading 'Footballer's New Job', in which it presented: 'Jack Cock the international footballer describing houses to prospective clients yesterday when he began work as an estate agent at Kidbrooke.'

And there he is on the page, describing houses. Not in some grisly and mildewed smudged-glass box in between Kebab Machine and Greggs the Baker, either. In 1930 being an estate agent had an air of aspirational purpose about it. These were the coming men. In *The Waste Land* T. S. Eliot described a 'house agent' as 'one of the low, on whom assurance sits like a silk hat on a Bradford millionaire'. Eliot could almost be a post-Victorian club director, sniffily taking note of the manager's new gold watch-chain, his uppity barrack-room confidence.

For Jack Cock, this was just another iron in his cross-disciplinary fire. Before managing Millwall for four years from 1944, Cock had previously been reported missing presumed dead during the First World War, won a medal for gallantry and played for England. In between his estate-agenting and football-managing portfolio, he also sang on the stage, making his debut at the Granville Theatre in Chelsea and going on to perform at assorted London music halls. He also acted in the films, *The Winning Goal* in 1920 and 1930's *The Great Game*.

Despite his humble Cornish roots, *The Breedon Book of Managers* described Cock as 'a sophisticated socialite who dressed in expensive clothes'. In April 1946 an article in the *Daily Mirror* noted the huge crowd of schoolboys mobbing 'tubby manager Jack Cock for his autograph'. 'I'm no footballer,' Cock told the *Mirror*, no doubt shrugging wearily and raising his eyebrows. But he's not fooling us. We know he loved it.

It was around this time that the relationship between the manager and the booming popular press was explicitly consummated. Newspaper readership was going through a period of rampant inter-war expansion. Suddenly circulation wars were the thing, with football a major weapon. The manager began, tentatively, to hold court. The entertainer, the man of parts, the demagogue was in the ascendant. The vinegary football sound-bite began to fill pages between games. Rivalries were fanned. Gossip was fostered and hoarded. Manager spake unto manager across the shifting plateaux of the news page, an original new media proto-celebrity.

Television, the century's great excitement, played its part here. The manager was a popular character actor in the thrown-together cast of the early televisual universe. And for a while the BBC became a pet managerial platform, his mini-*Pravda*. Always on the look-out for airtime-fillers and cultural populists, the Corporation groomed his profile, projecting him as a strident new voice.

In this role of early managerial TV celebrity and poseur, one man stands out. George Allison became Arsenal manager after Herbert Chapman's death. Of the two Chapman may be the managerial prom king, the quarterback kid and hot-rod. But in many ways Allison is more fascinating. Chapman had hard tactics and enduring on-field success. But Allison had something else. In the story of the manager's rise to crossover superstar, he's the hidden treasure, the forgotten pioneer.

His obituary in *The Times* after his death in 1957 described him as 'a born impresario'. Allison was also an opportunist and a high roller. At his peak his friends included the Hollywood actor Marion Davies and the homegrown glamour puss Anna Neagle. He hob-nobbed with Dwight Eisenhower and George VI, who laughingly boasted to Allison that he'd once scored a goal direct from a corner ('the wind blew it in'). Within living memory of the lurking dawn of the long-dead secretary, this was the manager in his fullest upwardly mobile bloom. Allison's portrait hangs in the National Portrait Gallery. 'He had become the prototype of the modern football manager,' reads the blurb beneath it.

And so he was. Heavy-suited and meticulously hair-oiled ('I am not tall, neither am I thin,' he wrote), Allison was a thoroughly modern man in many ways. Football management was just another counter in his splendid game of social snakes and ladders. Raised in the village of Hurworth, near Darlington, he came from a relatively humble background. As a boy he desperately wanted to become a footballer, or a journalist, or at least something momentously connected with the two. He took to sticking through the letter box of the *Evening Gazette* office anonymous reports of amateur matches in which he'd played, always violently critical of his team-mates but glowing in their praise of the right back, Allison.

Eventually these missives, love notes to his own brilliant future, got him a job covering football at the paper. From there he became the *Echo*'s man in Newcastle ('I think the editor was impressed by my morning suit,' he recalled). Aged twenty-one, he became assistant to the secretary manager of Middlesbrough FC, another stepping stone across the burgeoning media-football nexus. Soon afterwards he moved to London as chief sports writer for the Hulton group of newspapers, through which he would eventually get mixed up with Arsenal.

Before that, other extraordinary things had to happen to him. Allison's real big break came in 1911 when, as a junior reporter, he seized on a chance meeting to finagle a headline interview with Lord Kitchener shortly before the coronation of George V. The results of this were life-changing. For a start Allison briefly became world-famous. He was also appointed London correspondent of the *New York Herald*, an eye-popping fifteen guineas a week beano and a shoo-in to the life of the flapping, quaffing 1930s socialite scene.

Big things kept following Allison around. In 1912 he went back to Middlesbrough to get married to Ethel Swordy. The reception was interrupted by a curt telegram from head office – 'Titanic sunk: return immediately.' This was the Allison way. He surfed the currents of the global media happening. Kitchener, the *Titanic*, the unstoppable rise of the football manager: these were the kind of events that demanded his attention.

He duly became European manager for the legendary American publisher William Randolph Hearst's vast media empire. He was a popular guest at Hearst's 240,000-acre ranch in California, a pleasure palace he described as 'so vast, so fabulous, so wondrous, so bewildering'. For a while Allison was on the payroll of the BBC, together with working as Arsenal's programme editor and club historian.

And he still had irons in his fire. He had moves nobody had seen yet. He started getting his voice out there, a voice described in his obituary as both 'rich' and 'fruity'. For the BBC he commentated on the second-ever live football broadcast, a friendly between Corinthians and Newcastle; and then on the first broadcast FA Cup final. There followed further blue riband gigs, all live and exclusive with George Allison: England v Scotland from Wembley, the Grand National and the Derby.

The football commentaries in particular made a splash. Allison was famous for his habit of saying 'By Jove!' at moments of excitement, although one listener complained to the BBC that his voice had a habit of waking her parrot, which would shout, 'Damn you, you old bugger', before agreeing to return to its perch. Allison used to commentate over a bottle of port with Derek McCulloch, known as 'Uncle Mac'. Uncle Mac was the man who read out the number of the pitch 'square' the ball was in. These squares were printed in an accompanying numbered diagram in the *Radio Times*. Hence, some say anyway, the origin of the phrase 'Back to square one', the square in which the goalkeeper stood.

Allison even carried on with the commentaries after he became Arsenal manager in 1934. He had been a director during Chapman's reign. They didn't like each other. Allison was happiest hanging out with Lord Lonsdale and letting Chapman get on with the dirty job of managing the team.

Clearly, Allison was a fame-magnet. But was he really a proper manager? Or even a very good one? Under his direction Arsenal did win the League in 1934, 1935, and 1938 and the FA Cup in 1936. But this was basically the dead hand of the Chapman era. After that Allison stuck around until 1947 and the team drifted and decayed.

Really his talents lay elsewhere: in things like being famous, cropping up everywhere, and getting his face right in the middle of where it's all going down. He was principal guest at the annual dinner of Margate Chamber of Commerce, taking time during his address to praise 'the wonderful air of Margate'. He presided at the A-list-only Sports Night dinner of the London Press Club, alongside the likes of Douglas Jardine and Stanley

Rous. He had a speaking part in the film *The Arsenal Stadium Mystery*. His line, and it's a great line, was: 'It's one-nil to the Arsenal and that's the way we like it.'

Even his house being burgled made the papers, the *Daily Mirror* noting in June 1936 that 'Mr. George Allison, manager of Arsenal Football Club, returned from a holiday in Devon on Saturday to find that his home in Prince's Park Avenue, Golders Green, had been broken into.' The details tell us a great deal. Among the things taken were 'gold diamond-shaped studs, a gold fountain pen, cuff links, five silver cigarette cases, and gold-mounted note-cases'. What a haul. What knick-knacks. What spiffy bits and bobs.

This was the manager's early booty, his Rolex and Bentley Continental. Allison got there first. The manager was gilding his comfortable suburban semi, reaching out to the new world through the tentacles of the wireless transistor and ten-point type. Allison ushered him along this path, he piloted the early limousine. He bribed the doorman and cut the queue. The manager had his boots under the table.

CHAPTER 7

The Manager Gets Angry

In the middle of all this excitement it's important to make one thing clear. The manager may have had his moments. He may have dabbled with the liberal and the fancy. But the manager is nobody's gadabout. For all the curdled ambition of his own fevered rise, he fears change. He's intolerant, short-sighted and stubborn. In essence there are plenty of things he just isn't going to stand for.

For example, long hair. Bill Nicholson, Tottenham's double-winning manager of the early 1960s, wrote a long passage in his autobiography (*Glory Glory*) about the player Alfie Conn. It's only towards the end that he stops fannying about and cuts to the chase: 'There was another reason why I was unhappy with Alfie Conn. He wore his hair extremely long in an unbecoming manner for a professional footballer. Around that period a lot of players wore their hair long and it sickened me.'

Nicholson later tries to cast his horror of hipster androgyny (he also rails against players 'bringing hairdryers to matches') as a footballing matter, citing 'the risk of having hair fall across their eyes'. But hair in the eyes is only a tiny part of it. Alec Stock, manager of Oldham, QPR and Arsenal, was even more blunt. 'A boy who lets his hair grow below his collar-line or wears jeans or an outlandishly cut jacket, will soon be out in his place,' he wrote in his 1967 book *Football Club Manager*. 'I imagine this type of youngster standing in front of a mirror and thinking to himself: "Shall I wear my red or blue ribbons today" or "By golly, I think my hair suits me this way".'

Stock wasn't alone. In 1972 Alf Ramsey picked the Leicester City striker and all-round long-hair hipster Frank Worthington to play for England. Worthington duly turned up to join the squad at the airport dressed in cowboy boots, leather trousers and black leather hat. 'Oh Christ,' Ramsey growled. 'What the fuck have I done?'

This is the real voice of the football manager. Never mind the early dabblings with the stage, the fancy new friends and that oddly troubling sense of himself as part of the entertainment business. The manager is at heart a beetle-browed wallflower. He broods and fumes. He doesn't dance.

Even now he retains a sense of himself as forever in opposition to the present. Tottering heroically, he stands as the final bulwark against the intrusion of the new, of blue and red ribbons, of Frank Worthington's leather hat.

A notion of the manager as furious reactionary curmudgeon was crystallised in the years after the Second World War. By now he had a certain standing in the world, a set of net curtains to draw against the intrusions of New Elizabethan modernity. The forces that would thrust the manager skywards were transforming the world around him. The working classes had been mobilised in war: in peace they were still on the march. The welfare state and the NHS gave a sense of worryingly universal inclusivity. People talked, ominously, about the end of the age of deference. Newly ensconced in his small carpeted office, pocket-watched and three-piece-suited, the manager really didn't like the sound of all that.

Worse, some fool had invented the teenager. The manager has never got on with the teenager. What use is the curled lip, the giddy sense of rebellion, the oiled quiff to the manager? He had no desire to rock around the clock. He remained unmoved by the notion of scooting down to Brighton to get in a rumble with some greasers. For now at least he was defiantly un-beat.

The manager's own world remained brutal and unforgiving. There were over six hundred managerial sackings between 1945 and 1965. Football itself had become increasingly violent and cynical. Tackling was a major feature of the game. Hatchet men stomped the divisions. And from the dugout the cold water and parade ground bluster of the new Puritanism permeated to all corners.

The managerial bastard had arrived. Kicking over chairs, flexing his guns, he entered with fists bunched and ready to go war. Daddy was home. And he was deeply, inconsolably cross.

Bastardism, as an approach, had already been applied with some success. Major Buckley was notably scary. One of his players, Jackie Sewell, described him as 'a very frightening man . . . who could make grown men have tears in their eyes'. Herbert Chapman was fierce, and even heartless at times.

During the 1950s this mild managerial kick was distilled, refined and fermented into a high-strength super pilsner version. Cliff Britton, manager of Everton, once remarked that his ideal team would consist of 'eleven tee-total bachelors'. Tommy Docherty was a player under Britton at Preston. 'I don't think I have ever seen a man who appears less able to relax in my life,' Docherty wrote in his autobiography. 'He demanded great discipline and we would never dare be late for training. He was a cold man, difficult to approach and lacked a sense of humour.'

Coldness was in. Humour out. In 1963 Jimmy Hagan was sacked as West Brom manager after almost coming to blows with his first team over his unyielding – his deeply principled –

refusal to let them wear tracksuit bottoms on a frosty morning. Don Howe was West Brom captain at the time. Forty-five years later he remembered it vividly. 'That winter in 1963 was very severe,' Howe told me. 'It was properly freezing. Jimmy Hagan wanted us to go out and train. And we said, couldn't we have a tracksuit? And he wouldn't have it.'

This sense of vocation, a mission to fight cowardice and the effete, found its most successful embodiment in Stan Cullis, manager of Wolves during the 1950s. Under Cullis Wolves won the League three times and played a fearless and direct form of bicep-flexing Popeye football.

An aggressive centre half, Cullis had been captain of England at the age of twenty-two. Oddly given his reputation for belligerence, he retired from playing after suffering bouts of concussion due to a 'weakness in the forehead'. Cullis was always a man of contrasts. As a manager his delicate bald head and thin, high voice, were at odds with his imposing football teams. Cullis was also a devout Christian who never swore, relying instead on the word 'flopping'.

A former sergeant major in an anti-tank regiment, at Wolves he imported wholesale the military absolutes of order and command. The writer Arthur Hopcraft described Cullis as being 'without frivolous embellishments of manner'. That's one way of putting it. Another would be 'absolutely terrifying', the view of Ron Atkinson, a ground-staff boy at Wolves in the 1950s.

In *Stan Cullis: The Iron Manager*, the player Eddie Clamp evokes the sound of the slight, tweed-suited, furiously angry Cullis turning up for work: 'I sat scores of times in the dressing rooms while tough, fit professional players waited nervously. And above the tramp, tramp of his steps . . . I could hear the Cullis voice chanting: "I . . . Will . . . Not . . . Have . . . A . . . Coward . . . In . . . My . . . Team".'

Cowards were the real enemy for the bastard. He stood, Cnut-like, against the dilution of the eternally male qualities of pain and unhappiness. Cullis saw football as an absolute litmus test of human endurance. Once, during a match one of his players, Ted Farmer, was brutally elbowed in the stomach. At half time Farmer found he was passing blood. Cullis forced him to play on, telling the club doctor, 'Wait till it comes through his backside before you take him off.' Farmer was later diagnosed with a pierced bladder and spent five days in hospital. No one from Wolves visited him.

There were likeable bastards too. Alan Brown's 1996 obituary in the *Independent* mused: 'It is difficult to imagine any football manager being harder or straighter than Alan Brown', before casting him as 'a byword for truth, frankness and rigid discipline'.

Brown worked as a policeman before becoming manager of Burnley in 1954. He made an early impression by personally digging out sections of ground for the club's indoor training pitch. At Sunderland he insisted his players follow him around while travelling to away games, ready to drop their suitcases and line up in formation whenever he paused for a moment ('It's almost military,' he explained).

Post-war, Brown formed one half of a twin-pronged hard-man aristocracy. His tag-team partner was Harry Storer. Appointed Coventry manager in 1931 at the age of thirty-three, Storer was unyielding but also complex and extrovert. By 1950 he was being described in the *Daily Mirror* as 'the kind of man who meditates with Marcus Aurelius, daydreams with Omar Khayyam and shudders with distaste when a player shirks hard tackling'. That kind of man, then.

Storer's dressing room was a trench, a scrum and a mosh pit. A constant vigil was kept for 'skivers and cissies'. At Derby he would board the team bus shouting out to his trainer, 'How many hearts have I got today?', while thumping his own slabbed and beefcaked chest.

Storer was unrepentant to the end. After his retirement he was a scout for Everton. One of his final reports, on a player the club were considering signing, consisted simply of the word 'Coward' scrawled across the reporting form.

Stan Cullis was also steadfast in his refusal to mellow, but he did become one of the first real 'personality managers' sought out regularly by the BBC for post-match thoughts. He appeared on a weekly radio show called *Talking Football*, where, when asked a question, he would repeatedly describe himself as 'not having a crystal ball'.

Had he, though, he might have been able to glimpse the lasting effects of the new managerial Puritanism of the 1950s. This is still the manager's bedrock, the raw essence of his authority. It's his karate black belt certificate, the chiv in his inside pocket.

Co-opted and subsumed, the bastard still lurks beneath the pin-stripe veneer. The manager still needs to show off his biceps, but he needs to do it quietly. As Brentford's Andy Scott says: 'Looking back fifteen years it was a case of chucking the teacups and shouting and screaming. Since the academies have been introduced the players at younger levels are spoken to differently.

'If you shout at them they've never had that before. You have to mollycoddle them. You hear the stories about the likes of Brian Clough, but you just couldn't get away with it now. You'd get sued.'

Clough, a player under Alan Brown at Sunderland, was a convert right from the start. 'The first thing Alan Brown ever said to me was, "You may have heard that I'm a bastard . . . Well they're right",' he recalled, happily.

In fact football's joint hardest men were both huge influences on Clough: Harry Storer was Sunderland manager while he was a player there. He forced the first team to act as ball boys for the youth team. He made Clough brew the tea. Giddily he drank it all in.

Peter Taylor was so moved by Storer's flinty bloke-speak haiku-isms that he later claimed he and Clough owed their 'creed' to him. And certainly Clough would recite Storer's bons mots like a personal mantra: 'Directors know nothing about football'; 'Buy players who show courage'. This was his bastard inner music.

It was from Storer that Clough picked up the idea a manager could bypass his directors and thrust himself forward as the snarling gargoyle-totem of an entire club. It was also from here that he conjured his idea of an elevated form of managerial dictatorship.

The idea that the manager must retain at all times the capacity to inspire fear was smelted into the managerial chainmail during Clough's time. It was with a sense of fond nostalgia, almost a chuckle, that Roy Keane recalled an incident at half time while he was a player at Nottingham Forest.

'When I walked into the dressing room after the game, Clough punched me straight in the face. "Don't pass the ball back to the goalkeeper," he screamed as I lay on the floor, him standing over me,' Keane wrote in his autobiography.

This notion of the manager as playground tough has remained. In 1995 Leyton Orient manager John Sitton was filmed by a Channel 4 documentary team attempting to motivate his struggling side at half time in a game they were losing 3-0. Sitton's tactics included summarily sacking one of his players and challenging two others to a fight, an invitation he ended with the words 'and you can bring your fucking dinner too'. This last statement has been widely analysed. It's still not clear what it means.

The Wales player John Hartson wrote in his autobiography that his manager Bobby Gould had challenged him to a fistfight before a World Cup qualifier against Turkey in Cardiff, an incident Hartson described as 'embarrassing, weird, disturbing and totally undignified'. Hartson had criticised Gould's selections (i.e. not picking John Hartson). He later claimed to have relented during the fight, although Gould, then in his fifties, did end up with 'scratches on his face and hair all over the place'.

In a more keenly styled altercation in 2003, Alex Ferguson was reported to have caused a minor gash to David Beckham's eyebrow during a post-match dressing room bawling-out. Ferguson kicked a stray boot that caught Beckham in the face. No apology was issued. No complaint was made. Still something visceral was stirred. Cultural commentators recast the incident as a seismic collision of old and new: boot as the ancient managerial rite of the bastard-jungle; eyebrow as emblem of the preening, cosmopolitan celebrity soccer insurrection.

The modern manager can wield his iron-man ancestry with more subtlety. The appointment of spiffy-suited disciplinarian Fabio Capello as England manager in 2008 chimed perfectly with a national mood of self-loathing that followed the chaotic failure to qualify for Euro 2008 under Steve McClaren.

The appearance of the formidable Capello in succession had a rousing hair-shirt appeal, a pleasurably astringent effect. We thrilled to his 'Iron Sergeant' nickname, the talk of his iron fist inside an iron glove. We pitied the likes of Jermain Defoe marooned on the England bench as Fabio's iron fist rested, chillingly, on his tracksuited thigh. With Capello, the threat was in the aura. Initially he was unable to speak directly to the press in English. Mute, he seemed both excitingly primitive and supremely evolved, an Armani-clad raw, basic man, helicoptered in to glare and frown and gurn.

A similar early buzz surrounded the Chelsea manager Luiz Felipe Scolari following his unveiling in June 2008. For a while Scolari appeared daily in newspapers, projected in thrilling close-up: the no-nonsense nose-width moustache, the gaucho cowboy swagger. Meeting that cool, flat stare you could almost sense the grip of the Scolari headlock and smell the oppressively masculine Scolari bodily odour.

In a Premier League grown decadent on its own quadruple-garaged excesses, the re-emergence of the Manager Who Wants To Beat You Up seemed fresh and exciting. It looked like confirmation that even through the manager's more pigeon-chested recent incarnations – the Manager Who Wants To Be Your Friend, or the Manager Who Wants To Sell You a Photocopier – the bastard may have mooched and sighed and gritted his teeth in the shadows but he never really went away.

This is a good thing. You never know when you might need to yank him out of the car boot like an old, mud-encrusted pair of wellies and thrust your cashmere-socked foot into his spidery depths once more. Who knows, the bastard might even be properly back in fashion before long, cracking skulls, removing the 'duster from his executive briefcase, a borstal-screw enforcer ranged against that modern bogeyman, the Premier League yob-millionaire.

And if our man feels like putting together a crew, there's a little spiritual back-up about the place, a ghost posse of tasty geezers. Alan Brown, Harry Storer, Stan Cullis. They're all in. They're out of their chairs. They're taking off their watches and telling their wives to go home. They're still here. And they still fancy a piece.

CHAPTER 8

The Manager Fights Aliens

As has already been noted, the manager's relationship with abroad has often been a fraught thing. Bill Nicholson, the double-winning manager at Tottenham Hotspur, was convinced of the essential decadence of abroad. In his autobiography he warned sternly against English teams 'making the mistake of adapting to the Continental way'.

In fact Nicholson's book is shot through with mistrust of things 'Continental'. Here he is taking an England Under-23 squad on tour: 'We had a nerve-racking time in Ankara. The excitable fans were hostile at the start and their attitude worsened as the goals went in . . . That was one place we were delighted to leave.'

But not the only one. On a trip to Russia with Spurs in 1959, Nicholson found 'the food was awful and the facilities more rudimentary than we were used to'. Outrage piled upon outrage. 'When we ordered tea and toast one day there was no milk or sugar for the tea, no jam or butter for the toast . . . The next day I asked for rice pudding before a match. It came in cold slabs and the players couldn't eat it.'

Two years later Spurs were drawn against Gornik of Zabrze in the Uefa Cup. 'I arranged to fly there to inspect hotels,' Nicholson shuddered. 'The officials led me along the track and out towards a grubby-looking hotel . . . The hotel was filthy inside . . . "We can't stay here," I said. "It's so dirty. Look at that carpet."'

This is a common reaction. The manager stands, lip curled, wringing his hands, ranged against the alien and the fancy. Look at that carpet, he says. Boiled sausage for breakfast. The bread doesn't even toast. It's no wonder, is it? No bleeding wonder.

Nicholson actually did pretty well out of abroad. He was one of the progressives. His Spurs team won the Cup Winners' Cup in 1963 and dished it out overseas with some success. This is not the typical experience. In fact English football's relationship with the world beyond its borders is best seen as a series of crises. Terrible upsets, humiliations, scalding blows: this is what happens when you engage with abroad.

At the same time these brushes with abroad have also been oddly fruitful for the manager personally. After all, no crisis is complete without a crisis management team. Disasters tend to conjure their own unlikely hero, the lone figure rising from the rubble, padded sports coat caked with dust, a wounded puppy beneath one arm, and a look of furious destiny in his piercing, albeit rather bloodshot, blue eyes.

Abroad would come to play a crucial role in the manager's late flowering, although at the end of the Second World War this was all still to come. The manager had reached a professional plateau. The elevation from the primal soup of secretary-hood had been capped by the stunning advances of the Chapman-Buckley era. This was followed by a broadening of the role as the manager kicked up his heels and enjoyed a rather stiff-backed boogie. Finally, his position had been entrenched, his gains aggressively ring-fenced, by the bludgeoning presence of the bastard.

At the end of which, the manager had a certain standing. By the early 1950s he was a face. He was on the scene. He might even have started to wonder, at the end of another hard day of shouting, pioneering the plastic cone and giving interviews to BBC radio, if this was really all life had to offer him.

The manager needn't have worried. An iceberg was approaching. This was the big one, an event that would drop-kick him decisively into the foreground as master of disaster, office fire marshal and national emergency co-ordinator. It wouldn't be an easy process. But that was OK. The manager likes bad things and, it turns out, bad things like the manager.

English football's single greatest trauma was inflicted at Wembley stadium on 25 November 1953, the day the national team lost its unbeaten home record against European teams. It's hard to overstate the effect of the 6–3 defeat by Hungary. It wasn't just that it was a footballing thrashing. The real damage was a more visceral thing, a kind of mass revelatory freaking out. For English football this was the day the earth stood still.

Bobby Robson was one of many to have ogled uncomprehendingly from the Wembley stands. 'We saw a style of play, a system of play that we had never seen before,' the future England manager recalled. 'All these fantastic players, they were men from Mars as far as we were concerned.'

Bobby's Martians go right to the heart of the Hungary happenings. For English football, this was first contact. Abroad now existed. That much was beyond dispute. Not only was there intelligent life out there. It was hostile – and horribly advanced.

The early 1950s was already a golden era for the alien invasion. Shattering cosmic interventions were a daily fixture. Cinema films on release in the months leading up to November 1953 included: *The Flying Saucer, The Thing from Another World, Radar Men from the Moon, Cat-Women of the Moon, Invaders from Mars, It Came from Outer Space, Phantom from Space* and *The War of the Worlds*, which came out six months before the events in the

Wembley area of 25 November. It's hardly surprising, really, that Bobby had Martians on his mind.

Flying saucers in particular were everywhere. In response to a rush of public sightings in 1950, the Ministry of Defence had set up something called the Flying Saucer Working Party. Government psychiatrists published statements blaming the sightings on mass hallucinations. A tiny man-made saucer called the Ectoplat was displayed at the Festival of Britain. There were even newspaper reports of a daring new hairstyle called 'The Saucer', described in the *Daily Mirror* as 'a whirligig of real hair with a lace background, it can be pinned anywhere on the head. Price is two guineas'.

And all the while 'encounters' were being reported in the press. Just two months before the Hungary match the *Daily Mirror* reported that someone called George Adamski had 'talked with a man who pirouetted down to earth from the planet Venus in a Flying Saucer'. Adamski's alien had 'a voice slightly higher-pitched than an Earth-man's', plus 'his fingers were long and tapering, like an artistic woman's'.

Previously the same paper had revealed that a twenty-nine-year-old businessman called Peter Penrose 'believes he has the answer to the mysterious Flying Saucers which have been reported over various parts of the world'. Penrose had, the *Mirror* reported, been in daily contact with a being called Fezial, 'the Planet Master of Btrorp'. Sadly Penrose could give no hard news on what the saucers actually wanted, but he did reveal that 'Obeying Fezial's orders, I have cancelled a holiday I planned to spend in Ireland.'

One thing was clear. Aliens were hot. Hyper-evolved, semi-humanoid figures were stalking the inner atmosphere. And Hungary, missionaries from the Stalinist USSR, were at Wembley. 'Gentle sunshine filtered through the greyness and filled the vast arena with golden light as the players came out,' the *Guardian* noted in its match report, effortlessly conjuring the ethereal whine of the B-movie alien soundtrack.

Even the Hungarian players seem to have evoked something of the galactic traveller. They were small and unusually athletic, although much would also be made of their captain Ferenc Puskas's paunch and his short bandy legs. They dressed funny too. Billy Wright, England's captain, recalled, 'I looked down and noticed that the Hungarians had on these strange, light-weight boots, cut away like slippers under the ankle bone. I turned to big Stan Mortensen and said, "We should be alright here, Stan, they haven't got the proper kit."'

England were duly thrashed by the small-booted invaders. They were skeleton-rayed. Hungary scored after ninety seconds. Their third goal involved a drag back by Puskas so sublime one commentator suggested erecting a plaque at Wembley to commemorate the moment. And to prove it wasn't a fluke the two teams met again six months later in Budapest. This time the result was different. This time Hungary won 7-1.

Even the names of the Hungarian players had something thrillingly Martian about them: Sandor Kocsis, Nandor Hidegkuti, Vroxxar the Mighty. These were some scary names for footballers. The *Mirror* called Hungary 'a team the like of which has not been seen'. Walter Winterbottom, England's team manager, described them as being able to 'throb and pulse and surge as no other team has done'. Hunkered around their pick-ups, brandishing their pitchforks and blunderbusses, the townsfolk were duly terrified.

There had of course been signs that something like this was coming. Since the end of the war the manager himself had begun to engage with abroad on his own terms, venturing out alone into the California desert with just his home-made satellite dish and crackling FM radio.

George Raynor had managed Sweden to a gold medal at the 1948 Olympics, and would lead them to a World Cup final against Brazil ten years later. Two weeks before England's Hungary disaster Raynor took his Sweden team to Budapest and promised them he would 'paint Stalin's moustache red' if they won (they drew 2-2).

Walter Crook had gone from finishing bottom of the Third Division North with Accrington Stanley to helping establish Ajax of Amsterdam as one of the world's great clubs. And best of all Jesse Carver, a Newcastle player before the war, spent the years after it managing Holland, Juventus, Lazio, Torino, Genoa, Internazionale and Sampdoria. Carver then had a brief spell at West Brom, during which he revolutionised training and physical preparation. He left when the club refused to make him manager. It hadn't occurred to the directors that they needed one.

Wild-haired ramblers, alien abductees high on moonshine, the likes of Carver and Raynor had been shunned before the events of 1953. This would change. The second generation of managers to engage with abroad were welcomed gingerly back into the fold. FA Secretary Sir Stanley Rous even secretly offered the England job to Carver in 1954, a fact kept secret – in true conspiracy-theory style – by the journalist Brian Glanville for over forty years.

This was the tone of English football's first great crisis, the crisis of abroad. In retreat, the natives sought out their own grizzled resistance leader. One man presented himself. No prizes for guessing who. He's the one standing on the touchline, pointing and shouting at other people.

By now the manager was well established. An everyman, a climber and a missionary, a bully and a theorist, he had our sympathy. There was a sense of some *nouvelle vague* of coming managers, plugged right into the burgeoning notion of a very 1950s kind of modernity. Men like Vic Buckingham, debonair, happy-go-lucky, a former coach of Oxford University and amateur team Pegasus, who arranged a series of exciting friendlies against European teams when he was manager of West Brom. Buckingham would later manage Barcelona and 'discover' Johan Cruyff while manager of Ajax.

In England he was the most high-profile example of a subset perhaps best known as the Manager Who Talks On The Phone. Buckingham would invariably be pictured while frowning into a large Bakelite telephone. This showed that he was not just popular, but also modern. That he had associates and contacts. And that he knew their phone numbers.

So the manager had some heat. He had a gathering sense of some vital role yet to be played out. He also had a telephone. All he needed now was a storyline. Hungary 1953 gave the manager his 'what if'. Within living memory of the backroom secretary-nerd, the manager had received his call to action as leader of the intergalactic resistance, riding shotgun with his growing corps of sombre-faced coaches. He had a mandate. He had a sheaf of hastily drafted emergency powers. The only question was, what would he do with it all?

CHAPTER 9

The Manager Goes to School

After the shattering defeat by Hungary in 1953 there were really only two sensible approaches left to the problem of abroad. The manager, always ahead of the curve, became expert in both. The first method was the denial. The Wembley incident, even if we acknowledge such an incident did take place, has been greatly exaggerated. This was the essence of the denial. Yes, we all thought we saw something. But did we really? The denial involved an almost immediate back-track. It involved a burying of the head in the sand. The denial worked. It remains very popular.

The first great proponent of the denial was Stan Cullis of Wolves. Cullis had already made his name through a successful strain of managerial bastardry. The England team thrashed by Hungary at Wembley had been captained by his skipper Billy Wright. It had played the Wolves way, based around punting heavy-booted long passes to wingers or forwards, who would then jostle and chase their way towards goal.

Cullis wasn't about to give up on the good stuff. In tandem with his gimp and sidekick, the former RAF man Wing

Commander Charles Reep, he set about revising the Hungary happening. Reep provided statistical analysis of the match that seemed to suggest Hungary had only won because they were better at punting long passes in the direction of their forwards. And so Cullis maintained that the silken superiority had been a mass hallucination. The little green Hungarian men didn't exist. There was a perfectly logical explanation for all of this.

He did get his way, after a fashion. In 1954 Wolves hosted Honved of Hungary in a friendly at Molineux. This was a chance to shatter the myth. Ron Atkinson was one of the Wolves apprentice staff who, under Cullis's instructions, watered the Molineux pitch until it resembled a bog.

'Honved came out to play in their short shorts and T-shirts with lightweight boots,' Atkinson remembered. 'They were 2-0 up in no time, playing delightful football. Wolves with their billowy shirts, long shorts and big heavy boots seemed so ponderous in comparison. Yet Honved slowly but surely began to get bogged down in the increasing mud and Wolves with their characteristic long ball style gradually began to grind down the Hungarians. My club eventually won the game 3-2 in front of an ecstatic 50,000 crowd . . . There is no doubt in my mind that, had Cullis not ordered me and my mates to water the pitch, Honved would have won by about 10-0.'

The fact that only the second half was televised live capped Cullis's coup. Within a year of the Wembley happenings English football – with the decisive intervention of mud – had managed to obscure fatally the truth of the Hungarian invasion. Watched by millions of BBC viewers, the anti-conspiracy theorists had their flagship moment. The first ever grainy, dubious alien non-existence film had been put into circulation.

This strand of aggressive denial reached its fullest expression in Charles Hughes, the FA's zealous director of coaching between 1982 and 1997. Hughes was also a disciple of Reep, seduced by his abacus-level theorem, his roundhead simplifications. In essence Hughes was an isolationist. After the intoxicating victory for Pele and Gerson's team at the 1970 World Cup he famously declared, 'We have nothing to learn from the Brazilians.'

This represents denial fanned to an idiotic, cheek-puffing extreme. But there was another approach open to the aspirant managerial theorist, and an equally empowering one. If the manager chose not to deny, he could become an appeaser and a sympathiser. He could open his footballing doors of perception. He could tell us they came in peace.

The chief mover in this was Walter Winterbottom, England's first manager, and the man who had coached the routed 1953 team. In a big budget adaptation of the Hungary happening, Winterbottom represents the twitchy homespun boffin, the number-cruncher swishing about the fringes in his lab coat and thick specs. Winterbottom is Jeff Goldblum pointing at the skies, fiddling with his homemade walkie-talkie, waspishly schooling the stern-faced President in his post-Armageddon bunker.

In many ways Hungary 1953 made Winterbottom. This might seem odd, given that he was England manager at the time, but it was essentially a nominal post. One of the strange things about the fallout from that day is that not a single newspaper report on the match mentioned the England manager by name. No Winterbottom-must-go campaign. No morphing of his boyish features into a cauldron of goulash. Amid all the hand-wringing, he didn't get a look in.

The role was different of course. Winterbottom was director of coaching as well as England manager. In essence he was the nation's centrally appointed PE teacher. Tall, well-spoken and a little otherworldly, he was also an analyst and a dreamer. In 1961 he published a book called *Soccer Partnership*. His former captain Billy Wright is supposed to have been involved in this venture, but it's pure Winterbottom. Chapter 2 begins with the sentence 'Art is many things to many men.' Other chapter-opening zingers include 'The dynamic cycle of birth, life and death, with its attendant change and decay, is immutable' and 'Football is a wonderful game . . . a hundred flowers grow in its garden.'

Florid and misty-eyed he may have been, but Winterbottom believed in coaching. He believed in learning from the rest of the world. He believed in abroad. All of this attracted its share of lip-tightening scorn. As he noted of his own appointment in 1946, 'There was resistance to the very fact of having an England team manager, there was resistance to pre-match training sessions and meetings of players, there was resistance to the whole, new, ambitious Football Association plan for a national coaching programme.'

Here, as ever, the manager was surfing a tide of contemporaneity. The 1950s was in many ways a golden age of social mobility, working-class aspiration and hearty, ambitious men in shirtsleeves frowning over night-school books. Children from working-class families had begun to move on to study at college and university. By the mid-1950s, only one man in three had the same social status by occupation as his father.

Perhaps unexpectedly, this was all kicked off by Labour's defeat at the 1951 general election to a Conservative Party promising to 'Set the People Free'. A spirit of emancipation was in the air. Rationing was coming to an end. There were things to buy in the shops and a sense of a burgeoning kitchen-sink American consumer economy.

Televisions, refrigerators and record players were now considered a basic requirement. Between 1951 and 1961 car ownership rose by 250 per cent, as growth in professional jobs swelled the boundaries of middle-class prosperity. As Don Howe told me fifty years later, 'It was an exciting time. Just look at cars. At that time we were a car-manufacturing country. And all of a sudden the Italians started coming up with different model cars. They introduced the more streamlined car. Well, it was happening in football too. There was a streamlined way of playing, and a way of thinking about playing.'

Fancy cars, higher education, apprenticeships, night school, skiffle, vacuum cleaners, the winkle-picker and the milk bar. These were the kind of things the 1950s had produced. And for the manager, too, great advances were in the offing. Winterbottom had brought something new to the palette, the manager as chalk-squiggling Varsity egghead.

So neatly did he fit the role that Winterbottom's own pre-blackboard days are often overlooked. Before the war he had played briefly for Manchester United, using his wages to pay his way through Carnegie Physical Education College. Starting off at the FA his role was an advisory one, a go-between for the selection committee. Painstakingly Winterbottom would chisel his way further into the ossified sedimentary layers of the associ-ation, tunnelling ever closer to the distant oxygen of real power and influence.

In truth it was never enough. Before the Hungary match Winterbottom had overseen the other great shock for the national team, the 1-0 defeat to the part-timers of the USA at the 1950 World Cup. He knew then that something had to be done. And so it was. As he recalled in his book: 'Action was taken. At a meeting of the international Committee on that date, it was decided that a Technical Sub-Committee should be appointed consisting of the chairmen of each Selection Committee – Senior, Intermediate, Amateur, Youth – with power to consult directors, managers and players.'

Oddly, this radical action, the setting up of a subsidiary under-under-committee, failed to have any real effect. But other initiatives introduced by Winterbottom bore more fruit. He oversaw the first ever managerial coaching badge course. Through this he began to acquire his own disciples, a small, bright-eyed cult, a Dead Poets Society of similarly minded pro-gressives. Ron Greenwood later recalled: 'Walter was a leader, a messiah, he set everyone's eyes alight.' Bobby Robson called him 'a prophet'.

Don Howe, who played under Winterbottom many times, agreed: 'He was inspiring. He used to go round other countries looking at tactics, learning about them. It gave you confidence as a player. He'd do it on the blackboard, he'd use a lot of lines showing where players ought to be. I found it fascinating.'

Wavy-haired in flannel trousers and heavy brogues, the prophet continued to preach his anti-apartheid of learning for all. In 1959 he led a managerial course at Lilleshall country house that featured Tommy Docherty, Frank O'Farrell, Bob Paisley, Malcolm Allison, Billy Bingham, Peter Taylor, Dave Sexton, Les Cocker and Malcolm Musgrove. The manager was tarting up his CV and presenting himself as a card-carrying professional. Hungary had made this possible, and in Winterbottom the manager had found a teacher who was both kindly and zealous.

Unfortunately he was also enduringly naive. His players often saw him as donnish; an intellectual, but also a nerd, killjoy and twit. Winterbottom didn't always help himself. He railed against the presence of billiard tables at football clubs, suggesting their replacement by 'a large indoor gymnasium and a recreation room with a library of books'. Sure thing, Walt. The boys are going to go for that one.

During one England trip he took the squad to see a Grecian ballet at the Konzerthaus in Zurich. Winterbottom recalled that the ballet's opening scene featured a woman dressed in Greek robes slowly sinking down between two tall candlesticks while 'a solitary piano played insidiously'. After several long minutes of hushed silence Raich Carter announced in a loud voice, 'There goes big Swift on his knees again!' Winterbottom's players were ejected from the theatre for excessive giggling ('There was no controlling them'). Unfazed, they headed upstairs, gatecrashed a private party and 'before long Mortensen was doing two-finger exercises on the piano with the others "Lambeth-walking" around the floor as they commandeered the whole party'. And no doubt the Konzerthaus extended an open invitation for the FA to return any time.

In truth Winterbottom's disciples were in the minority. Egged on by the competing ideology of the denial, there were many who found his mania for self-improvement disconcerting, wrong-headed and vaguely irritating. Stan Cullis talked darkly about his players coming back from England meetings with 'funny ideas', at a stage in English football history when, to be frank, any idea was a funny idea.

And so for a period Winterbottom became a lightning rod for a strain of boffin-bashing, the sneering anti-intellectualism that still lurks within English football's dark heart. Tommy Lawton openly ridiculed Winterbottom's blackboard, on which he drew 'so many lines and squiggles you couldn't see the pitch. I got a migraine looking at the diagrams.'

In an interview with the BBC Lawton recalled one meeting in particular: 'Finally me and Stan [Matthews] had enough of it. I shouted from the back of the room, "Look, Walter, let's stop all this guff. It's simple. Get the ball out to the wing to Stan, get him to cross it and I'll head it into the net and then we can go home". Stan and me got up and walked out of the team meeting.'

This kind of thing would linger on even into the 1960s when the young Graham Taylor, future England manager, became the youngest-ever FA qualified coach at the age of twenty-two, while he was still playing for Grimsby Town. Taylor was a grammar school boy himself, and would go on to complete his English A-level at night school. 'The FA ran these courses, but there was still this feeling that if you were being coached by people who hadn't been professional footballers there wasn't much acceptance of that,' Taylor told me.

'English football is still scared of theory. And yet we all know there's a major difference between being a good player and being a good coach. The very top player, there was this feeling they did things by instinct. There hasn't been that willingness to accept that you can actually improve people by coaching them.'

If the classroom sulk was scarcely in the managerial grand plan, there was at least a sense here of some polarised intellectual turf war being fought, the battle of the chalkboard-ideology and the no-bleeding-ideology-at-all-thank-you-very much. It took the manager into places he'd never been before, into the realm of the theoretical, the abstract and the Zurich ballet.

And whichever side you lined up on, the defeat by Hungary had given the manager his mission. He now had a belief system, some prejudices, and a crazy dream. The growing anxieties of the new world would do the rest, fostering that sense of the manager as change-maker and tracksuited saviour with his blackboard, his scowling patriotism and his magic transformational sugar lumps.

Before Hungary he was merely an angry man telling other men how to kick a ball. After Hungary he became a keeper of the flame and a shepherd. Walter Winterbottom may have blazed this trail, but in the end he proved no more than a popgun theorist. He spread his wings to fly but found himself immobile, weighted down by the clutching hands of the FA International Selection Committee, the Technical Advisory Committee, the Snuffling Post-Lunch Snooze in the Smoking Room Committee and his own failure to strike the right folksy, populist notes.

In the aftermath of the Hungary defeat Winterbottom did succeed in staging a redesign of the England kit, opting for a Magyar-style V-neck shirt and replacing the baggy shorts. Sadly, this would remain his most visible achievement. Six years later he finally got the chance to pick the England team. An experimental XI lost 3–2 in Sweden. After that it was back to the committee.

It would take another man to build on Winterbottom's tactful manoeuvrings within the Football Association. He may have introduced the broader notion of the manager as egghead, but

Winterbottom did almost nothing to speed the development of the England manager's job into what it would become, the defining gloss on the notion of manager as international states-man and mass media lightning rod.

Alf Ramsey, his successor, was the real mover here. Ramsey played in the 1953 Wembley defeat by Hungary. It proved his final international. Prior to that Ramsey had also played in the humiliation at the hands of the USA in Belo Horizonte. Winterbottom may have emerged relatively unscarred from these traumas but Ramsey bore a deeper mark. Unlike Winterbottom, he fed on this kind of thing. In fact he carried his own personal swag-bag of grievances and black-eyes, something that would provide a thrilling turbo-charge to his advances as England man-ager.

Incidentally, they still talk about that match in Hungary too. It even has its own filmic resonances. In 1999 the Hungarian cineaste Peter Timar wrote and directed a film called *6:3*, aka *Past Plays Itself*. It's set in London in 1953. A strange creature called Tutti goes to watch the big game at Wembley and ends up befriending a street cleaner called Helen, who takes pity on him and allows him to live inside her rubbish bin.

We get grandiose national alien invasion fantasy. They get cheeky arthouse cinema short. But then, we got the manager too, with all his trapped energy, and his ultimately destructive sense of dramatic personal empowerment.

CHAPTER 10

The Manager Is No Longer Becoming
a Newsagent

In any history of the manager Matt Busby is an overpoweringly central figure. He's not so much a keystone as a vast, looming monolithic Stonehenge all of his own. Every manager has his own distinct place, and all tend to support one another in the vast superstructure that is manager hood. If we were attempting to construct a house out of managers, Herbert Chapman might be the front-door handle, Jimmy Hogan the outside light, Ron Atkinson a briefly fashionable 1980s Habitat salt shaker, Alec Stock the relentlessly jabbering radio in the bathroom and Jose Mourinho the expensively quilted invitation to an exclusive Eurotrash yacht party propped up on the mantelpiece.

Busby, for his part, would be the entire one-piece steel frame holding the ground floor together. Not to mention the wiring, the plumbing, the wallpaper, the smell of fresh bread in the kitchen, the external damp course, the attic conversion and that vital, indefinable sense of being a house rather than a home.

The strange thing about Busby, in the middle of all this professional quintessence, is that he isn't a particularly vivid figure in himself. There is no distinct Busby twang, no circulating internet list of Busby witticisms, no enduring sense of the Busby physique, the Busby hairstyle or even the Busby voice. He's just there, opaque, all-enclosing and immovable.

It would be easy to say that Busby's achievements speak for him. This is a man who became Manchester United manager in 1945 with the club bankrupt, the ground a bombsite and the trophy cabinet last troubled in 1911. As Bill Shankly later recalled: 'I happened to be stationed in Manchester when the blitz came to the city and I saw Old Trafford a few days after it had been blitzed. When I looked at it I thought that's the end, there'll never be another football team again.'

But there was. Just over a decade after Busby took charge United were among the most powerful clubs in Europe. Within twenty-five years they were installed, in perpetuity, as the most popular club in the world. So much for Busby's achievements, then. They do tell a story but not the whole story. What endures is a presence, tenacious and all-pervasive, something abstract and unapproachably grand.

You find it in little details. Busby is the only manager ever to feature in a Beatles song lyric. In 'Dig It', on the album *Let It Be*, John Lennon sings:

> Like the FBI and the CIA
> And the BBC, BB King
> And Doris Day
> Matt Busby
> Dig it, dig it, dig it
> Dig it, dig it, dig it, dig it, dig it, dig it, dig it, dig it

Looking at this again, the first thing that strikes you is, what's Doris Day doing in there? The second thing is, did they really need so many 'dig its'? But then you read the list: BBC, BB King, FBI, CIA, Matt Busby. That sounds about right. 'Dig It' was written in 1970. By then Busby already had the air of an ancient and much-valued institution, something stoical and comforting, like the World Service, or milkmen, or the Natural History Museum.

Other managers might have worked at bringing the manager thrillingly, albeit sporadically, into the mainstream. Busby didn't really care about that. He communicated, through his slow-burning presence, the idea that a football club could be something important, central to a community or even to a nation's concept of itself.

Outside of that he just got on with being Matt Busby and the world quivered in his presence. In 1969 Busby was voted the UK's seventh most popular man. Not its seventh most popular taciturn Scottish football manager: the seventh most popular male human in the country, cutting it with the big boys, the Prince Charleses, the Mick Jaggers, the John Betjemans. This despite the fact that he rarely gave interviews, never sought the glare of the walnut-veneer TV analysis studio and basically kept himself to himself.

This would be a strange phenomenon in any history. For the manager it represents a triumphant combination of individual force of character, and an answering communal need. Busby achieved great things. His story was tinged with crushing, heart-wringing tragedy. But the world was also ready for him. Half a century on from the tentative shedding of the secretary's stammered consonants, his dusty backroom desk, the manager had evolved sufficiently to stand centre stage and feed the national appetite for a certain kind of public figure.

In many ways the interesting thing about Busby is not so much what he did, as what he meant to other managers. Pre-Busby, the job had a certain substance. But it wasn't, strictly speaking, a vocation. Between the end of the Second World War and 1968, 25 per cent of all serving managers had changed jobs at least once a year. In Arthur Hopcraft's book *The Football Man* he notes the existence of two types of manager: the 'most respected' and 'the ill-equipped kind who flit from one club to another for a few opportunist years before giving up for good and settling for the used car trade or the dance hall business'.

This sounds about right. Before Busby the job of football manager didn't really stick. It was a temp thing, a hot-desk thing, a gap-year thing. Being a manager wasn't what you did; it was just what you, you know, *did*. Charles Foweraker, Bolton manager between 1919 and 1944, started off working as the club gateman. Bill Beer was a sheep farmer for several years in Australia before coming back to manage Birmingham City. Archie Macaulay, manager of Norwich in the 1950s, was a tactical innovator, widely credited as having invented the 4-3-3 formation. He left the profession to become a traffic warden in west London. Eddie Hapgood was manager of Bath City until 1956. He retired to run a youth hostel.

Joe Mercer, later caretaker manager of England, worked as a butcher before getting his decisive break at Sheffield Wednesday. According to Hopcraft he was 'busily boning bacon' when a journalist came in and suggested he apply for the vacant position. Mercer phoned the club and was offered the job. Colin Veitch was manager of Bradford City for two years in the 1920s. It's easy to see why this might not have diverted him completely. Other assorted Veitch occupations included scholar, playwright, theatre director, conductor, composer and personal friend of George Bernard Shaw.

It wasn't all literary friendships and pork-based meat products for the massed ranks of the occasional manager. For several decades there was a notable subset of manager-newsagents. Fred Cox, one-time manager of Portsmouth and Gillingham, retired in 1970 to run a newsagent's in Kent. Edmund Goodman resigned at Crystal Palace in 1933 to run a grocery store in Anerley. Norman Dodgin, Oldham manager between 1958 and 1960, left football to run a tobacconist's in Exeter. Henry

Johnston, who played in the famous 1953 Matthews FA Cup final, went from Blackpool manager to the next-best thing, running a newsagent's in the town.

After Busby this kind of thing just dried up. The manager-dilettante, the half-manager, no longer fitted the template. The big thing about Busby, looking at that set jaw, those steely eyes, the overwhelming sense of personal destiny, was that he wasn't about to retire to become a traffic warden. Opening a newsagent's in Stretford never figured in his plans. Busby was manager to the core. Cut him and he bled manager. Open him up, take a look at his entrails, you'd see, not jobbing sheep farmer, but manager, manager, manager.

This was Busby's gift to those that followed. He gave them a calling. He induced a collective doing-up of the top button, a sucking in of the gut and a hardening of the ambitions. He made the manager not so much a star, as a fixture, an unavoidable feature of the quotidian, like the minister for agriculture or the Pope.

The job got harder, and also longer. It became a matter of obsession. During the 1978–9 season the Southampton manager Lawrie McMenemy travelled over a hundred thousand miles, spoke at more than a hundred functions, moved house five times and had a total of three days off.

In his 1967 book *Football Club Manager* Alec Stock, manager of Fulham, described a routine of working all day every day ('I rarely have lunch: I'm a one-meal-a-day man'). By Wednesday he'd be discussing players' personal problems with his chairman ('One has income tax trouble, another has a sick son, a third is thinking of getting married'). The sixteen-hour days were capped with a trip to a match every night of the week: '4 p.m. Match out of town (Leicester, Swindon, Portsmouth, anywhere) so prepare to leave. Chairman so keen that unless a match is on the schedule I feel I'm cheating. And if I go home I'm like a bear with a sore head and my family, too, start wanting to know why I'm not at a match.'

Besides his gruelling obsession, Busby also gave the manager his narrative arc. As Eamon Dunphy wrote in his excellent biography *Strange Kind of Glory*: 'His was the great football story.' So Busby provided football with its first great Arthurian legend, its rom-com template, its Bronze Age holy book. His emergence was perfectly timed. Busby got there first, seized his moment and he'll never be shifted. He's ours now. And those that have followed, even those who achieved more, have simply been expanding, referencing or generally riffing on the Busby role.

This was a story that began on the road. Busby arrived in Manchester Dick Whittington-style, carrying a suitcase with just a pair of football boots and a slice of his mother's homemade cake. Hard-earned success as a player with Manchester City and Liverpool was curtailed by war. After which Busby set about his true calling as a crusader, the first manager to transform single-handedly an entire football club.

Looking back it's a story made up of romance, tragedy – the Munich air crash that killed eight members of his young team – and almost unbearably cathartic triumph as United won the European Cup ten years later. That his team should fall sharply into decline after his own retirement the following year was an unintended final twist. This was Busby's gift to the manager: a never-ending story, immaculate in its details.

And after Busby you were either in or you were out, no half-measures, no ice cream parlour on Bournemouth sea-front, no south London sweet shop empire. This was serious. This was a calling. The manager was on Busby time now.

CHAPTER 11

The Manager Is Your Dad

Busby gave the manager his vocation. He lent him a lasting air of the seeker and the follower, the disciple of Sir Matt of the ideal managerial life. This is the Busby-shaped RSJ that spans the length of the haphazardly extended managerial mansion.

So much for the bigger picture. Busby also bequeathed the manager something else, a quality bound up with his own unusual presence. Busby has been described often as paternal or as a fatherly presence. He wasn't just the daddy of the early managers. He was also the first real managerial daddy. He might not have looked like your dad. He might not have sounded or acted anything like your dad. But, even now, he still reminds you, oddly, of your dad. Or someone else's dad. Or the ideal dad you kind of wish you'd had instead of your own dad, who has, as yet, shown no indication he might quietly and single-handedly create one of the world's great sporting clubs.

The manager-as-your-dad is a powerful archetype. In his book *Fever Pitch* Nick Hornby writes about the unusual similarities, even physically, between the long-serving Arsenal manager George Graham and his own father. Most football supporters have felt this. It's deeply uncomfortable, vaguely embarrassing, and bound up no doubt in some forbidding Freudian nightmare of projection and yearning. But it still keeps happening.

It does a job for the manager, too. The manager-as-father is also a source of his power. The manager plays on this. He twitches the thread. He toys with our finer feelings. He mercilessly plunges in the knife and wrings out every last ounce of terrible guilt-by-proxy. This is the manager's nature. He does whatever is necessary to survive. If we want him to bear an uncomfortable resonance of the paternal and the dad-ish, he'll do it. But it's going to hurt us a lot more than it's going to hurt him.

Barry Fry, an original Busby Babe, was at Manchester United for four years as a junior and reserve team player in the 1950s. Fry is one of the most cheerful and garrulous people you could ever hope to meet. But mention Busby's name to him and his voice changes instantly. Weirdly, and unexpectedly, he gets serious.

'Matt Busby had an aura,' Fry says. 'He was just totally different. He had total respect as soon as he walked into a dressing room, or any room for that matter. Everybody wanted to please him. He always took care to see all the apprentices were OK. He took care of you like a father. I know [George] Besty felt the same way too. He was there for you like a father.'

How did this happen? Pre-Busby there wasn't much in the manager's bearing to suggest such an explicit paternal quality might be within his emotional range. It seems to have come down to an issue of personality, and to that unique Busby presence. Former United player Eamon Dunphy described his first meeting with Busby after the then-Manchester United director had finally agreed to have him act as his biographer. Dunphy finds the great man 'immensely charming'. He has 'a remarkable

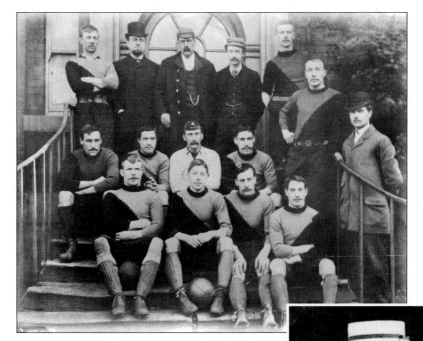

Above: Wolves' 1893 FA Cup winners. Manager Jack Addenbrooke is on the periphery (right). (Colorsport)

Right: The tragic Syd King, 1905. (Colorsport)

Below: A time traveller from the distant future, Herbert Chapman in 1932, with Alex James (right) before the FA Cup final. (Getty Images)

George Allison (second right), football's first great managerial impresario, pursued by journalists before the 1936 FA Cup final. (Colorsport)

The wandering Jimmy Hogan (right) as Aston Villa manager, standing next to Scott Duncan of Ipswich Town in 1939. (Getty Images)

Wolves' Major Frank Buckley, and his dogs, in 1939 managerial finery: cheerful, raffish and dictatorial. (Getty Images)

Jack Cock, estate agent, war hero, music hall singer, film actor, restaurateur and, in 1947, manager of Millwall. (Colorsport)

Alec Stock in his office at Yeovil, 1949.

(PA Archive/Press Association)

Walter Winterbottom tries his best not to look like a PE teacher, England training in 1950. (Topfoto)

Stan Cullis, Wolves' Iron Manager between 1948 and 1964. (Topfoto)

Alan Brown in 1964: 'a byword for truth, frankness and rigid discipline'. (Topfoto)

Above: Alf Ramsey stays seated as England win the World Cup, 1966. (Gerry Cranham/Offside)

Right: The manager as your dad. Matt Busby escorts George Best along a train platform, 1971. (Action Images/MSI)

Below: Heavyweight personas: Brian Clough and Muhammad Ali, Madison Square Garden, 1971. (Popperfoto/Getty Images)

At the snooker table in 1972, family manager Jock Stein and players, including Kenny Dalglish (left), Danny McGrain (third left) and Billy McNeill (right). (SMG/Press Association)

Patriarch to a strict and unforgiving family. Don Revie at Elland Road, July 1972, with dossier in the foreground.

(Gerry Cranham/Offside)

A unique personal electricity: Bill Shankly communes with the Anfield crowd, April 1973. (Topfoto)

Sunderland's Bob Stokoe prepares to launch into the most famous managerial sprint of all time at the 1973 FA Cup final. (Colorsport)

Right: The love-god template: Malcolm Allison, 1973. (Getty Images)

Below: Back row from left, Derek Dougan, Malcolm Allison and, right, Jack Charlton; front row, Brian Clough and Brian Moore; some of 1974's woozy, kipper-tied ITV World Cup panel. (Getty Images)

face'. He's also 'handsome as a knight should be'. His is 'a strong and imposing physical presence', which carries 'something graceful, almost feline about him as we walk down the short, carpeted corridor to his office'. Busby was eighty-two years old at this point.

This remarkable, and remarkably reserved, brand of magnetism was something Busby had from boyhood. He grew up in great poverty in a mining community in Lanarkshire. His father was killed by a sniper's bullet in the First World War when Busby was just seven. His mother saved her pennies to send him to grammar school, although he left and worked in the mine when the family threatened to emigrate en masse to America. Even then he stood out. Dunphy described him as 'an unusual boy, composed and mature, serene, he had . . . an élan that was extraordinary in a teenage boy'. And later: 'Barely twenty he was mature beyond his years with an indefinable quality that set him apart from the others, a certain graciousness, almost feline.' This was always, even as a boy, his great quality: some indefinable great quality.

As a footballer Busby became known for his Crombie overcoat, trilby and pipe, the uniform of a prosperous small-town sawmill and wood chippings business magnate. And also, let's face it, the uniform of the universal dad. This was Busby's lot, born to look like your dad. He never fought it. He never pushed it. It just happened.

Later, as United manager, Busby's presence was described by Arthur Hopcraft: 'To watch Sir Matt Busby move about Manchester is to observe a veneration,' he recorded. 'Small boys rush towards him holding up their picture books for autograph . . . Adults shout his first name and grab his hand . . . They wave at him in his car.'

This was Busby complete. Here he is as Manchester's dad, the dad half-glimpsed in his motor car erect and unsmiling, oblivious behind his steering wheel, untouchable in his holy dad-hat and dad–coat. Busby was aware of this effect. He attributed it to the early death of his own father, a shock that created in him 'some paternal, protective feeling to other unfortunate, sensitive young people'.

This isn't to suggest there was anything soft or new–dad about Busby. He was above all an out-of-bed-and-on-with-it type of patriarch. Busby had nurtured his idea of a benevolent pater-dictatorship while coaching a British Army team in Italy towards the end of the Second World War. His charges included the future managers Joe Mercer, Frank Swift, Tommy Lawton and Cliff Britton.

There was something of the *Dirty Dozen*, or the *Escape to Victory* platoon about Busby's team. He gave them all specific jobs. Mercer became food-gatherer and scrounger-in-chief. Lawton and Swift were the baggage men. Britton got transport. Together they talked endlessly of their experiences in the game, concocting in their midst a kind of ideal state of familial travelling team. It was from these experiences that Busby decided not so much on the tactics or methodology of his future career but on the tone. It would be supportive and generous. This was a big shift in emphasis.

The pre-war football Busby himself had played in was a brutish thing. Clubs were presided over by boardrooms of distant grocery magnates and a secretary-manager whose loyalty was to his directors. Huge squads of minimum-wage players were bullied about the premises by the semi-Neanderthal figure of the trainer and a medical staff of sadists and quacks. In 1902 Manchester City captain Di Jones cut his knee in a pre-season friendly. He was treated, after a fashion – the nip of brandy, the cotton wool bandage – by the club doctor and then sent home. The wound turned septic. Jones died a week later.

As a player at Liverpool Busby had marvelled at the terribly traumatised figure cut by his manager George Kay, who was notorious for sitting on the bench moaning and holding his head in his hands. Busby recognised that for young players often 'the manager was a man sitting at his desk and you saw him once a week'. This was the slack Busby would take up in spectacular fashion.

The first hint of his appointment as Manchester United manager came in December 1944. Busby, still serving in the Army, received a letter from United's chief scout and Mr Fix-it, Louis Rocca. It began, 'Dear Matt, No doubt you will be surprised to get this letter from your old pal Louis' and ended with the words 'I have a great job for you if you are willing to take it on'. Within two months Busby was United manager, signing a five-year contract in his Army uniform and becoming the club's first proper manager since 1937.

The Busby method may have been patience but his success was instant. From the start his team played with great verve and purpose. There was an injection of panache, a lightness about them. In time Busby's United would come to bear the imprint of the new Elizabethan age, the rather hopeful – even fanciful – notion that a tired, post-imperial society might reinvent itself as a white-hot technological powerhouse.

Perhaps with this in mind Busby's youth policy became a national fixation. Busby didn't invent the initiative to nurture home-bred young players. This was already in place, presided over by a director called James Gibson, who first had the idea of producing a community-based all-Manchester team. But Busby certainly got most out of it. His evolving team of the 1950s was like a lab experiment. This had never been done before. Busby – kindly, taciturn, overcoated – was raising rug-rats up there. And while attendances dwindled elsewhere United began to draw huge crowds, cementing their status as national obsession, a shared sporting jewel.

In part, the process of scouting and grooming that would spawn the legend of Busby's Babes was born out of necessity. United were in debt. Times were hard. The club didn't move back to Old Trafford until 1949. Until then Busby shared an office at Gibson's cold storage firm. It took him two bus rides and over an hour to get to the training ground.

No matter: it was during this period that Busby began to embed his paterfamilias new world order. The club became 'like a family'. This was his mantra. The manager's door was always open. Nobody was shouted at or humiliated in public. And Busby wanted to know everything about his players' private lives, to share, intrude upon and stick his noise right into any problems they might be having. This was management Busby-style, a pastoral hand on the shoulder, a heavy hand even, but a supportive one too.

This cut something of a dash in post-war England. In 1947 the *Manchester Evening News* reported on Busby's methods: 'He never browbeats a player . . . He takes him to a quiet corner, gives him a fatherly chat and a pat of encouragement.' Perhaps it seemed almost mawkishly considerate or foolishly fond. But no one ever doubted that Busby was in charge. Barry Fry recalled that he could still be frighteningly tough when he needed to. 'Oh yes,' Fry told me. 'If he tore you off a strip he cut you in half. But he wouldn't do it unless he really had to. And when he did you knew he meant it.'

Once, when a director, Harold Hardman, made a comment questioning the selection of his captain, Johnny Carey, Busby followed Hardman into the gents and told him, sternly, 'Never dare say anything like that to me again in front of people.' And you just wouldn't, would you?

Success came quickly. In 1948 United won the FA Cup. There's a picture of the team posing with the trophy. Busby is loitering at the back on the right. We're used to finding the early manager in these pictures, a lurking presence, ill at ease and sallow. Busby looks almost uncontrollably pleased with life, glowing with pride like some half-cut, sleep-deprived young dad awkwardly cradling his first-born.

In 1952 United won the League. Four years on, Busby still looks proud, but he's already become the tolerant patriarch, white-haired and inscrutable. By this time his ability to nurture young players had begun to flower. United won the FA Youth Cup in each of its first seven seasons from 1950 onwards. In 1956 and 1957 they won the League title using many of the same players.

By the time 1958 came around, a team with an average age of just twenty-one was progressing in the European Cup. Busby had defied the Football League to enter United in European competition, the first English club to do so. In a way this makes the events that followed even more perverse and cruel. Eight of Busby's players and three of his coaching staff died in the Munich air disaster in February 1958, when the antiquated plane they were travelling in crashed at a slush-covered Munich-Riem Airport. The crash is still the most shocking single event to affect any English football team. Busby himself was given the last rites by a priest.

No good could come of such a tragedy. Drawing on all those reserves of quiet dignity he seemed to have been storing up for just some such moment, Busby did manage to make what he could of it. He built another great team and a decade on from Munich won the European Cup. It's a poignant, almost symmetrical piece of narrative completion. Even in his moment of triumph at Wembley Busby remained as always, reserved, straight-backed and generous to his players. This was real grace. He was knighted a few days later, but this still seems slightly beside the point.

Matt Busby lived out the greatest managerial story ever told. And he introduced the most emotive of the many managerial personae and subtexts. With Busby the manager-as-father always reflected a very specific kind of fatherhood. This isn't the golfing buddy dad, the clowning dad or the soft touch also-likes-a-go-on-the-Nintendo dad.

As Barry Fry says: 'Five years after I left Manchester United I went to watch them play Chelsea. I hadn't seen Matt for five years. But I still called him "boss". You always called him "boss". He was the boss.'

This is not an easy role to play. We think of other managers who have played the dad card over the decades. Brian Clough incessantly telling people off and even clipping a pitch invader around the ear after a League Cup tie in 1989. Terry Venables singing 'What Do You Want to Make Those Eyes at Me For' on the Russell Harty show in 1974 and conjuring the embarrassing dad, the dad making a spectacle of himself at your cousin's wedding.

Busby's presence is cooler and more refined. He's your dad at Christmas, your dad in old photos. With his immobile features and his sense of lingering always in some more adult atmosphere, he's almost an absent dad: much-loved but duty-bound and departed. Before Busby the manager might occasionally have seemed a rather comic figure: a jester, a hustler, a buffoon even. Busby gave the football manager depth. And he proved that he can also make you – if not exactly cry – then at least come over slightly gruff and hoarse and brave.

CHAPTER 12

The Manager Goes Platinum

For the manager the 1960s was a decade of sudden, giddy and life-changing public success. This would be his moment, his perfect moment. The glass elevator was poised to transport him out of his cobble-close backstreets and up into the celebrity nimbus. It might have taken eighty years of sullen and incremental ascent. But the manager was on the verge of being an overnight success.

Celebrity autobiographies tend to lead up to these watershed moments. It's the big gear change. Suddenly private concerns give way to public. Personal ambition is subsumed by the tidal force of historical ascendancy. It's Elton John going from writing lyrics on napkins to playing the Troubadour in Los Angeles, or Elvis on the Jimmy Young show. Before these moments all we have are signs, preciously guarded indications of a gathering destiny. Young Elton's precociousness at the piano. The pigtailed Britney rocking out on the Mickey Mouse Club. In retrospect, we feel we always saw it coming.

The manager, primed and ready to launch, leaves behind him the usual paper chase of clues: Herbert Chapman and his silk hat;

George Allison's fruity voice crackling out of the Bakelite transistor. Stringing them together is strangely satisfying. It's like laying the glasses out before a party, plumping the cushions and putting the crisps in a bowl. Then, finally, the moment comes. The tone changes, the chocks are away, and we go from reading Aunt Fanny's yellowing biro'd letters to interpreting our man through the *Daily Mirror* front pages, the *Top of the Pops* appearances, the drugs busts, the knighthoods. And we're pitched head first into all the old stories, the dalliances and the anecdotes that have already long ago become public property.

It's a rhythm shift in any story. So let's just take a few deep breaths and have a moment. Let's remind ourselves to break a leg before we head out, hand in hand, on to the manager's Live Aid set. The days of flowering unseen, of playing the pubs and the clubs and the hops and bops, are now decisively over. From now on we're working the crowd, punching the air and yelling, 'Make some noise Detroit', while we bask in the manager's supernova.

In many ways the 1960s is the most boring decade. It's boring by dint of repetition and jaded superlative. Everything happened in the 1960s. Everybody experienced their personal epiphany. If you can remember the sixties, you probably weren't there. You've just been told about it, endlessly, by people who were. It's the same for the football manager. These would be his personal rock and roll years.

We've already heard from Matt Busby. Crucially – and unlike Herbert Chapman, an isolated north London pioneer twenty years before – Busby wasn't alone. There were others. This would turn out to be the decade of the super-manager, as the 1960s brought us stadium-rock management, touched by a perfect storm of opportunity and talent

Busby, Shankly, Stein. This is our managerial supergroup. They're like the members of Cream, if Eric Clapton had been joined not by some other excellent 1960s musicians, but by Mick Jagger, Jimi Hendrix and Liberace. Busby, Shankly and

Stein are our Beatles, Stones and Kinks. And by 1965 all three were in situ at their big city powerhouse clubs, Manchester United, Liverpool and Celtic. An enduring iconography was in place. These were the days of the manager's life.

Not that he didn't meet some resistance along the way. Like any wild-eyed long-hair, any love-beaded freedom-seeker, the manager was destined to tangle, in his own way, with the forces of The Man. So visible was he during the early 1960s that some among the retreating mandarins of the FA and Football League chairmen voiced concern over this uppity new superstar presence. Old rules about managers not being allowed to coach from the sidelines were morosely reinforced. In December 1964 managers were even instructed not to sit on the bench any more, to conceal their incendiary presence from public view. The rule was ignored and eventually rescinded.

In the middle of all this an ideal standard was being founded. The managerial David was being vigorously chiselled out. And not from some glistening block of sumptuous Tuscan marble. But instead from a romanticised notion of the beautifully fertile Lanarkshire coal face.

Busby, Shankly and Stein were all Scots. They were also all from mining communities. Busby and Stein worked as miners before becoming professional footballers. They were all proud, and vocally so, of their background. And so the communities they came from, or at least some abstract notion of these communities, has been woven into the managerial-legacy DNA, fused into its molecules at the point of the manager's most vigorous ascent.

Scottish mining communities are now a thing of the industrial past. Tight-knit, cobble-close and profoundly socialist, we have a picture of these communities. Perhaps it's an idealised picture, bound up as it now is with the generous and wonderfully self-propelling success of Busby, Stein and Shankly. There are echoes in all of them of those great Calvinistic values, the seam of moral urgency that dictates gifted individuals use their talents to enlarge their social horizons and to bring greater wealth to all. And there's the enduring sense of being rooted in your own community, of never leaving it all behind.

These are still football's most tenderly nursed values. As Eamon Dunphy wrote in Busby's autobiography: 'The team ethos that was supposed to exist in football really did exist among miners . . . You depended on each other. The camaraderie was real. There was no place for vanity, selfishness or greed.' Graft, solidarity, community and triumph in adversity. Busby, Shankly and Stein. It's a heady cocktail, and one on which the figure of the manager, in the reflected glory of his most definitive trilogy, would become gloriously drunk.

The idealised 1960s stadium-rock manager has many common features. The bedrock of all this, the entry-level spec, is the incredibly hard upbringing. Great managers have hard lives. So much so that, at times, these uber-Scots can sound a bit like Monty Python's four Yorkshiremen sketch, with its lumps of coal for Christmas and cardboard boxes for shoes. Busby grew up in a hundred-year-old, two-room miners' cottage with a cold-water tap outside. All seven family members slept in the same room. The communal toilets were seventy-five yards away. That's nothing, says Stein, I used to come home bleeding from crawling down mine seams and my favourite food was tripe. Call that hardship? says Tommy Docherty, a post-Busby Glaswegian at Manchester United. Docherty grew up in the Gorbals where, as he recalled, 'illness and malnutrition were a constant threat to family life . . . The Gorbals was not only impoverished and deprived . . . It was also home to the notorious razor gangs.'

In the public eye this kind of hardship, a side-effect of industrial life in the first half of the twentieth century, gave the manager his soul, his bluegrass roots. It became a defining feature for these men who would lead so hungrily. Even now the perception of Sir Alex Ferguson is backlit by his own sense of Jazz era authenticity, the base element of embattled Scottish industrial working community. Ferguson was famously a shipyard steward in Govan while establishing himself as a player at Rangers. He once led a semi-walkout over pay and conditions. He remained, in the centrist salad days of Blairism, a visible and active Labour Party member, wheeled out on the conference platform to lend his invincible brand-association of old values and progressive success.

Busby, Shankly and Stein were the godfathers of all this. Each brought something different, his own virtuoso guitar solo, drum break or shrieking signature vocal. Busby gave the preacherly and the paternal tone, father and Father rolled into one. Shankly brought an urgently vocal presence, of which we will hear more later. Stein was the Big Man, the beacon, the lighthouse. Lawrie McMenemy – himself a Big Mac on occasion – remarked sagely after Stein's death, 'There are a lot of "big men" in football but there was only one Big Man – that was Jock.'

Stein's achievements are among the most striking. In 1967 his Celtic team beat Internazionale 2-1 in Lisbon to become the first British team to win the European Cup. The most remarkable aspect of this was the comparison between the two teams. Inter were international all-stars, considered unbeatable by many in Europe. Stein's Celtic team was drawn entirely from Glasgow and its suburbs. They were small, tenacious and largely ginger-haired. As Bobby Murdoch, one of the Celtic players that day, recalled: 'They were sleek and tanned, like film stars. We had quite a few with teeth missing, with blobs of Vaseline on our eyes to block out the sweat. It was quite funny really.'

This was an unrepeatable success, and also one that still reeks of pure, untainted footballing socialism, the pit village principle writ large, projecting the super-manager's shadow on to a global screen. Stein also embodied the furious energy of these new men, something that would be characteristic of the demob-happy post-war manager. He got the Celtic job in 1965, after which he didn't stop working for thirteen years. He took training, then stayed late at the club furiously combing his network of contacts. Stein travelled everywhere. He drove himself at great speed around Scotland, watching matches, meeting contacts, secretly scouting players, obsessed with being absolutely on the cusp.

This was a man saturated with football, a football maniac. When there wasn't any football left to gorge himself on, Stein went for the next best thing, talking to journalists about football. He was always available to the press, always prepared to chat, banter, chide and befriend. In Glasgow he was pretty much a consultant to the football editor's desk. He was known for phoning late at night, just to keep the football talk going, unable to let it drop. After his death Alex Ferguson said, 'When that phone rings late on at night you still think that the Big Man is going to be on the other end.'

There was a vaguely kooky side to Stein's involvement. Once, when a party of Welsh miners on their way to a rugby international came to look around Parkhead, it was Stein who appeared at the gates to give them a two-hour tour around the ground. On another occasion a Celtic away game was cancelled. Who was that large middle-aged person standing at a major road junction outside Glasgow flagging down supporters' cars to save a wasted journey? It was the Big Man himself.

During the celebrations after the 1967 European Cup victory Bill Shankly, who was present, famously turned to his old friend and said, 'John, you're immortal.' It's a lovely line. How ironic, then, that the crowning epithet of Stein's crowning moment should point directly to his sad end.

Unfortunately Stein wasn't immortal. In fact he is the only manager, and one of very few public figures, to have died live on television. Stein had a heart attack at the end of Scotland's 1–1 draw with Wales at Ninian Park in September 1985, a match that saw his Scotland team qualify for the 1986 World Cup. He collapsed after the final whistle and died shortly afterwards.

It was a truly shocking end. And also, away from the immediate sorrow of friends and family, a beautifully poetic one. A full seventy-five years on from the largely unreported death of Spen Whittaker, secretary-manager of Burnley on a train platform at Crewe, what better way to go for the super-manager? This, by tragic association, was the clenched fist of solidarity, the ultimate tribute to all those cold, stretched, bacterial pneumonia-infected secretaries of the distant past. Stein is in good company.

The 1960s had to end. The come-down was inevitable and the morning after prolonged. The cult of the manager would be co-opted, as movements always are. Before long they would be selling manager wigs in Woolworths. By historical accident, and by force of the communal will, for a period of some years from the 1950s through to the 1960s football managers – as embodied most clearly by Busby, Shankly, Stein – did come to represent something important. They spoke directly to those on the terraces. They loomed as middle-aged working-class heroes.

This kernel of something vivid and authentic has since been repeatedly mimicked in synthetic form, occasionally almost as parody. The media got hold of it. Vested interests – the canny director, the would-be demagogue-manager – played on this lingering memory. And so managerial rock and roll has been sold back to us in sanitised form. Since the golden age of the stadium-rock original, we've had more than our fair share of pop idols, air guitar heroes and mime-acts.

A hint of something real, something with feeling, lingers among the assorted big men, showmen, Special Ones and unsmiling inspirationalists that followed over the next thirty years. But if you want the real thing, the manager in all his bigger-than-Jesus splendour – and much as it might be painful to hear it, yet again – it turns out you really do have to go back to the sixties.

CHAPTER 13

The Manager Learns to Talk

Bill Shankly was the first football manager to earn the accolade of pop star-style single-name status. There he is, in among an A-list platoon of poster boys and T-shirt icons: Sting, Prince, Banksy, Whitney, Jimi, Janis, Shanks. This is elite company for the football manager.

In fact it's tempting to wonder exactly what Shanks thinks he's doing in there. Even in our more tabloid short-cut-friendly times only a handful of managers have succeeded in joining the single-name club. Jose perhaps. Sir Alex and Arsène. But Shanks will always wear the yellow jersey. He may not be the most successful, or even the most famous of the elite stadium-rock managers of the 1960s and 1970s. But Shanks is the most pop.

Why did this happen? Undoubtedly Shankly had a unique personal electricity. It's accepted practice at this stage in any potted Shankly history to use the word 'genius'. In 1997 a plaque was unveiled in Glenbuck commemorating the fifty-five footballers the Scottish mining village produced during the last century. Among them was Shankly: 'The legend, the genius, the man.' This is the standard line. 'I watched his genius unfold,' Tom Finney sighed in 1993. 'A great man, a great manager and a great psychologist,' was Kevin Keegan's verdict. The greatest, the genius, the undisputed, the granditudelissimus. When it comes to Shankly, we all turn into Don King.

This is a funny thing. On paper Shankly's record as Liverpool manager is very good, but it isn't unique. Between 1959 and 1974 he led the team to three League titles, the Uefa Cup and the FA Cup twice. This involved transforming from within, turning a messy Second Division club into one of the most powerful football institutions in the world, not to mention giving the manager his most irresistible nudge yet out from the musty, velveteen wings and into the centre stage of mainstream celebrity.

His peculiar managerial gunpowder, his special move, is hard to pin down at first. Certainly he brought a sense of something political. Shankly often talked about socialism and football, not just as an expression of working-class solidarity but as a means of playing the game, the perfect socialism of the perfect team. This was intoxicating stuff, an ideological head-rush in a game already fluffed and gingered up with its own competing excitements.

Shankly also had a vivid connection with the city of Liverpool, something he nurtured feverishly, becoming a found-ing father of the popular notion of fan culture, of a mass communion between supporters, team and geographical place. Occasionally, before matches, he would even allow himself to be passed around above the heads of the Kop, returning to the dressing room before kick-off with his clothes torn and hair askew.

This idea of manager-as-political-firebrand would flower as a separate branch of the Shankly legacy, hot-housed in the 1970s by the popular notion of the Arthur Scargill-style left-wing inspirationalist. Shankly kick-started this brand of managerial activism. But that still doesn't quite explain the cult of Shanks. Shanks came from somewhere else.

With Shankly it was really all about one thing: his voice. This was the gift that would decisively implant him among the blue-riband, pound-for-pound heavy-hitters of the managerial division. Matt Busby may have been great but he was also largely mute. Shankly was great too, but he was at his best when he opened his mouth.

Before Shankly the manager spoke in halting fashion. He was stilted. He had no flow. Partly this is a class thing. Unaccustomed as they were to speaking in public, managers developed a habit of putting on posh voices. Tommy Docherty recalled his manager at Preston, Cliff Britton, adopting a horribly affected accent for his first TV interview in 1957. 'One doesn't like to estimate how a football game will go, but suffice it to say, we shall strive our hardest,' Britton told the cameras, coming on like a man doing an impression of someone doing an impression of someone being posh.

This was the football way pre-Shankly. Nobody had yet given these men the confidence to speak freely. Stan Cullis would pose as a genial minor public school housemaster during his radio spots in the 1950s. The Newcastle forward Jackie Milburn famously induced disbelieving laughter at a benefit dinner by addressing the crowd, in all seriousness, in a halting parody of a plummy accent.

Shankly couldn't be doing with any of that. In a profile in the *Guardian* in 1968 he was described as 'firing his words as if with a Gatling gun'. So impressed was his interviewer he even tried to render that voice in print ('Ah was always daft about fitba'. Ah went tae Carlisle whan ah was 17 an' a half', etc.), ending with the observation 'the sayings of Shankly are as forthright and weighty as the sayings of Mao'.

In a way, this has turned out to be about right. Weighty, portentous, Mao-like, Shankly's voice has simply refused to go away.

What survives now is a zombified anthology of quips, aphorisms and gags, still staggering from biography to website to after-dinner speech after all these years. These old favourites, these best-ofs – 'I want to build a team that's invincible, so they'll have to send a team that's from Mars to beat us'; 'Me having no education, I had to use my brains' – they are like a motorway service station CD tracklist of classics, faves and drummed-in-with-a-hammer Christmas number ones.

For the post-Shankly generation, it's even tempting to wonder exactly why all these quotes have been feverishly transcribed and jealously hoarded for the past forty years. At times the Shanklyisms can sound glib. Take this: 'The trouble with referees is that they know the rules, but they do not know the game.' It's the kind of thing you might expect from some punditry third-rater during another bog-standard Sky Sports Saturday afternoon jabber-athon.

And how about: 'If he had gunpowder for brains he couldn't blow his cap off.' Is this really funny? Or was Shanks just a compulsive wise-cracker, a footballing David Brent? The regular introduction of Jimmy Tarbuck to the pre-match Liverpool dressing room – described in the *Daily Mirror* in 1965 as 'manager Bill Shankly's secret "ease the tension" weapon' – doesn't do much to quell the sense of unease.

This is what we've done to Shanks. These are the debilitating effects of the Shanks heritage industry. What was once new and startling has become diluted by layer upon layer of repetition. On the page, the genius eludes us. To get that freshness back, you really need to listen to the voice itself. Fortunately you still can: the gatefold double album *Shankly Speaks* is a recording of a two-day interview at the Adelphi Hotel in Liverpool in 1981. Shankly's first topic on the track listing is 'Producing great teams', and straight away, he's off, speaking. The content might be occasionally bland, but the voice has an unstoppable rhythm, not to mention a sandpaper effect. It makes you bristle. At one point he laughs and it's a childish, gurgling, lovable thing. You want to hear that laugh again.

Above all the voice communicates a sense of street-level grandeur. It's not the voice of the terraces but a personalised hybrid of everyday speech and the punchy, wisecracking theatricals of a movie gangster. This is another thing about Shankly's managerial voice. It's a transatlantic thing. Reared on depression-era Hollywood, men of his generation were often in thrall to the heroes of American cinema. Shankly had his eyes fixed on this larger horizon, the bluff exterior of a South Ayrshire James Cagney, the wise-guy patter of an Anfield Jack Benny, even the gag-cracking feistiness of a Football League Groucho Marx.

It seems fitting that Shankly's great number-one hit, his 'Blue Suede Shoes' and 'Mull of Kintyre', was borrowed from the great NFL coach Vince Lombardi. When Shankly said, in jest, 'Some people say football is a matter of life and death. I'm very disappointed with that attitude. It's much more important than that,' it was towards the end of a long interview and meant as no more than a throwaway line.

But it gave us the high-water mark of the new managerial voice. This remains his big T-shirt-shifting moment, and perhaps also the words we can expect to find etched on the manager's tombstone. It was also the manager's great moment of liberation, his bra-burning epiphany. The manager could now be funny. He could kid and he could riff. No longer would his words emerge through the chimera of the faux-BBC accent. Post-Shankly the manager was unashamed and defiantly regional.

It was this verve for one-liners and the Gatling Gun zinger that drove Shankly's own rise to popular fame after his appointment as Liverpool manager in 1959 at the age of forty-six. Shankly's quotability may have been limited to the quip and the pungent put-down, but this was perfect for the nascent tabloid press.

With the rapid evolution of 'personality' sports journalism, by the mid-1960s the medium had caught up with Shankly's message. Creaking, rumbling and finally spurting with the violence of a long-dormant geyser, the manager's ancient voice came pouring out of Shankly in bullet-hard, silver-plated, ready-made manager-speak.

Shankly wrote the pocket translation guide. From here on in every half-pint pundit, every bus-stop know-it-all and studio talking head would aspire to the Shankly model. And like some long-dead pirate captain whose oaths are resurrected among the chattering parrots of his marooned treasure island, Shankly and his Shanklyisms still follow us around in bastardised mimesis.

At Liverpool Shankly would inspire Kevin Keegan in the dressing room by telling him to 'go and drop some hand-grenades out there'. As England manager Keegan offered the same advice to Paul Scholes in June 1999 before a vital Euro 2000 qualifier against Sweden. In the first minute of the game Scholes launched a vicious lunge at the Swedish midfielder Hakan Mild that left him needing stitches. Early in the second half Scholes became the first-ever England player sent off at Wembley. This is, it's fair to say, a mistranslation of the original Shankly, Shankly as reinterpreted by some foghorn mono-linguist, loudly informing the local Manuel that his gazpacho is bleeding well cold.

At other times the Shankly inflection hits exactly the right spot. In November 2008 Arsène Wenger had become embroiled in a spat with Stoke manager Tony Pulis over some heavy tackling in a Premier League game. Pulis, usually a remote figure in baseball cap and glasses, replied with a timeless Shanklyism of overblown rhetoric: 'As Mr Wenger is such a learned professional . . . I would like to remind him of Abraham Lincoln's great quotation: "You can fool some of the people all of the time, and all of the people some of the time, but you cannot fool all of the people all of the time".' After which, there's not really anything left to do but graciously accept the applause and leave the room.

At other times the manager's post-Shankly vocal range has been more of a mixed blessing. The waffle merchant, the rent-a-gob and the Shankly-tribute act would become familiar. The manager had found his voice. Now the question was: would he ever shut up? This would receive its most striking incarnation during Shankly's own lifetime in Alec Stock, manager of Orient, QPR and Yeovil. Stock remains the master of the purple phrase and the gnomic epigram: 'Managers need success like other men need food and drink'; 'What a manager thinks today, he may not be thinking tomorrow'; 'There is never a flame in a football club unless its manager first provides the spark'; 'A good manager follows his nose'. And the faintly troubling: 'A manager is naked.'

Stock was by no means restricted to the pithy. In fact he was at his best when allowed to ramble and to jam. He could be frank: 'I know this will not win me any friends in the valleys, but Welsh players are among those I am reluctant to sign. They worry me.' He could be a polemicist: 'A referee once complained to me of a missile being thrown on the field at Loftus Road. I pressed the point with him and kept on pressing it. Do you know what the missile turned out to be? A paper carton. There is a mixture of danger and liberalism about.'

Stock could also be righteous. Once he was asked by the mayor of Luton how much impact a football club could have on its community. 'None at all on the lady who owns the little hat shop at the corner,' was his instant reply. He was something of a verbal phenomenon, a man who felt not just a duty but an irresistible impulse simply to talk. One 1972 interview in *The Times* was introduced with the words 'Stock is no Trappist monk, no piece of garden statuary . . . words gush out of him like a waterfall.'

In the preface to Stock's *Football Club Manager*, ghosted by the journalist Bryon Butler, Butler writes, wearily, 'This book did not have to be squeezed out of Alec, idea by idea, word by word. It flowed out of him.' This was the way of the managerial rhubarb-merchant. In the Shankly era it seemed about right to claim, as Stock did, that 'all a manager has, his only instruments, are words', even if this does tend to overlook other things like training, tactics, signing players and occasionally stopping for a think.

Stock left the Army aged twenty-seven and became player-secretary-manager at Yeovil. There is a loneliness to the early Stock, something that perhaps fostered the urge to shout his way to the top. At Yeovil the only other member of staff was a groundsman. Stock himself mixed the cement to repair the terraces. On the day of a match he would mark out the pitch and mow the grass, after which he would be physically sick at half time 'out of worry'.

He eventually became manager of Leyton Orient, where his thirst for verbiage would flower. 'A manager is the best thing a football club has to a public relations man,' he said, in the days before most clubs had an entire platoon of public relations men called Gavin with heavily gelled hair who say things like 'top banana'. Stock became a regular figure on *ITV News*. He cultivated reporters, made free with his phone number and would often be woken by newspapermen ringing him at home after midnight in order to flesh out a quote.

Like Shankly, Stock was a self-proclaimed and very public football obsessive. 'I cannot begin to visualise myself doing any other sort of job,' he wrote in his book, although he does go on to imagine himself, quite weirdly, becoming 'an auctioneer. Or I might even have had a go at farming in a small way.'

But Stock's farming career was destined never to take flight as he became instead the acme of the insatiably verbose manager, and at times an inescapably comic figure. The notion of the manager as caricature, or pastiche was given its early impetus by Stock. His story has an unusual afterword, as he became the chief inspiration for Paul Whitehouse's Ron Manager character on the

BBC sketch show *The Fast Show*. In the process Stock found a rare managerial immortality, living on in the 'Jumpers for goalposts, Giggsy-wiggsy' impersonations of a million teenage schoolboys, and in the process finding his own single-name niche, as the archetypal Ron, the cartoon Ron of the managerial imagination.

Shankly himself would retire suddenly as Liverpool manager in 1974. The Charity Shield game at Wembley against Leeds, who were managed by Brian Clough for the first time, became his farewell match.

'It's Shankly's moment, and Brian Clough is well aware of that fact,' Barry Davies announced on the BBC as the two men walked out at the head of their teams. Shankly, in light-grey Italian-style suit, peach shirt and purple and magenta tie, didn't look like a man destined for retirement. He still looked constantly on the verge of saying something delicious and true. He looked like he had plenty left to say. And he would be heard again, too, if only through the mouths of those yet to come.

CHAPTER 14

The Manager Learns to Swear

If you're going to San Francisco
Be sure to wear some flowers in your hair
If you're going to San Francisco
You're gonna meet some gentle people there

This is an idealised and rather fanciful interpretation of the 1960s. Or, as Alf Ramsey might have put it, a load of balls. It isn't just the wishy-washiness of the lyrics to Scott McKenzie's 1967 number-one hit, or the reality of what it might actually be like to be surrounded by gentle people with flowers in their hair. It's more the sense that the 1960s was a decade composed solely of billowing kaftans, daisy chains, joss sticks and above all fun. This might have been the case in San Francisco. But Alf Ramsey wasn't from San Francisco. He was from Dagenham. All right?

Ramsey's own wonder years as a manager came between 1962 and 1970. As England manager he led his team to victory at the 1966 World Cup, an occasion that can often seem rather jolly and sepia-tinted. The June sunshine at the Empire Stadium. The Queen's white gloves. People on the pitch. Hats off all round. But beneath the pristine veneer something more pungent was afoot. Dark forces drove the man who gave England its sole headline triumph in international football: ancestral resentments, ancient slights, and a fascination with the zombified class structures of the pre-modern Football Association.

Elsewhere this may have been the superstar DJ era of Busby, Shankly and Stein, but the England manager remained in many ways a remedial figure. Ramsey spent much of the 1960s hunkered in his tiny office at FA headquarters in Bayswater, a room described in the *Daily Mail* as looking like 'part of the servants' quarters'. It was from here that he would wage his own guerrilla campaign against the forces of blazered historical ascendancy.

Like it or not – and you can bet he wouldn't have – Ramsey was fighting a class war. The battle might have already been half-won elsewhere, but within the Football Association things were still pretty much as they had been in the summer of 1959 when Jimmy Greaves found himself changing planes at Heathrow to join the England Under-23 team in Italy. At the airport Greaves bought a cup of tea and a piece of cake. He was about to take a bite when Stanley Rous, FA secretary, walked by. 'Greaves,' came the barked voice. 'Put that cake down this instant. You will be fed on the plane.'

This was the way of things pre-Ramsey. His predecessor Walter Winterbottom took training and carried the string bag of balls while an FA committee picked the team. At the 1950 World Cup in Brazil Winterbottom even ended up cooking dinner for his players. Two tournaments later in Sweden the squad was accompanied by a middle-aged businessman called Chalwyn, a friend of Rous, who joined in team practice games as the fancy took him.

Ramsey was appointed in 1962. Immediately he set himself cussedly against all that had gone before. Not that you'd have known it by looking at him. Like much of British society in the 1960s, Ramsey was basically Edwardian in appearance. He wore immaculate suits and developed a zealous interest in the correct degree of visible shirt cuff (before collecting his MBE he insisted his tailor seek instruction from Buckingham Palace on the precise detail of the required outfit. He turned up wearing an extraordinary hat and three-piece combination. Warned that nobody else would bother reaching such heights of sartorial correctness, he told his tailor, 'It's not important. I'll know I've got it right.')

Ramsey was fighting for the right to be considered proper. This was his silent agenda. And while other high-profile revolutionaries may have looked to the petrol bomb, the covert Russian missile base or the flaming guitar, Ramsey had only one weapon in his armoury. His really quite funny-sounding voice.

Ramsey always denied having had elocution lessons, claiming his voice was a product of imitating the officers he met during the Second World War. There seems no reason not to believe him. For a start, no instructor could have come up with such a bizarre hotchpotch of BBC radio announcer diction and tortured malapropism, an effect reminiscent of a minor public school teacher in the presence of the wife of the Fourteenth Earl of Egham, momentarily disorientated by one too many dry sherries and trying very hard to remember whether it's 'envelope' or 'onvelope'.

At times Ramsey seemed a comic figure, a brilliantly realised fusion of Rigsby, Steptoe jnr and Hyacinth Bouquet. During a BBC radio interview in the early 1960s, he was asked: 'Are your parents still alive, Mr Ramsey?'

'Oh yes,' he replied.

'And where do they live?'

'In Dagenham, I believe.'

The real key to his voice, however, was what he did with it. As Don Howe, who was picked to play for England twice by Alf Ramsey, told me: 'Alf was a first-class man, but he did have this thing about being posh. He had a posh way of talking in certain situations. But he was different when he was just with the players. He was straightforward. The way he put things across was very very down to earth.'

Howe might be too much of a gentleman to mention it, but a large part of this was the concussive power of Ramsey's swearing. He was a world-class swearer. He swore with venom and timing. This was a man who swore right. He could be savage. On a 1965 European tour Gordon Banks conceded a sloppy goal to a Yugoslavian free kick. 'I have just been up to his room,' Ramsey told his players. 'I told him "One of these days I shall lift up a dagger and fuckin' well kill you".'

He could also be playful. The Chelsea striker Peter Osgood once described arriving for England training in 1969: 'Alf greeted me with, "Ossie, how do you fancy training today?" "Not a lot, Alf," I unwisely replied. "Well, you're going to fucking well enjoy it!" he told me in those clipped plummy tones. I was shocked. It was like catching the Queen kicking one of the corgis up the arse.'

He could also be funny. In 1967 Alf was in Canada with England. As he stood by the team bus a TV newsman accosted him. 'Sir Ramsey,' the presenter smarmed. 'It's such a thrill to have you and the world soccer champions here in Canada. I'm from one of our biggest national stations, going out coast to coast live. And, coach Ramsey, you're not going to believe this but I'm going to give you seven whole minutes all to yourself on the show. So if you're ready, Sir Ramsey, I'm going to start the interview now.'

'Oh no you fuckin' ain't,' came the reply as Ramsey boarded the team bus.

The magic never deserted him. Ramsey was once asked to pick an England team to compare with a Brian Clough XI for an episode of *On the Ball*. The commentator Martin Tyler recalled, 'Alf was very dismissive about some of Clough's choices, saying "There's a right couple of wankers in there!"

Brian Moore said to me, "Did he really say wankers?" We had a right chuckle about that. We were like two little kids.'

This was the brilliant surprise of Ramsey's swearing. Togged out like some terrifying Victorian dad, his oaths, his lingering Dagenham-isms were like a peck on the cheek when you were expecting a clip round the ear. Terse, stern-faced, potty-mouthed, these were Ramsey's own revolutionary sounds of the sixties.

It's worth noting that swearing was still a very big deal. In November 1965, seven months before England won the World Cup, Kenneth Tynan became the first man to say 'fuck' on English television. The big moment came during a late-night satire programme called *BBC3*, Tynan claiming, rather nervously, 'I doubt if there are very many rational people in this world to whom the word "fuck" is particularly diabolical or revolting.'

Amazingly it turned out there were. The BBC switchboard was jammed for days. The Corporation publicly apologised. The *Daily Express* called it 'the bloodiest outrage the country had ever known'. Conservative MPs immediately tabled motions in the House of Commons calling for Tynan's prosecution and for his removal as literary director of the National Theatre. Mary Whitehouse wrote a letter of complaint to the Queen (it was forwarded on to the attorney general in mute support).

This was the kind of swear-power Ramsey was tapping into, and employing, sparingly, as a form of extreme motivation for his players. As Gordon Milne observed: 'I think his accent somehow worked in his favour . . . It was so funny when he would say "Fuck it". It was great for morale.'

Roy McFarland recalled playing against Scotland in a Ramsey England team in the early 1970s. 'Just before we went out on to the field, as we were going out the door, he'd say, "Come on boys, let's beat those Scots fuckers." It was a bit of a shock to me. Christ almighty, I thought.'

Perpetually at war, not just with West Germany, Brazil and Argentina, but with the corporal-class of the FA, Alf's swearing came right from the heart. His own origins were almost pre-industrial in their poverty. He grew up in a wooden hut with no hot water or electricity. His father drove a dustcart and raised pigs. Ramsey described his occupation, stiffly, as 'general labourer' and there has periodically been reference to a 'hay and straw dealer', but he was basically a rag-and-bone man.

Excitingly, Ramsey also had a ne'er-do-well brother called Bruno, a local gadabout who wore a rakishly angled trilby and earned a living gambling on greyhounds in the company of someone called Charlie Wraggles. Ramsey was protective of his brother, albeit perhaps slightly ashamed too. The only relief from all this, and from the daily slights and snubs of his Bayswater maid's quarters, would be in unimpeachable success on the field.

Ramsey taught the manager to swear like he meant it, and even now there is great power in that lingering divide between the public man with his TV platitudes and the private one with his training-ground oaths. It's a delicate balancing act. At Brentford's dank and boggy Osterley training ground on London's western fringe, Andy Scott tends to finish training with what he calls 'a run-through'.

This turned out to be a detailed preview of their next opponents, Shrewsbury Town. 'They'll fucking bang it at you,' Scott told his players. 'Boom! Set pieces are major for them. They'll be in your fucking faces. You've got to let them know you can bark and bollock and bite!'

This is also a skill Scott himself has had to work on. 'Yes, you do swear a lot,' he says. 'It's part of the job. But it's best if you use it for shock effect. It's like if you ever heard your parents swear. You weren't expecting them to. And if they did it really shocked you.' Has he ever had a manager who didn't swear? 'No. Never.'

This isn't something that looks like going away. In 2008 the Newcastle manager Joe Kinnear swore fifty-two times during one five-minute press conference, which began with the following exchange:

Kinnear: Which one is Simon Bird?

Bird: Me.

Kinnear: You're a cunt.

Other passages included: 'I am not fucking about. I don't talk to fucking anybody. Everything I fucking say or do. It is raking up stories. You are fucking so fucking slimy.'

Plus the more reflective: 'Fuck off. Fuck off. It's your last fucking chance.'

Kinnear had only just started in the job after four years out. Wandering around St James' Park he looked at first like a hairy-knuckled throwback, perhaps even a terrible mistake. He needed a way back in and he found it in swearing. After his tirade something seemed to give. The managerial ranks opened up. Here was someone who still talked the talk.

This is something the manager guards jealously. He reserves the right to swear. And he keeps it all to himself too. Premier League players have been transferred as a punishment for swearing at the boss, an act of insubordination described by one manager, in all seriousness, as 'a fucking liberty'.

Back in 1966, Alf's England duly won the World Cup. They were probably not the best team at the tournament. But they were mercilessly well-prepared and rigorously drilled, all of which came directly from Ramsey and his luminous will to succeed. In the process he also propelled the creaking, work-in-progress figure of the England manager irreversibly into the foreground. At the final whistle of England's 4-2 defeat of West Germany the Wembley crowd began to chant, 'Ramsey! Ramsey!' This had never happened to an England manager. Although, given that it would have meant repeatedly shouting the word 'Winterbottom', perhaps it's not entirely surprising.

That final Wembley whistle was also the moment that things started to go wrong for Alf. There's a famous picture of him sitting on the England bench as his trainer Harold Shepherdson leaps up to celebrate. Next to him Ramsey is still seated, and looking for all the world like a man who has just been told his connection at Clapham Junction has been delayed by nine minutes and we're terribly sorry for the inconvenience. In fact Ramsey was in the process of whispering the immortal line 'Sit down man, stop making a spectacle of yourself.'

Alf had exercised his will. But his triumph was also an act of bloody-minded self-immolation. Immediately after the World Cup he cloistered himself, exhausted, inside his house in Ipswich with his wife Victoria. 'We put the telephone in a little room where it was difficult to hear and we determined that we wouldn't answer it for a week . . . We could hear a faint buzz all day every day and there was a television team camped outside the door for forty-eight hours but we didn't want to see anyone.'

His job done, almost overnight Ramsey seemed antiquated. Brilliantly stubborn in adversity, in triumph he became pointlessly stubborn. Later he grew a high hedge around his front garden. 'Occasionally,' he said, 'we see coaches stop outside our house and go slowly past the windows. We get a lot of people peering in but it doesn't worry us because they don't see us anyway.'

This dinosaur-like quality became more pronounced as his career intersected with the side-burned, cowboy-booted geezer-maverick players of the subsequent decade.

At the 1970 World Cup, as his players sunbathed by the pool, Ramsey arranged for Shepherdson to blow his whistle after fifteen minutes as a signal that they should turn over and lie on their other side. Before leaving England he had negotiated with Findus to ship 140 pounds of beefburgers, 400 pounds of sausages and ten cases of tomato ketchup to Mexico. At the docks the Mexicans refused to grant Alf's ready meals entry and the whole lot was burned on the quayside. He was more successful in shipping across the team bus. Unfortunately it kept blowing up in the heat.

Old antipathies resurfaced. The FA chairman Sir Harold Thompson is said to have never forgiven Alf for asking him to put out his cigar while the players were having breakfast during a trip to Prague. England failed to qualify for the next World Cup in West Germany and on 1 May 1974 Alf got it. He was summarily sacked with just a laughably inadequate pension to see him on his way.

Quietly martyred, Ramsey retreated to Ipswich, his own post-revolutionary Elba. This was where he remained almost undisturbed until his death in 1999. At his funeral the World Cup-winner George Cohen described him as 'a great football manager, but also a great Englishman'. This is fitting. Ramsey was greatly English. Driven by his own sweary revolutionary fire, Ramsey blazed brightly. He gave the manager his industrial language. And he spoke, albeit rather rudely, to the immediate milieu of the beaten-down ordinary Alfs; the swearing generation with, not flowers, but an enduring layer of Brylcreem in their hair.

CHAPTER 15

The Manager Becomes Incredibly Famous

So much for football, then. Next up, the world. By the early 1970s the manager was almost famous. He was a name. He was a face. But he wasn't yet a global media event. He was still to be flown across the Atlantic by a national newspaper in order to be presented to Muhammad Ali. Nobody had yet thought of producing the film of the novel of his life. He hadn't gone truly mainstream. And this after all is what really counts. Madonna once said she couldn't be happy 'until I'm as famous as God'. Madonna needn't have set her sights that high. She could have started off with simply trying to be as famous as Brian Clough.

The big thing about Clough was that he didn't really seem to have a big thing. Nothing, in fact, beyond simply being Brian Clough. No training ground gimmickry, no seaweed supplements or holistic warm-down routines. Quite the opposite in truth: Clough's teams were often packed off on potentially ruinous pre-match benders and team bus booze-ups. Clough's management – and indeed his entire public presence – was all about personality: the Brian Clough personality, an entity that would project him not just into the nation's living rooms on a Friday night but in time into a kind of supra-football folk hero status.

The Clough personality has by now been relentlessly analysed. At least twenty Clough biographies, autobiographies and personal scrapbooks have been published. In 2009 a cinema film about his forty-four-day reign at Leeds United was on general release. Refracted through its many narrative prisms, the Clough personality feels like public property.

There seems no need to rehearse the ossified anecdotes, the moss-encrusted back-story: to talk again about his father working in a boiled-sweet factory, about his terrible depression after retiring from playing through injury. Or to dwell on late, drunken, wizened Clough, the man who would retire after seeing Nottingham Forest relegated, exiting with a woozy embrace of a pitch-side policewoman.

In the story of the manager's rise Clough romps home in a dizzying variety of cross-disciplinary fields. The first young manager. The first pop manager. The first manager to take a small-town team out of the Second Division and win the European Cup twice. The first manager mimicked by a million playground humorists. The first manager to have an identifiable hairstyle.

From a distance he looks like a moderniser and a populist, not to mention an egomaniac and drunk. We picture him as a time-traveller, a footballing proto-punk wrenching the bootroom door off its hinges and ushering in a brilliant new future of Clough-clones, Clough-descendants, Clough upgrades. This is half of his story. Bill Shankly gave the manager his voice. Clough expanded on it, introducing a whole new range of public intonations. Shankly had jokes. But Clough had good jokes.

'Strike action by the players? Don't be daft, man! My players have been on strike for bloody weeks – we can't win a game!'

'Our team is so young every away game is like a school outing. Our big problem isn't injury – it's acne.'

This is solid material from Clough. It's an Eric Morecambe kind of voice: hectoring, acerbic but affectionate also. It was put to good use. The lasting triumph of the Clough personality is that it provided us with football's first mainstream pop culture figure. As a manager his impact seems bound up with modernity and progress. But in the wider world of light entertainment Clough arrived as an instantly recognisable figure. Here was another working-class iconoclast and provincial braggart, a hybrid of Alf Garnett, Muhammad Ali and bigger-than-Jesus era John Lennon.

The level of Clough's wider celebrity at his peak is still shocking. Suffice to say that for a period of several years the manager of Derby, Brighton, Leeds and Nottingham Forest was one of the most famous people in the country. Football management had spilled out from its narrow demarcations of back-page splash and terrace demagoguery. This was the football manager commandeering the beige leather chat sofa, nonchalantly conducting the studio guffaws. When Clough was sacked by Derby in 1973 he appeared inside the City Ground, having bought a ticket, to accept the applause of the crowd. After taking his ovation he left to appear on Parkinson.

There was an element of serendipity about this. Clough's emergence coincided with a notable golden era of TV light entertainment. Television was in the process of spawning its first generation of chat-show faces and for a period of several years Parkinson's sofa was like an express elevator, rocketing its incumbents up into the heady, brown leather-upholstered VIP lounge of an unblinking three-channel small-screen consciousness.

It was here, in the pubescent televisual infrastructure, that Clough danced his antic jig. He seemed to burn with a vital energy. Watch him talking to David Frost on *The Frost Interview* on the night of his departure from United a year after Parkinson and Derby. Pale, Duke-like, unstoppably lucid in matching orange shirt and tie, he's got Frost in the palm of his hand, the audience on a string. He's edgy, unignorable, moreish.

Clough's rise was bound up with the rise of other northern, left-wing working-class voices. For the first time the mainstream was jammed with a new kind of patter as comedians, trade union leaders and football managers all emerged from the shadows. In December 1979 the *Daily Mirror* carried a festive round-up centre-spread written by Bernard Manning, in which he gave away 'special prezzies' to deserving celebrities. It's a beautifully aged distillation of the late 1970s tabloid celebrity universe. Manning's gift list included: 'Ernie Wise, often seen on his own these days, a survival kit. Joan Collins a bottle of something that fortifies the over-forties. Charlie Williams, an autographed photograph of Enoch Powell.'

And halfway down a brilliant moment of Clough/Scargill synchronicity: 'Brian Clough, a gift voucher for a course of lessons at a charm school', followed by 'Arthur Scargill, a dustbin for all the rubbish he talks'. There they are, twin prongs of the uppity, attention-seeking, northern new man. Clough was flying. That same year he was listed among a roster of famous donors to the Labour Party. The Tories got Eric Sykes, Les Dawson, Lulu, Tom Jones, Rod Stewart and the Bee Gees. Labour hit back with Clough, Parkinson, Billy Connolly, Magnus Pyke, Melvyn Bragg and 'about half the cast of *Coronation Street*'. By 1980 his name was even being bandied about the floor of the House of Commons, with Michael Foot suggesting 'my old mate Brian Clough' be approached to run the British steel industry in place of Ian MacGregor.

Above all for Clough these were the Mike Yarwood years. Yarwood was TV's premier impressionist of the 1970s, regularly drawing over ten million viewers and famously trouncing *You Only Live Twice* in a cross-channel face-off in 1977. His shows were all about the impressions. He did Harold Wilson. He did Robin Day. He did, controversially, Prince Charles, crystallising for the first time the familiar 'hhhnnnyesss, welllll' nasal intonations of the street-level Windsor mimic. And he did Brian Clough.

Interviewed by the BBC in 1975 Clough said of the Yarwood impressions: 'He's got me, you know. It's too good.' He said later he found the whole thing not just flattering but inspiring. And no wonder. In many ways Yarwood made Clough as a mainstream heavyweight. It was his moment of formal coronation. Post-Yarwood, everybody in the country could 'do' Clough, just like everybody could 'do' Frank Spencer or Margaret Thatcher. The drawling 'young man' with woozy stab of the finger was now a staple.

In 1981, as his memoirs were published, the *Mirror* revealed that even Scargill himself, 'an expert mimic', could do 'a very believable Brian Clough'. Clough had been presented with a cartoon effigy of himself into which his public persona would slowly bleed. His triumph, and the manager's great leap sideways, were complete. So much for Clough the personality. He could also back it up with peerless success in the day job. He won trophies at clubs thats had no history of success: a League title at Derby County, a title and two European Cups at Forest. In doing so Clough came to represent the ideal of the football manager as a head man and lead player, singularly inspirational, football's Hamlet.

Central to all of this was the way Clough made people feel. He had a freewheeling, playful quality. In partnership with his co-manager and best friend Peter Taylor, Clough seemed at all times to be engaged in something buoyant and rakish. There was a lot of kissing and grabbing. Gary Newbon once interviewed Clough live on ITV. Asked why his players had not been more committed during a 4-0 defeat at Everton, Clough paused, kissed Newbon on the cheek, and said, 'Because they're just like you and me, Gary – a bunch of pansies'.

Newbon got off lightly. There's a famous picture of Clough

grabbing Peter Taylor's crotch as the two men posed with the League championship trophy. Taylor doesn't look particularly alarmed or even surprised by this. Clough grabbed Diego Maradona's testicles before a pre-season friendly in Barcelona. He regularly punched his players in the stomach as a half-time cure-all for underperformance. The rest of the time he appears to have spent kissing everyone, male or female, he could get close to.

From the outside life looked like a bit of a scream. From a week spent in dizzying luxury in Iran pretending to mull over a job offer from the Shah. To singing Sinatra songs as he wrote out his team sheet on a Friday afternoon. This was the frolicking anarchy of Clough, the spontaneity and the fun. It's a sense of unpredictability that was perhaps his only real footballing inno-vation. Clough would get bored after ten minutes of training and shout, 'Right, let's go through the nettles', at which point the players would have to run off the pitch and plough their way through a twenty-five-yard-square area of nettles and long grass. Sessions would often finish with Clough trying to cram the entire squad into one of the goals, with the last man in getting a fine.

There are many stories of his loopy approach to team prepara-tion. For example, the massive drinking session after Clough had decided his Forest players looked nervous getting off the bus the night before the 1979 League Cup final against Southampton. A private room at the hotel was filled with 'a vat' of champagne. Clough then theatrically turned the key in the lock and announced that no one was leaving until they'd drunk the lot. Forest won 3-2 the next day. That same year, before the European Cup semi-final against Ajax his players were marched around the Amsterdam red-light district, at one point watching as their co-manager attempted to negotiate a group discount into a sex club.

It all started for Clough at Hartlepool in 1965. He had retired from playing the previous year after suffering a serious knee injury playing for Sunderland. It was a bitter blow. Clough had scored 251 goals in 274 games in the Second Division and had played for England twice. He was already married with children. The year that followed had been terribly depressing. Clough had put on weight and begun to drink. Temporarily buffered by the proceeds of a testimonial match, he'd wandered and wavered, his prodigious energy stilled.

His appointment at Hartlepool was announced via a tiny panel in the *Guardian*. Clough took his team-mate from Middlesbrough Peter Taylor with him, nominally as trainer. The two years they spent there still seem thrilling and portentous, pregnant with eerie momentum. As Clough later said, 'We didn't have time to stop for a piss.' They painted the stand and mended the roof, which leaked so badly Clough would often be dripped on while taking phone calls in his office. Rummaging around the main stand, Taylor once came across a stash of poultry feathers. He later found out that Fred Westgarth, one of their predecessors, had kept chickens up there, taking them out only on match days.

With Clough the pictures tell the story. Shortly after his appointment he took his public service vehicle test and announced that henceforth, as a money-saving initiative, he would be driving the team bus. He duly appeared as a spread in the local paper, immaculately groomed, lip slightly curled, hair oiled into a gleaming semi-Ted. He looks luminous and milk-white, frail almost.

It's impossible not to make the Cliff Richard comparison. *Summer Holiday* had been released in 1963. Four years earlier, in June 1959, the Queen Mother had been briefly menaced at a royal theatre appearance as, according to the *Guardian*, 'more than five hundred teenagers besieged the stage door chanting "We want Cliff Richard".' They were eventually dispersed by mounted policemen. Early Cliff, like early Clough, was fresh-faced eye-candy. And like early Cliff, early Clough had a camera-ready glow. He looked like a man out of his time, like the only modern person in the world.

It's a comparison that doesn't go much further. Cliff would rapidly atrophy, while Clough retained his air of edginess and his heat. On that first day in charge as the youngest manager in the League he told a newspaper reporter: 'Age does not count. I know I'm better than the five hundred or so managers who have been sacked since the war. If they had known anything about the game, they wouldn't have lost their jobs.' This isn't Cliff Richard. This is a man coiled with a sense of his own destiny. Welcome to the Fourth Division, Johnny Rotten.

There was a compelling DIY energy to all this activity. Clough worked without pay for two months, earning his first precious gobbet of notoriety in the national press. And while Hartlepool prospered, mildly enough, rising to eighth in Clough's final season, it was the manager himself whose fortunes were irresistibly on the rise, his magnetism stoking from deep in the Fourth Division the embers of the rising cult of the manager, a fascination with the messianic, self-propelling Clough figure that would mushroom so dramatically in the 1970s.

This, then, is how Clough has come to be seen. He looks like a gift from the future, a great leap forward like Copernicus, or Chuck Berry, or the internet.

And he hasn't stopped yet. The Clough personality is still out there. His presence remains almost tangible, safe from the uncharitable revision or the gradual slip beneath the waters. A Clough revivalist industry thrives on the internet. Replica green Clough rugby jerseys can be bought. Fund-raising dinners are organised. To date two English city centres, Nottingham and Middlesbrough, have installed Clough statues. Derby is set to follow. Campaigns for a posthumous knighthood come and go, doomed, but still stoking the fire of his anti-heroism. We're not finished with him.

There is a good reason for this. In death Clough has something of the popular folk hero about him, reconfiguring a distinctly English archetype around the props of players, chairmen, goals, saves and trophies. Here we have football's contribution to the lineage of the Athena poster outsider, this time clad in manager's clothes: football's Robin Hood, its Oscar Wilde, Bugs Bunny, its Batman and its Zorro.

The lineage of the charismatic, picaresque hero stretches right back to the Green Knights of medieval literature. It's a preoccupation that was later transplanted to America, with its frontier criminal outsiders, its Jesse James and Davy Crocket, its Geronimo. Clough stands in this tradition. He is football's contribution, bright-eyed and eternally confrontational.

The Robin Hood parallel was unavoidable given Clough's Nottingham connection, particularly in the footballing press with its mania for the folksy analogy. *The Times* described Clough and Taylor's Forest testimonial match as an occasion for 'The modern Robin Hoods who have filched rich soccer prizes from the old baronial halls of Liverpool and Manchester'. So well-grooved did this Clough/Hood connection become that one national newspaper's review of the 1993 film *Robin Hood: Prince of Thieves* described Alan Rickman's famous turn as the Sheriff of Nottingham as 'a passable impersonation of a bloody-minded Brian Clough'.

It seems fitting that included in Clough's revolving swarm of anecdotes are many tales of his kindnesses. It turns out he also gave to the poor. The journalist Duncan Hamilton wrote that Clough sent people flowers 'as often as others posted letters'. He was once approached by a child with old, worn shoes, who asked him for an autograph. Clough gave the boy two twenty-pound notes. Among his acquaintances debts were repaid and rent arrears quietly cleared. He would pay for strangers' groceries in the supermarket queue. He bought meals for people in restaurants. There are no corroborated records of Clough actually riding through the glen. But somehow it wouldn't surprise you.

Sadly, Clough also stuck to the other side of this tradition, the fatal flaw and inevitable decline. For Clough the fall from grace began in 1980 shortly after Nottingham Forest's second European Cup final victory. In 1982 Taylor resigned, the relationship between the pair having broken down fatally. Clough was still only forty-five. Within two years his Forest team would sink into an unrecognisable mediocrity.

As a manager it was Clough's own much-heralded idiot savant simplicity that would betray him. He was a tactical minimalist. He liked to lay a towel on the floor in the dressing room and place a ball at the centre of it. 'This ball is your best friend,' he would tell his players. 'Love it, caress it.' This kind of thing was frankly unsustainable. The hands-off svengali, glimpsed only briefly at the training ground, had a limited shelf life. For one thing it was rapidly overtaken by a need for more detailed tactical planning. And for another it rested on the undiluted focus of that compelling Clough personality.

Which, to be honest, showed some signs of waning. Clough's drink problem is widely documented. For many years he drank whisky during the day. Later he switched to vodka. Physically, the signs began to show. Clough aged rapidly. He became gaunt and erratic in his pronouncements. The voice remained the same. It was just the unwavering judgement that had gone.

There were times when he seemed to struggle to remember his Forest players' names, often referring to them in public as things like 'the big tall lad'. At one stage in his final season he was spotted making v-signs at his own fans. Towards the end he could sometimes be found asleep in a ditch near his home. Even before this Clough became maudlin and prone to bouts of sorrow over his falling-out with the now-deceased Taylor. 'If only we could go back,' Clough told Duncan Hamilton. 'Relive it . . . see the way things used to be, we'd be more grateful for what we've got now. I know one thing: we'd never have fallen out.'

Nostalgia and death: both become Clough. After the white heat of his youthful ascent, this end period of sadness and retreat is essential to the lasting quality of his legacy. This is what we expect of our English heroes. No story is complete without a beginning, a middle and a sad end. Just as the round table disintegrated, just as all must die young, just as Christopher Robin grew up and left his bear and his hundred-acre wood, so Clough faded out, leaving just a brilliant imprint of his brilliant personality.

Clough

Managers Who Can't Play Any More

Brian Clough's career also raises more strictly football-centric questions. Over the years it has become axiomatic that great players rarely make great managers; that no swag-bag of playing honours can prepare a middle-aged footballing man for the dizzying leap into management.

In fact the opposite would seem to be the case. Failure as a player is key. Failure will do nicely. The one thing you need on your CV is: failure. Alex Ferguson was a cumbersome centre forward, who played semi-professionally until he was twenty-three and then spent four disappointing years at Rangers. The most notable part of his time at Ibrox was being made scapegoat for a 4-0 defeat by Celtic in the 1969 Cup final.

Arsène Wenger began his playing career in the French Third Division and eventually had three years at Strasbourg. Rafa Benitez played at a low level in Spain before retiring through injury. Malcolm Allison retired after losing a lung. Unfinished business, an amateur psychologist – or indeed a professional one – might suggest was the common denominator here.

Jose Mourinho, who also played only at amateur level, has a simpler answer. 'More time to study,' Mourinho shrugged when he was asked about this. And he might have a point, particularly in the era of the Benitez-style technocrat, the stat-master and tactics Ph.D., the dawn of a movement we might call 'The Manager As Geek'.

The corollary of all this is the well-rehearsed list of famous players who turned out to be poor managers. Stanley Matthews, the first player to be knighted for services to the game, took over at Port Vale two years after retiring. Vale were abruptly relegated and the great man caught up in an illegal payments scandal.

Bobby Moore took Southend into an acrimonious relegation to the Fourth Division in his only full season as manager. Bobby Charlton oversaw Preston North End's relegation to the Third Division in 1973. Stories would circulate of Charlton spending training sessions showing his players how he could hit the crossbar nine times out of ten from thirty yards, and advising them to spend most of the coming game picking one another out with immaculate cross-field diagonal passes.

There are of course exceptions. Many excellent players have had moderately successful careers as managers. But it is still hard to pick out an example of a really top English manager, one of the true elite, who didn't have a playing career interrupted or even mildly unfulfilled due to either injury, world war, lack of talent or random acts of misfortune.

You could probably write an entirely separate book geared solely to examining this phenomenon. But you can be certain you'd get bored fairly quickly by the stock responses: a combination of 'you don't have to have been a horse to be a great jockey' (a favourite line of Benitez) and the general notion of instinctive greatness, the idea that those who are truly exceptional at something are often utterly incapable of explaining how to start actually doing it.

Perhaps it's even simpler than this. Being a manager is incredibly difficult. Many come. Very few succeed. Great players, mediocre players, quite good players, they all fail. But there are only ever a handful of great players out there giving it a go. Statistically, what are the chances one of them was going to make it?

Mainly though it's impossible to study the manager's thwarted and occasionally desperate history without coming to the conclusion that being a manager is just a completely separate business. That success as a manager is wholly unrelated to talents such as being good at kicking a ball or being able to run fast.

And perhaps some galvanising sense of incompleteness does help. As a manager you have to want success with a reckless and self-destructive fervour. You have to feel a need to prove yourself every day, to carry around with you a sense that failure and oblivion are always just a breath away.

And perhaps when you've won the World Cup, or when people will keep on insisting on shaking your hand in the street, this kind of quivering, wild-eyed desperation tends to ease off a little. And easing off, that won't do. The manager doesn't ease off. Ease off? He doesn't know how to.

CHAPTER 16

The Manager Falls in Love

We like our heroes to be fully formed. We want them to have a sense of humour a nice car and their own home. But we also demand that they have a softer side: if not exactly flaws, then issues, hobbies, hidden depths. This has always been the way. The concept of the Magnificent Man was formulated by Aristotle. The Magnificent Man was an early notion of the ideal: a jock, a quarterback, but also a brain and hip cat. He fought, he debated, he made music, he burst into tears at the sight of a bunch of peonies. Truly, he was magnificent in many ways.

Later the thinkers, dreamers, posers and fops of the Italian renaissance embraced this idea. Here the Magnificent Man was upgraded to *L'uomo universale*, or the Complete Man. The Complete Man was a scholar and a gentleman. He discoursed knowledgeably on music, painting and sculpture. He dressed nice. He drank deeply. The Complete Man was manly and athletic. He was handy in the saddle, tasty in the wrestling ring, a flier on the track.

The Complete Man was also a sensualist and a rake. He sang,

he danced and he loved prodigiously. This was what it was all about for the Complete Man. He had needs. Complete needs.

And so, with a sense of grim inevitability, it would come to pass for the football manager. Even during the great flowering of his cult of personality, the glory years of the 1960s and early 1970s, the manager had yet to emerge to Completeness. He had yet to show us that, besides innovating, inspiring and shouting, he could dabble in affairs of the heart. But really, in the end it was only a matter of time.

Tommy Docherty has been described – notably by himself – as 'the only manager sacked for falling in love'. Put like that there's still something faintly shocking about it. It's not so much being fired. That sounds fair enough. It's the other bit. Even as he bestrides the contemporary skyline the image of the manager in a romantic swoon is troubling. More than troubling, it's even a bit upsetting.

But still, it happens. Love flowers on the most barren soil. Even in among the touchline-bound quasi-psychosis of the managerial mindset, there is room, apparently, for the brilliant surprise of romantic love. It's all part of the manager's unashamed – and fully realised – propulsion into the light during the second half of the twentieth century.

We already knew he could be angry. It turns out he's capable of finer feelings too. And like a litter of oedipally challenged children of divorce, goggling in silent revulsion as some heavy-bosomed step-mum comes shimmering into the paternal bed chamber stinking of middle-aged sex, the question is, can we really handle this?

It's tempting, still, to say no. No thanks. But this would be going against the tide. The manager has needs, just like anyone else. In Docherty's case, the forbidden fruit of managerial love was flushed out into the open almost by chance, or at least by a combination of historical inevitability and something in Docherty's personal publicity-magnetism.

In his time Docherty was box office. A lively, charming and witty Glaswegian, he was appointed Scotland's first full-time manager in 1967. He had built his reputation on a successful spell at Chelsea, and during his fourteen months in charge of Scotland Docherty became more or less a permanent fixture on television and newspaper back pages.

His presence within the managerial pantheon is more a testimony to this sparky charisma than trophies won and entire clubs single-handedly hewn from the dust. In a *Guardian* newspaper interview in 1980, already some years past the heat of his prime, he was described as having 'the world weary air of the old rake who no longer expects true love every time eyes meet across a crowded room'.

If there was something rakish about Docherty it was a kind of sublimated professional promiscuity, grounded in the dugout-hopping free managerial love of the 1970s, when managers of his ilk – the big personality merchants – would flit from club to club on an insatiable decade-long *grande bouffe*.

Docherty was frisky. He just couldn't help it. Even from beyond the TV lens, or in the pages of one of his many auto-biographies, he seems always to be gripping your shoulder, tickling you, whispering crackerjack one-liners in your ear and buying you a plastic rose from a passing gypsy. His description of trying to get to sleep before making his debut as a Celtic player is uncomfortably sensuous: 'Like most people I have a little routine where sleep is concerned. I settle down in a particular position, only to turn over when I feel I am ready for sleep. I must have done that routine a dozen times . . . I looked at the clock . . . I couldn't get comfortable. The blankets tickled. When I turned on my favourite side the bed covers didn't lie right across my back. There was a draught . . . The pillow was too hot so I flipped it over in order for my face to lie on the cool side.'

You can almost feel the Doc's hand, warm and insistent in the small of your back. No, Doc. Not now. It's too soon. Don't spoil things, Doc. Not that the Doc was really like that. In fact he was a furiously domestic figure, very much the marrying type, the housewife's managerial crumpet. While a Preston player he opened a café called the Olympic. There's a picture of him with oiled hair and wearing an apron, rolling out dough on a board. It's a peculiarly seductive image: the manager as proto-Nigella, a domestic god with freshly ironed pinny, floury fingers and playful sideways glance.

This is where doomed managerial love first starts to intrude. Any history of Docherty has to put up with him falling in love – proper mistily recounted love – not just once but twice. This is a central theme in his story. So first up we get him meeting 'the girl of my dreams in Girvan' in October 1948.

'It was for me at any rate, love at first sight,' Docherty wrote of meeting his first wife. 'I had never set eyes on such a beautiful girl, nor one with the personality to match. Agnes was vibrant, had a keen wit and her conversation never failed to enthral me . . . Every street which contained memory of her became like a shrine to me'.

This is wonderfully fulsome, tender stuff. It just doesn't sound, you know, like a football manager. Before Docherty, managers' life partners – the MWAGS – were not exactly taboo. They were just discreetly shoved into the background. Managerial wives were mute and forbidding, a faithful lineage of invisible Ednas and Noras. Bill Shankly's wife Ness provided the archetype of the football widow: an uncomplaining makeweight, silently tending her husband's distant furies and passions.

According to popular myth Ness and Bill had only two nights out during the entire twenty-five years of his career. Certainly Shankly was the main impetus behind the managerial wife's emergence as football's equivalent of the Les Dawson mother-in-law figure, an invisible straight-woman for the manager's one-track gags and funnies. Shankly was said to have taken Ness to watch a football match on their honeymoon. He later denied taking her to see Rochdale play as an anniversary present. 'It was her birthday,' he explained, deadpan. 'Anyway, it was Rochdale reserves.'

Basically the manager was supposed to be in love with only one thing. Football was his libido and his life partner. Sexless, one-dimensional, his needs utterly sated by a single overriding obsession, the manager seemed safely preoccupied. When it came to matters of the heart, he simply didn't have one. Or if he did, it was full up with things like zonal marking, scouting systems and 4-3-3 formations. Alf Ramsey once introduced his wife to Spurs goalkeeper Ron Reynolds at a club social. 'You won't mind having a dance with her, will you?' he asked Reynolds. So Reynolds danced Mrs Ramsey around all evening while Alf sat down and talked football.

Major Frank Buckley's wife famously — and reassuringly — never called him anything other than 'the Major'. Jimmy Hogan was rarely seen in the company of his wife and children by either friends or relatives, so much so that it was often a shock to find out, years later, that they even existed. Most tellingly, Alec Stock's wife Marjorie wrote the definitive job description for the early managerial wife in Stock's book *Football Club Manager*. 'I must have spent more hours than anyone in Christendom looking out of a window with food ready and waiting in the kitchen. He never rings me to say he will be late, and if the team loses he slips into long silences or sleeps restlessly.'

This is what we had come to expect. We wanted Ness, dignified and distant. Or we wanted Marjorie Stock, long-suffering, curtain-twitching, and resignedly not up to any funny stuff. Imagine our shock, then, when from Docherty we got this instead: 'Despite the distance between us and the brief periods we spent together, our love flourished . . . we set a date to be married'. Whoa there. Why, you wonder, hands over your ears, humming loudly, are we being told all this?

It's really not Docherty's fault. The reason he feels forced to tell us these things – and you do feel terribly sorry for him – is that he's right. He was fired for falling in love. This would become the defining feature of his memorable managerial life. In 1972, after a successful spell as Scotland manager, Docherty was tempted back into club management at Manchester United. It was the peak of his ascent. It might have been the spur for a decade of crushing, era-defining success. But it wasn't. Because before we knew it, he was falling in love again – in forbidden love this time – with Mary Brown, then wife of the United physiotherapist.

This remains the most high-profile of all managerial love affairs. Unfairly, irrationally, it still makes you cringe slightly too. Docherty got to know his future second wife when they were both visiting her husband in hospital. And soon the whole thing is unfolding in the classic style. 'We found conversation came easily . . . We felt ourselves being drawn closer . . . There was no denying our feelings . . . I sat Agnes down and told her'.

This is also a story with a happy ending. 'Thirty years have passed and Mary and I are still very much in love and gloriously happy,' Docherty tells us, making us blush and cough uncomfortably. The Manchester United board took a dimmer view. Docherty was sacked and, to all intents and purposes, his career would never be the same again.

In a saner, more rounded world, the Doc would have kept his job. Everybody would have been very civilised about things. Eventually they might even have gone on holidays together, enjoyed wonderful dinner parties, joked about it. But this isn't a civilised world. This is the manager's world. We might have thought the manager couldn't shock us any more. We were wrong. The manager's quivering awakening, the warmth of his managerial bed, this is all, still, frankly a bit much to take, even from the friendly, frisky, husbandly Doc.

There is another side to this story, however. The managerial world is not entirely without love. We do find tenderness there.

We find the right kind of love. We find manly love. And manly managerial tenderness. Around about the same time Docherty was being sacked, Brian Clough and Peter Taylor were giving football its first great in-house love story.

This was love between manager and manager; both an exalted and a wonderfully productive thing. We always needed a love story in here somewhere. The moving Hellenic friendship between Clough and Taylor is a main source of the manager's furrowed emotional depths. He can feel. And he can also have close male friends without there being anything funny about it.

Clough and Taylor worked together as co-managers at Hartlepool, Derby County and Nottingham Forest. They stuck it out through the bad times. They chinked champagne flutes in the good times. 'You don't normally find pearls in Middlesbrough,' was Clough's verdict. 'I did, the day when I met Pete for the first time.'

Taylor was Clough's soulmate and his failsafe. They met as players at Middlesbrough and quickly became inseparable. They talked football and politics obsessively. Taylor, the older man, took Clough to listen to shadow chancellor Harold Wilson speak at a Middlesbrough working men's club, the two emerging 'burning' with a passion for change. 'Nothing separated us in those early days,' Clough said. 'It was the closest we came as friends.'

In many ways the lasting image of their relationship was its eventual break-up. By 1982, two years after Forest's second European Cup victory, things were falling apart. Taylor had become paranoid and exhausted. He was convinced his phones were tapped. There were creeping dissatisfactions, not least with the galling failure to provide an extra gallon of Bell's whisky, the prize whenever the pair (although namely Clough) won manager of the month. His low-key revelatory book, *With Clough By Taylor* – with its casually dropped suggestion that working with Clough might have been the cause of Taylor's recent heart attack – was the final straw. It was all over.

As Clough biographer Pat Murphy noted, tight-lipped, 'the break-up was civilised enough'. It was also played out in public. The two came dramatically face to face shortly after Taylor's return to football as Derby manager, as his team were drawn against Forest in the FA Cup. After the game Clough said, 'I've missed Peter Taylor since the day he walked out on me.'

There was bitterness there too. Clough wrote in a newspaper column that if he saw Taylor hitch-hiking along the A52 he would run him over. But more than anything there was regret. 'Brian and I had some great times together, travelling the world,' Taylor recalled. 'We laughed, we bullied, we cried and succeeded.'

At times, as his powers waned, Clough would say to his captain Ian Bowyer, 'Get me down the tunnel, pal', because he couldn't bear walking out before a game without Taylor. Lawrie McMenemy once recalled finding Clough alone in the team bath after a match during his first season of sole charge. 'He was very low. I sat on the edge of the bath and he told me a few things about the break-up'. After Taylor's death, a grief-stricken Clough dedicated his autobiography to him with the words 'Still miss you badly.'

This is wonderfully moving stuff. From Edwardian tight-ass, through his mid-years as John Wayne, the unflinching tough guy, the manager had now become loved-up, saucer-eyed and overflowing with the more delicate emotions. And this, apparently, was fine with everyone. The story of Clough and Taylor's enduring love is one of football's most tenderly guarded tales. This kind of male companionship – manager-on-manager action – is safely within his range. We're cool with that. So Brian and Pete gave us a royal couple, a double act to sit alongside the great male friendships: Horatio and Hamlet, Sal and Dean, Boswell and Johnson, Sebastian and Charles.

The *Brideshead Revisited* parallel is worth lingering on. Sebastian Flyte and Charles Ryder, the pair of languid, youthful toffs at the heart of Evelyn Waugh's novel, provided one of the most popular models for the notion of doomed male love. In Clough and Taylor football gave us a working-class *Brideshead*. This was Charles and Sebastian reimagined amid the baroque glories of League championships, European Cups, the Baseball Ground, Michael Parkinson and TV adverts for East Midland Electricity.

It's not an entirely fanciful parallel. The peak Clough years came in 1979 and 1980. Clough and Taylor, at this point, bestrode the sporting universe. A year later, in 1981, the lavish ITV adaptation of Evelyn Waugh's *Brideshead* was screened to a rapturous reception. And as the extended drama of Clough and Taylor's break-up swirled around the old First Division, so *Brideshead* hit America and went double platinum.

Plus, Clough just seemed to have this effect on people. If you spent enough time around him, you inevitably began to swoon, to yearn to brush, tenderly, the stray lock from his collar. In the *Brideshead* parallel Clough was always Flyte, the mercurial, teddy bear-toting maverick. All he needed was a Ryder: quieter, more reflective, a perfect foil.

Twenty-six years after Clough and Taylor broke up, the journalist Duncan Hamilton published his widely fêted account of his time reporting on Clough for the *Nottingham Evening Post*. Like Taylor, Hamilton was powerfully drawn to Clough. He followed his star, becoming his amanuensis, his straight man and his travelling companion. And he kind of loved him too. Hamilton's book, *Provided You Don't Kiss Me*, is brilliantly written and a compelling story. It won prizes. It reinforced the powerful Clough mythology. And it has at its centre another genuine love story. Like *Brideshead*, like Clough and Taylor, Clough and Hamilton gives us the manager recast as object of the most tender, and Platonic, reverence.

If you thought Taylor and Clough was a bit like *Brideshead*, just check out Hamilton and Clough. The story begins with the young Hamilton yearning to breach the confines of his narrow world. 'I longed to escape across the river Trent. That was where you found Brian Clough . . . And after that one season covering Notts County my wish came true.'

Compare this with *Brideshead*'s Charles Ryder longing to escape the provincial boundaries of his college rooms. 'Even in the earliest days, when the whole business of living at Oxford, with rooms of my own and my own cheque book, was a source of excitement, I felt at heart that this was not all Oxford had to offer.'

Then comes the gut-wrenching, low-comic, opening encounter with the Flyte/Clough love object. Hamilton: 'The first words Brian Clough ever said to me were: "So who the fuck are you then?" . . . A queasy apprehension filled my stomach.' Ryder: 'He looked at me for a moment with unfocused eyes and then, leaning forwards well into the room, he was sick.'

This exciting new friend is also a bit of a looker. Hamilton: 'He was just a few weeks short of his forty-second birthday, fit and vigorous. His hair was healthily thick and swept back, his face lean and virtually unlined.' Ryder: 'He was entrancing, with that epicene beauty which in extreme youth sings aloud for love and withers at the first cold wind.'

Before long our narrator is whisked off his feet. Ryder: 'It was an aesthetic education to live within those walls, to wander from room to room, from the Soanesque library to the Chinese drawing room, adazzle with gilt pagodas and nodding mandarins, painted paper and Chippendale fretwork.' Hamilton: 'I saw the stubby-framed Diego Maradona perform juggling and conjuring tricks in a pre-season friendly . . . I saw Forest claw back a two-goal deficit in the European Cup semi-final . . . Gary Birtles and Tony Woodcock seemed to be running on silk.'

At one point our hero even finds himself cast out into exile from the place he loves most. Leaving Flyte's mum, Lady Marchmain: 'I don't understand how we all liked you so much.

Did you hate us all the time? . . . As I drove away and turned back in the car to take what promised to be my last view of the house, I felt that I was leaving part of myself behind.' Clough to Hamilton: 'Take your fucking portable typewriter and stick it up your arse. You're banned . . . You come into this club and we treat you like a friend . . . And you fucking insult us. You know fuck all about this game. Fuck all. Don't stand there, just fuck off!'

Only to be welcomed back into the fold in giddy fashion. Flyte: 'You've got to come away at once. I've got a motor car and a basket of strawberries and a bottle of Chateau Peyraguey.' Clough: 'Come down and we'll have a drink. I've got a story for you. Fancy a glass of champagne?'

Undercutting all this, in both stories, there lurks the ever-present tinge of tragedy. Hamilton eventually drifts out of football, crippled by 'acute disillusionment' as Clough, his inspiration, is reduced to a shambling, drunken figure, much like the handsome, alcoholic Flyte, who ends up in exile in a Moroccan monastery.

Tender feelings for the manager, then. This is his emotional register: noble, doomed, non-touchy-feely love. This is his territory. At least, it's all we're really going to let him get away with. The manager's myth did always require some hint of vulnerability, some suggestion he had a heart as well as biceps, fists and a big mouth. And secretly, perhaps, we all feel the manager might like us – you know, in that way – if only he knew us better. Like a million teenage groupies, our walls plastered with fan junk and centre-spread, perhaps some tiny part of us imagines the manager might yet pick us for his special friend and soul brother. If only we could sit down and have a proper chat some time, tell him what we really think, and impose some tiny part of ourselves on his thrillingly vital and raw managerial world. We're available, anyway. If the manager ever wants to talk or anything. Maybe get some coffee. Go for a ride in a punt. We're just saying.

CHAPTER 17

The Manager Embraces the Dark Side

At times the history of the football manager can seem like a bit of a one-note affair. Plaudits are handed out. Garlands are strewn. Extended all-star ovations are solemnly endured. The history of the manager, just like the history of everything else, is written by the winners. And at times it can resemble a sheep-skin-coated Baftas, an unceasing round of backs slapped and tearful eulogies delivered.

Happily, the manager resists this tendency. He rails against it. Because the fact is, the manager does not always embrace the light. Occasionally he seeks out the sinister. When he's good, he's very good. When he's bad, he's innocent of any charges until somebody proves otherwise. And when he's really bad, he's Don Revie.

In many ways, Revie is the most interesting of the super-managers of the 1960s and 1970s. Revie was our super-villain. Large-scale, cartoonish, a hunched and fidgety silhouette, he was hugely successful at Leeds United – but also creepy, furtive and seemingly always on the cusp of some explosion of nervous hysteria.

'It has always riled me when I see the career Revie has had. He was always an evil man to me,' Bob Stokoe once said. This is the kind of language Revie has attracted. It just seems to fit him. When Leeds beat the champions Derby 5-0 in October 1972 the *Guardian* match report noted: 'Don Revie, the Leeds United manager, scarcely could conceal his delight', but mused that 'there was a sinister side to the game which overshadowed all. The forces of evil were greater than those for good'.

Two years earlier, Revie himself, wringing his giant hands, had railed against 'this reputation for being a dirty and a "method" side. Nearly everywhere we went we were booed on to the field and again at the end . . . One bloke at Everton threatened to shoot me as soon as I sat on the trainer's bench.'

Revie fulfilled a need. He brought us the notion of the managerial dark side, of something epic and treacle-black within the depths of his trench coat. A Two-Face to Brian Clough's avenging Batman, Revie brought a sense of epic internal battle. The feud with Clough, in particular, was thrillingly personal. For a while, around the time of his own doomed attempt to succeed Revie at Leeds United, Clough's hatred for his counterpart was almost his defining feature. This antipathy was based in a suspicion that Revie bought off referees, based on covert conversations Clough claimed to have interrupted once after a match at Elland Road.

It was a two-hander played out in cinematic widescreen. And a public face-off that had the incidental effect of catapulting the manager ever deeper into the public consciousness. Most famously, they met in a televised head-to-head on the BBC, which centred on the correctness or otherwise of Clough's sacking at Leeds after just forty-four days. This was a managerial presidential debate, Clough and Revie trading high-speed verbal blows in extreme, sweaty close-up. For the occasion Revie was squashed into an electric blue blazer and dark tie. He snorted and fretted and silently shook his head as Clough, sprightly in light-grey suit and striped shirt, goaded and joked and mugged to the camera.

'I wanted to win the League but I wanted to win it better,' Clough announced. 'That's impossible,' Revie muttered. 'We'd only lost four matches.' 'Well, I could only lose three!' was the haranguing, victorious reply. Most agreed that Clough had won the debate. But, then, that was what we wanted to hear. Fresh-faced and televisual, Cloughie was our fine-featured JFK next to Revie's bulky, sweating Richard Nixon.

Revie's super-evil was a curious kind of thing. In *Paradise Lost* Milton's Satan is, it's generally accepted, a far more sympathetic character than the assorted blameless paragons of the God squad. We warm to Satan's mischief. This is often the way. The devil always gets the best tunes. With Revie, for some reason, the sympathies ran dry. A genuinely great manager, he remains marginalised, uncared for and peculiarly unattractive.

Partly this is because he was up against a more charismatic – and equally flawed character – in Clough. Partly it's because of football's overriding geographical tribalism. And partly it's because Revie just doesn't try to make you like him. He simply doesn't care about that. Like all comic-book super-villains, he had his own agenda. He had his own super-neuroses, his super-sorrows, his super-flaws. This is a man without a mask, just a series of twitches and tics.

Like Clough, Revie was born in Middlesbrough. He endured the standard terrible managerial upbringing among the terraced cottages of the new industrial poor. His mother died when he was twelve. He left school at fourteen to become an apprentice bricklayer. He first played senior football at Leicester City, where he was so keen to learn – while spending half a day lugging bricks around – that he would occasionally burst into tears from exhaustion.

Even as a player, Revie was stalked by the incidental and the bizarre. He missed the 1949 FA Cup final after suffering a burst blood vessel in his nose. Five days after picking up the injury his nose began to bleed incessantly. He was taken on an eight-hour taxi ride from Plymouth for treatment at Leicester Royal Infirmary. He bled all the way there in the car. Another hour, he was told, and he would have died.

This kind of peculiar luck would stoke Revie's enduring beliefs in fortune and fate. The wheel would duly spin full circle at the 1956 FA Cup final. Dropped from the Manchester City side, Revie found himself recalled when on the morning of the match winger Billy Spurdle developed boils. Revie, showing an early glimpse of his supernatural hunch-antenna, had kept himself fit on a diet of sherry and eggs. He was man of the match as City won the Cup.

Revie moved to Leeds, where he captained a team that teetered close to the shambolic. Training consisted of long runs, at the end of which senior players would arrive back with ice lollies in their hands. Before one vital away game at Blackburn Rovers during the relegation season of 1959–60 Leeds stopped in a huge hurry at a café near the ground and ate beans on toast as a pre-match meal.

Revie was eventually appointed manager by board member Harry Reynolds, a self-made steel magnate. Together they set about reconstructing the club, consciously aping the patriarchal Matt Busby formula at Manchester United. Leeds became a family affair, almost to a creepy and intrusive degree. The players' wives were hugely involved. Revie sent flowers on their birthdays. He found houses for players' families and even jobs for their fathers.

This was a strict and unforgiving family. Revie sacked twenty-seven players in his first two years. Junior players were taught about bank accounts, table manners and sex, what Revie described as 'keeping their hair short and their clothes smart and not getting caught up with loose girls'. He would even shun friends who had marital problems. In the early days Mike

O'Grady, the only single first-team regular, was continually asked when he was going to get married. He eventually left. 'The family [Revie] wanted was the football team. They were his children,' Peter Veitch, the chairman's son-in-law once said.

Leeds began to develop an aura. The sense of some powerful, insular force abroad in the game was palpable. Players leaving to go to other teams found their new team-mates fascinated by them, and even slightly afraid. This was, after all, the era of the gang. Suedeheads, skinheads, mods, greasers and rockers: these were the tribes that stalked the fringes of football's urban milieu. In concentric circles beyond this lay the endlessly fractured ideological boot-boys of the 1970s. The hard left and the far right, the Trotskyites and Living Marxists of the Tooting Popular Front, and its ongoing fatwa with the Streatham Nationalist Liberation Army. Positions were taken, kickings handed out and train carriages bloodied. The miners and the Met. The IRA in London and Birmingham. And feral, pack-like Leeds, stalking their way towards a position of ascendancy in the old First Division.

In the middle of this Revie was the managerial Don, a blue-suited Teddy boy king. This was the era of Dirty Leeds. As Jack Charlton – pictured relaxing 'with a good honest pint' – wrote in the 1969 *Charles Buchan's Soccer Gift Book*, 'Yes, we were respected and feared wherever we went.' Revie told his players to hunt in packs, to surround the referee whenever captain Billy Bremner committed an assault on another player. He told them to feign injury, to waste time when they had the lead. During one infamous victory at Everton the referee took the players off the field and told them to stop kicking each other or he would abandon the match.

Even in victory, they could be wicked. There was the ruthless 10-0 defeat of the amateurs of Lyn Oslo at Elland Road. And, famously, the televised 7-0 defeat of Southampton in March 1972, during which Leeds players kept the ball with disdainful –

and brilliantly skilled – élan, humiliating their opponents as Barry Davies on commentary cried out, 'Every man-Jack of this Leeds team is turning it on . . . It's almost cruel!'

This was a rare excursion into the gratuitous flamboyance of the showboat. Above all Leeds had a mania for victory. Throughout the Revie era they carried a strain of something wild and introverted. In his second season at the club they were battling relegation. For the last three months Revie barely slept. He stayed up drinking endless cups of tea and brooding, hyper-sensitive and fixated.

Revie's England captain Mick Channon would later call him 'a very nervous man . . . You could see that in him. He would sweat through nerves. I don't think he could trust anyone.' This was his peculiar villainous tic: the rivers of sweat, the deadly fidget, the lethal endless muttering.

'He was a big man with big hands,' the winger Eddie Gray recalled. 'I remember the hands because when he brought his fist down on a table – something that he often did when upset – the whole room seemed to reverberate. If we had not played well, the other warning signal for us was his habit of storming into the dressing room after the match, briefly combing his hair in the mirror and then going out again without saying a word.'

This was Revie's strength: his maniacal super-energy. He would often drive to Scotland in the mid-afternoon to talk to the parents of a player he might be interested in signing, then drive back through the night and be first out on the training field at 8.30 the next morning. His dossiers became legend, obsessively compiled profiles of opponents, testimony to his Mekon super-brain. Before one FA Cup tie against non-League Sutton, Revie's dossier was utterly thrown by some minor issue of seating around the pitch, leading to a pointless and bitter pre-match wrangle (Leeds still won 6-0). He couldn't stop, though. This was his terrible burden.

The dossiers – with their scrabbling insistence that the truth was out there somewhere – were the thin end of Revie's lurking paganism, his super-flaw. For all his fact-finding, Revie was a terribly superstitious man. He believed in magic. He read the entrails. He consorted with the unseen. The spirits would come to him at moments of great tension. During the famously bruising FA Cup final against Chelsea in 1970 Revie had a premonition. Leeds had just taken the lead with six minutes to go. Watching his players celebrate Revie was overcome with a sudden sense of disaster. He had to be physically restrained from rushing on to the pitch. The equalising goal came almost immediately, followed by a replay lost late in extra time. Revie would later let it be known he blamed defeat on Princess Margaret for wearing green as she watched from the Royal box.

This was the way of Revie's Leeds. The veil between the visible and the invisible was stretched thin. Before Leeds won the League Cup, the first trophy of the Revie era, Terry Cooper had dreamed he would score the winning goal. Revie was totally unsurprised when this came to pass. Every player had his good luck charm, his pre-match ritual. And Revie himself would personally supervise a ceremonial Thursday 'soap massage', rubbing the players down vigorously with his own huge healer's hands.

His odd habits included sending all his players congratulatory telegrams whenever they played an international. Even when he moved to Birmingham Gary Sprake kept receiving well-meaning telegrams from Revie, including while he was in hospital recovering from a back operation.

Revie always walked the same route to his dugout and continued wearing his lucky blue suit even when it became terribly shabby. Ludicrously, he had a fear of ornamental elephants. Also of birds: he once visited the chairman's daughter's new house and refused to go into the bedroom because there were pictures of birds on the wall. 'You don't have birds in your house. You don't have birds anywhere,' he explained.

Perhaps unsurprisingly, Revie also believed a gypsy curse had been placed on Elland Road. In 1971 he duly invited a gypsy from Scarborough to visit the club and ordered her to lift whatever lingering hex still hovered about the ground. Unsurprisingly because the gypsy curse remains football's chief enduring superstition, the must-have for every managerial star-gazer. As long ago as 1946 Derby County paid off some descendants of Romany gypsies evicted from the site of their Baseball Ground, supposedly in return for the lifting of an accompanying curse. The next season they won the FA Cup for the first time.

Revie codified all this, bringing it under the managerial wing so much so that it's almost part of the job description now to have some quirk or phobia. For a hundred years, until its formal expiry in 2006, Birmingham City had laboured under their own gypsy curse, placed on St Andrews by Romanies evicted from its site in 1906. Following Revie's lead, Ron Saunders tried to banish the curse in the 1980s by putting crucifixes on top of the floodlight pylons and painting the bottom of his players' boots red. Clearly an expert in the paranormal, Ron told *Match of the Day* the club had brought in 'a healer, and . . . Madame Rossini, who is . . . a horoscope person'.

Barry Fry, in charge of Birmingham from 1993 to 1996, would take the advice of a clairvoyant and attempt to lift the curse by passing managerial water in all four corners of the pitch on the stroke of midnight. This is one of those stories that gets repeated so often that you start to wonder if it's just a part of the ongoing myth kitty of the dugout. But apparently not. 'Yes, I weed in all four corners,' Fry confirmed. 'To be honest it was the club secretary who told me about the curse, and about how Ron used to put crosses on all the doors. I said to him, "Well what happened after that?" He said, "He got the sack." But I had to try something. We were on a terrible run.'

I asked Barry what happened after that. 'The next day we lost

4-0 to Wolves,' he said. 'But really it was just a laugh. I'm not superstitious. Most managers are. But I'm not.'

This is a common theme among managers. It's not me. It's them. But someone out there must be a believer because this kind of thing is still going on. Southampton's move to the St Mary's ground in 2001 involved the excavation of some pre-Christian tombs. After a miserable start at their new home, the club employed a white witch to exorcise lurking unhappy spirits.

More recently this kind of wand-waving has incorporated imported orientalism. In 2007 Manchester City attempted to transform their City of Manchester Stadium into 'a hub of positive energy and harmony' with the use of feng shui, immediately dubbed 'Sven Shui', after the manager Sven-Goran Eriksson. Sven Shui involved burying magic crystals beneath the pitch and hanging club offices with Buddhas, three-legged money toads and lucky fortune trees, one of which, it was reported in the magazine *When Saturday Comes*, still had its price tag (£24.95 from B&Q).

Happily, the managerial superstition has even survived the transition to the enlightened modern era of the overseas polymath. While he was Newcastle manager Ruud Gullit was seen shouting at the FA Cup's sponsors to remove the trophy from Newcastle's training ground when they turned up to ask the players to pose for a photo with it. Tottenham's Spanish manager Juande Ramos brought with him not just a strict grasp of modern nutritional trends but a set of beliefs that involved avoiding using the telephone on the day of a game and putting his right foot first on to the turf before each match.

Revie was the first to flush all this out into the open. By the time Ramos turned up, with his by now almost standard refusal to look at the Carling Cup before Spurs' victorious final appearance in 2008, it was pretty much the norm. A belief in the obscure magic of the ritual and the hex was a part of the richly textured managerial presence.

For Revie, however, this was no mere flirtation. Revie was living it, bedevilled by the drip-drip of his own super-neuroses. And it was Revie's inevitable torture to find himself in charge of an almost-great team of nearly-Invincibles. Leeds were runners-up in the League on five separate occasions, winning it just twice, and were beaten finalists in Cup competitions on five occasions. It's impossible not to see in this fragility that underlying skein of hysteria, fear of the sun-god and the magpie, the runes, the tea leaf, the stink-eye.

Revie never quite escaped his fears. In 1974, having just won the League with Leeds, he took the England job. This would finish him. Following his patterns, arranging his soup tins in a straight line and furiously refolding his towels, he tried to recreate the dense and cloying family atmosphere of Leeds. He decreed that 'Land of Hope and Glory' should be played before matches and song sheets handed out to the crowd. The dossiers were wheeled out again. Pre-match games of bingo and carpet bowls were foisted on the cowboy-booted swingers of the maverick-era England squad.

Denied an outlet for his restless energy, Revie sank into tinkering with his team and travelling with a top-heavy entourage of hangers-on and flunkies. Against Wales he picked Peter Taylor, who was playing in the Third Division with Crystal Palace. For the home international against Northern Ireland he made nine changes to his first eleven. Throughout Revie gurned on the touchline, a large, peculiar-looking man in a black raincoat, flailing, lip-chewing, fatally distracted by his own periphery of magic spells and secret codes.

Eventually he fled. On 12 July 1977 news broke of Revie's guerrilla gaol-break. It was a ludicrously cloak-and-dagger affair. Supposedly scouting future England opponents, Revie instead flew under an assumed name – disguised beneath a flat cap and accompanied by Jeff Powell of the *Daily Mail* – to Dubai via Switzerland and Athens, there to coach the UAE. Powell had left behind his scoop story of Revie's exit in an envelope, which was also delivered to FA HQ. Disaster almost struck: Revie was spotted at Athens airport by a British man who called the papers. Luckily he called the *Daily Mail*.

Revie would find some happiness in the employ of Sheikh Mana bin Khalifa Al Maktoum, coaching Emirates club Al Nasr and lounging on the sheikh's beach, with its quarter of a mile of private sands. His final activity of note in England came with an appearance in the High Court, at which Revie overturned the FA's ten-year ban. The case was most notable for the terrible scorn poured on Revie. Mr Justice Cantley, in his summing up, described him as 'prickly', 'utterly selfish', 'lacking in candour' and – most notably – 'brooding on imagined wrongs'.

Those imagined wrongs, the rabbit's foots and lucky lumps of coal, the terrible shrinking horizon of his own capacities – this was Revie's desert peninsula. Even as he suffered from Motor Neurone Disease in his final years, he was still stalked by the crankish. As his condition declined a sensational story appeared in the *News of the World* that Revie had found 'a miracle cure', which would be paid for by the sheikh and administered in a Moscow hospital. Sadly this was simply more Revie-guff and Revie codswallop. He remains one of the great managers, and perhaps the most fascinating of all the big-personality merchants of the 1970s. Decked out in Real Madrid white, Revie's Leeds played black. And in the middle of it all, it's impossible not to like him just a little bit, isn't it?

CHAPTER 18

The Manager Gets Laid

So much for love. The manager, we knew now, had a heart. Still there was the lingering suspicion that he might have other needs too. That he might need something a little more than simply companionship and the odd hot meal. We could cope with him falling in love. But could we cope with the hot funk of his managerial pheromones?

Throughout the majority of the twentieth century the manager had a guileless quality. He was an innocent. Alf Ramsey used to greet his wife in public by shaking hands with her. He once said that after an argument they liked to 'shake hands and make up'.

And frankly, we'd have been quite happy just leaving it at that. When Marjorie Stock wrote in Alec Stock's *Football Club Manager*, 'A lot has happened since the night I woke Alec up in the small ours and told him: "I hope you break your leg tomorrow",' there's something confusing even in that brief glimpse between the managerial sheets. Stock himself is far more reassuring on this front: 'I do get irritated when I, say, go to a dinner and businessmen around me turn the conversation to women. They start telling jokes, dirty jokes, and they start to giggle, and I say to myself: "Where do these children come from?" I am told that they are "successful business-men" and I am left to conclude this is probably what they do in business. Yet I very rarely hear blue stories in dressing rooms. If anyone tries, he is almost cold-shouldered. A barrier goes up. That is the way of football.'

And so it was, from the outside at least. Many years on from the media's discovery of sex in 1963 – around about the time of the Chatterley ban and the Beatles' first LP – we were still fairly safe on this front. The notion of the kiss and tell story had made its first appearance with the publication of Regency courtesan Harriette Wilson's memoirs in 1831, a shag-saga that included among its personnel the Prince of Wales, the Lord Chancellor, four future Prime Ministers and the Duke of Wellington, who famously advised 'publish and be damned'.

It would be another hundred years before the kiss and tell reached the popular press. The early randy reverend tone was set by the story in the *Empire News* of the Rector of Stiffkey and his vicarage-based adventures in prostitution. It would take the 1970s to elevate the sex splash to an authentic daily celebrity staple, not just a badge of office but a way of actually becoming famous in the first place.

The front rank for the new era of tabloid head-hunting was predictable enough: pop stars, actors and members of the House of Lords. Britt Ekland. Rod Stewart. Pamela Des Barres. Lord Lambton. If these were all fair game, the football manager was at first kept chastely out of sight. The spectacle of the thrusting managerial hip, the sweep of his sweat-beaded comb-over, was all still some way off.

In part this was because football managers still weren't quite famous enough to carry the dirt-digging splash. But on the whole it was because football reporting remained a tight-knit business, a divvying-up among friends, with flights and hotels shared, home telephone numbers given out, secrets kept and backs scratched. The manager still had some favours to call in here. The dam broke towards the end of the 1970s, as the manager's celebrity, the rising tide of his importance, became too much to contain. Sex sold newspapers. Managers sold newspapers. As football became the territory of the showbiz hack and newshound, the conclusion was reached that a combination of the two might just do the same. The manager was about to leap – tight-lipped, ashen-faced and clad in just a pair of leopard-print club-colour bikini briefs – on to the Sunday front page.

This was in many ways an inevitable side-effect of the rise of the Showman. A big-haired, showbiz-inflected figure, the Showman arrived in football management in the early to mid-1970s, with the flowering of Malcolm Allison's unignorable Big Mal persona. As Big Mal, Allison managed Manchester City, Crystal Palace and Middlesbrough with varying degrees of success, but always with a dandyish sense of bravado.

Allison also introduced sex into the managerial repertoire, the casual, good-time, swinging sex of the 1970s, the kind that usually involved that other 1970s species, the dolly bird. Not to mention such 1970s sex props as fur coats, the reek of male cologne and some confused sense of personal empowerment. Allison was a face on the London nightclub scene. He revealed in his memoirs that he had a brief fling with Christine Keeler, the call-girl who had been involved in the Profumo affair. 'We went out a couple of times and I recall that we made love,' Allison wrote, languidly (Keeler later denied this last bit).

Allison left his wife for a Playboy bunny girl called Serena Williams. 'Mal is a terrific lover,' Williams told the *Daily Mirror*, in the first recorded example of far too much managerial sex-life information. 'He is the sort of man women come up to and freak out over on the spot.'

The high water mark of Allison's freak-out-inducing love god status came at Crystal Palace in 1976. He found himself in much hot water after inviting the glamour model and actress Fiona Richmond – star of *Electric Blue* and *Let's Get Laid* – to join him in the team bath after training. Allison and Richmond were captured frolicking by lurking photographers. A line had been crossed. *Daily Mirror* readers responded with 'a sizzling postbag'. The paper's £10 star letter described the picture as 'an affront to public decency . . . Allison should be sternly reminded that he holds a position in football which usually calls for a modicum of dignity'.

But did it really? The manager was out there now. He was making the scene. The definitive managerial sex scandal of the 1980s would arrive with the *Sunday People's* 1984 splash on Manchester United boss Ron Atkinson's two-year relationship with his 'blonde mistress Maggie'. This was a landmark affair for the manager. The big thing here was that Atkinson kept his job. Unashamed and unapologetic, he hung in there.

It was a proper warts and all job, too. Even the neighbours were called in, eyewitnesses to the spectacle of blooming managerial courtship. 'He even used to leave his Mercedes on her front drive — and you don't get many Mercs round here,' commented one notably uncensorious onlooker. 'Maggie is a beautiful lady. She jets around the world on business and has a permanent tan.'

Widely desired, a big man having a big affair, Ron seemed to float above it all. The manager had arrived at another docking point within the mainstream. He was now quarry to the sleaze-merchant, a staple of the love-rat splash, whether we liked it or not. Ultimately we would endure the writhing embarrassments of Sven-Goran Eriksson's reign as England manager, which was punctuated by a series of explicitly recalled sexual encounters. Eriksson's recumbent, eerily placid demeanour made these additionally bizarre.

His most brilliantly postmodern affair of the heart was with the TV celebrity and fellow Swede Ulrika Jonsson. Sven and

Ulrika were introduced to one another by Alastair Campbell, at the fiftieth birthday party of the *Express* newspaper owner and pornographer Richard Desmond. Ulrika immediately confided her attraction to Vanessa Feltz. The ensuing fling was reported in Ulrika's own serialised memoirs, the star detail the stack-heeled shoes left by the England manager outside her bedroom door as a do-not-disturb sign for the nanny.

Primed and ready, it seemed we might even be able to ride out the arrival of Jose Mourinho at Chelsea in the summer of 2004. Brilliantly handsome, by March 2005 Mourinho had installed himself as chief sexpot, the most widely lusted-after manager of all time. A year after his arrival he was being described over a whole spread in the *Mirror*'s main pages as 'a Portuguese man of PPHHWWOOAAAARR!!'

'He's ruggedly handsome, intelligent, rich, suave, sophisticated,' the paper frothed. 'But Jose Mourinho is a dark and brooding enigma . . . From his "smouldering eyes", his "cleverness" and his dark good-looks, no one doesn't fancy Mr Mourinho.'

Part of Mourinho's appeal was his doe-eyed fidelity to his wife, Tami. Three years later he would duly appear in the *Sun* calling '[his mistress] Elsa Sousa his "Princess"'. Even worse, 'hunk Mourinho lived up to his nickname the Special One as he and his mistress made love for hours — to the music of rock star Sting'.

This turns out to be a constant feature of the Mourinho boudoir. As the paper reported separately: 'A pal of thirty-four-year-old Elsa said: "He particularly likes making love to Sting."' And elsewhere again: 'Elsa said he loved making love to soft rock music like Bryan Adams and Sting.' It can only be hoped that this isn't the start of a libidinal trend among football managers. At the very least, listening to the music of Sting appears to be no longer an option.

There are good reasons why we squirm slightly at all this

stuff. The managerial role carries with it a delicate balance of the more austere virtues. The fatherly, the political, the pastoral, the comic: there is a subtle interweaving of roles at work here. Our feelings for the man in the padded overcoat can often be ambivalent and conflicted. Until suddenly the spectre of the managerial shag-marathon, the managerial boner or the managerial romp comes ya-hooing in through the door and the whole thing falls to pieces amid baffling feelings of embarrassment and disappointment.

By way of final confirmation of this, the first-ever managerial internet sex tape emerged in 2008 featuring the former Wigan manager Paul Jewell and a female friend. This, then, is the final frontier of managerial sexuality. There's really nowhere left to go from here. This is hard core.

CHAPTER 19

The Monks of the Bootroom

The 1970s was a period not just of vaulting managerial ascent but of fevered change everywhere. The politics of sex, the politics of class, even the politics of politics: these were the ideological turf wars of the decade. The sense of old meeting new penetrated everything. In 1973 *Carry On Girls*, the twenty-fifth *Carry On* film, was released. Set in the seaside resort of Fircombe, it paints a picture of a society in flux, of old values being challenged and cast aside like an outdated combine harvester.

The film is set around a beauty contest organised by district councillor Sid Fiddler, played by Sid James, in a bid to boost tourism. Backed by the incompetent Mayor Bumble, the contest faces fierce opposition from middle-class women's liberationist Augusta Prodworthy (June Whitfield), and a kind of twittery, horn-parping collaboration from chief contestant Hope Springs, a bee-hived, arse-waggling Barbara Windsor. Ultimately Prodworthy's lipstick feminists succeed in sabotaging the contest, although not without the compensatory – and ultimately conciliatory – wag-wag-wag of the James laugh as events take in a titillating all-female bikini fight, and a titillating bikini itching powder and sprinkler system attack.

The *Carry On* films had first tackled the hard-left sensibilities of the 1970s two years earlier in *Carry On at Your Convenience*, where shop-floor politics met sexual politics in a heavily unionised lavatory and bidet factory. The key moment of *Convenience* came with the *Girls*-style intervention of the all-female anti-strike demonstration. Here they come: an indignant, placard-waving, gor-wouldn't-mind-a-bit-of-that mob, the forces of modernisation reduced to caricature, but still on the advance, still strangely stirring.

For some the likes of *Carry On Girls* would act as a kind of distant alarm call, a codified acknowledgement that battle had been joined between the old, dark, caveman male and something else a little more enlightened; and perhaps as a harbinger of change even within the cloistered, ball-scratching complacency of the 1970s male, with his birds and booze and football, his burping, grunting hierarchy of pleasures. On top of which, like Christ adorning the Sugar Loaf, stood the football manager: arms spread in absolution, cultish, irresistible and unapologetically male.

Of course this is all the product of hindsight. In 1973 the world of the manager seemed entirely isolated from the violent revolutionary forces at work in *Carry On Girls*. The emergent power at this time was Liverpool. Bill Shankly's club had been reinvigorated with the finessing of his second great team. It was about to be handed over to the peerlessly shrewd Bob Paisley, who would ultimately become the most successful English football manager of all time.

This was the era of the Liverpool bootroom, the revered managerial brains trust, with all its burgeoning mythology. Never mind the unprecedented success. Never mind that with the bootroom staff in place Liverpool won the League title in 1964, 1966, 1973, 1976, 1977, 1979, 1980, 1982, 1983, 1984, 1986,

1988 and 1990 and the European Cup in 1977, 1978, 1981 and 1984. The bootroom was always about something more, even, than these worldly riches. The bootroom was about a certain tone of voice, a sense of liturgy and ritual, of tiny virtues magnified into an overarching piety. It was a holy place from the outset. We gaze at its lined and taciturn old men, captured in epic black and white, with a childish potato love. This is football's liniment-infused managerial altar.

The notion of the holy manager was nothing new. Among the various messiahs and evangelists, Matt Busby provided the first really convincing figure of this type. Busby gave us the manager as impossibly senior Vatican official. In Arthur Hopcraft's *The Football Man* he described Busby being greeted in the street by strangers, his treatment the same as 'middle-aged priests of compassionate nature'. Eamon Dunphy wrote in his biography, in all seriousness, 'The quality Matt possesses reminds me most of Pope Paul VI.' This was the Busby way. His funeral service was attended by one Archbishop, two bishops and a total of twenty-three other clergymen.

The men of the Liverpool bootroom took this further. In the bootroom we find the monk and the holy hermit. It's a place of primary virtues, of small truths tearfully recalled. Which isn't bad going for a shabby 12ft by 12ft bolt hole under the main stand. The bootroom stank of dubbin and quietly mouldering kit. There were baskets and empty beer crates to sit on. Its companionable squalor was closely guarded. There was superstition around the bootroom, an idea that the club's fortunes were somehow bound up in its miscellany of old bandages, pens, newspapers, bottles and notebooks. Tommy Smith once tried take an old rug out to give it a sweep. He was ordered to put it back.

When Bill Shankly arrived at Liverpool in 1959 the bootroom was a place for the staff to hang their coats. In time it became a kind of snug. Opposition coaches would be welcomed in – although only rarely players – and in the later years even the odd passing celebrity. Ronnie Moran, bootroom royalty, claimed to have seen up to forty people crammed in there after European games. Shankly didn't create the bootroom but he allowed it to happen. The first thing he did on joining Liverpool was to guarantee the jobs of the existing backroom staff: Bob Paisley, Joe Fagan, Reuben Bennett and Albert Shelley. This was the founding line-up, the A-team. And like a boyband or a superhero collective, they all had their own special powers.

Paisley was the tactical brain, the deep thinker and, as a qualified physio, the healer. Fagan was the psychologist, the nice guy, the normal one. Shelley was the old one, the ancient geezer, janitorial and revered. This is a staple figure in the male environment, a fixture of the sporting club, the boozer and the university senior common room. Shelley retired as first-team trainer in the late 1950s but still kept on shuffling in, sweeping up and wheezing out his one-liners. One of his main jobs was painting the white ball that they used in the second half in midwinter. For a while he was also the physio. This involved remaining in his seat and shouting, 'Gerrup!' whenever a player was hurt.

Ronnie 'Bugsy' Moran was the drill sergeant. He shouted. He belittled. No egos was the rule, no stars. Bugsy said the horrible things that needed to be said. 'He is deliberately antagonistic,' Graeme Souness would observe later, thrumming with manly admiration. Reuben Bennett was the biceps. He was the living legend that every group of blokes worthy of the name concocts around one of its number. Bennett was superhuman. He drank entire bottles of Scotch. He could karate chop a brick in half. Bill Shankly once described him as 'the hardest man in the world'. Roger Hunt recalled, 'In the afternoon you'd see him standing outside Anfield in shirt sleeves when it was ten degrees below. He used to say he didn't feel it.'

Bennett claimed to have taken the longest goal kick in the

history of the game while a player at Crewe, the ball landing on a passing train and ending up in Southampton. He once publicly cleaned out a large gash on his knee with a wire brush. There was a story that when he was in the Army doing bayonet training a stray blade went right through his forearm. He yanked it out and shouted, 'Next!'

Looking back at photos of them, the thing that strikes you about all these bootroom boys is just how old they all were, right from the start. They had prodigious wrinkles. Paisley seemed barely able to open his eyes. Shoe-horned into skin-tight Gola tracksuits, bundled up in woolly jumpers, the monks of the bootroom twinkled and sat on their beer crates, sated with unutterable wisdom. What did they actually do in there? As Joey Jones, a Liverpool player of the 1970s, noted, 'Everyone knew about the bootroom and wanted to know its secret.' It's still not clear if we ever really found out. This was a self-defining myth. Its secret was its secret. Its mystique lay in its impenetrable mystique. Shankly, with his mania for religious imagery, likened the bootroom to a confessional. By which he meant a place of honesty, of simple mantras and almost mawkishly minimal creed.

'The branches of our system sprouted out just like a tree,' Shankly said. 'It has been tried and tested and is so simple anybody can understand. But if you think it is so simple it is not worth doing, then you are wrong. The simple things are the ones that count.'

And there it is. The little things. Wax on, wax off. Imagine you are lotus flower growing on hillside. Consider the tiny ant. Empty your mind. Don't give the ball away. Don't talk much. Keep on winning. This was the holy secret of the bootroom. The football manager had concocted something new here. It was his new Unitarian church, his old-aged new-agey-ness. Ranged against the spiky heathenisms of Clough and the furtive manoeuvrings of Revie, the bootroom seemed like a square of clean white light. Sammy Lee called it 'sacrosanct'. It even had its own holy book, the widely whispered-over notepads in which Paisley and his muckers would write down details of training, what the weather was like, haikus, single words, ink dots. Here was wisdom. Here was a small room in which sat ancient men in cardigans.

This is one way of looking at it. Another is that the bootroom wasn't so much a ninja collective as one towering genius and some other blokes. Paisley was the main man, an unprecedented trophy-hog, a towering statistical presence as manager between 1974 and 1983. And a man who, right up to his retirement, retained both the mannerisms and dress sense of someone who had just popped out to the shop for a newspaper and needed to get home sharpish to catch the snooker. Mark Lawrenson, now a *Match of the Day* pundit, described his first meeting with Paisley after signing for Liverpool in 1981. 'When I got in the car I saw Bob was wearing slippers and a cardigan. They'd just won the European Cup and there's this fellow, who everyone in football thought was an absolute god, driving me to the ground in his slippers and cardigan.'

Those slippers: they even got a mention in his obituary. Paisley was a manager blessed with an inspirational anti-glamour. Originally the team physiotherapist, for a while he appeared on the edge of Liverpool team photos dressed in a long white coat. He was also a bricklayer by trade. When he first came to Anfield in 1939 he helped build the manager's bench in his spare time, the same bench the bootroom would occupy throughout the glory years.

'I never wanted the job, but you've got me and that's it', were his first words to his players on being appointed manager. Tortured by his subsequent first solo public appearance, walking out at Wembley ahead of the teams for the Charity Shield, Paisley responded in his own way to the beige leather glare of 1970s managerial celebrity. Not for Bob, the Parkinson sofa. Instead he sought ascetic oblivion in the ranks. Paisley allowed the bootroom to bloom around him, the jungle fortress from which he would rule.

Hunkered in his cell with his smocked and tonsured brothers, he was free to concentrate on what he called 'feeling it', a predictably mystical version of 'reading the game'. Paisley's training as a physio had given him depth. It was crucial to his aura. In time he was credited with having a kind of sixth sense. Players said he could 'see' where they were injured. Sitting in the dugout he would witness a player going down and say quietly, 'Cartilage, six weeks.' 'Bob was never wrong,' was the word.

Paisley learned his basic medical skills by sitting in the casualty department at Liverpool's Royal Hospital and watching what the doctors did. A few years later he also took a correspondence course. At one point, in the Shankly era, he got hold of what he called 'an electrical machine' (in the press it was described as 'a magical machine'). For a while Shankly would go out into the streets and drag pensioners back into Anfield, where he would beg Bob to set his machine on their aches and pains. The final straw came when Shankly brought back an old man with a whippet and tried to get Paisley to work his miracles on the dog.

As manager Paisley retained this sense of having X-ray specs. Described as 'almost incomprehensible' in his team talks, even his awkwardness in public became a part of the bootroom shtick. In truth he was a brilliant judge of a player, with an almost no-miss record on successful signings, and a tactical deep-thought, a problem-solver nonpareil. These were his secret skills. And the bootroom was the pillbox from which he lobbed his bombs and picked off his bulls' eyes.

But still there's more to it than this. We admire Paisley. But we love the bootroom. The 12 ft by 12 ft holy cave outgrew even its main man. It's still the bootroom we really want to know about. It's the bootroom, rather than Bob's special powers, that became Liverpool's lucky charm as they grew steadily into a bastion of invincibility. The bootroom seemed to mean something. But what exactly? And here the lurking spectre of Augusta Prodworthy and the all-girl strike-busters of *Carry On at Your Convenience* appear on the edge of our vision. Here they come, placard-waving, fist-clenching, the frontline infantrywomen of the progressive and the grown-up. The bootroom was the opposite of all this. It was a man hole.

The man hole is a recurrent theme throughout the entire varied history of men sitting around doing stuff. It's chauvinistic, primal and apparently unavoidable. From the striped, plastic workman's tent, stretched above his pavement renovations, and reeking of tabloid, fried egg and hairy arse. To the warrior halls of medieval literature that would spawn the Camelot myth. The man hole has always been there.

The snooker hall, the pub backroom, the Bullingdon Club, the officer's mess. This is where men do the small, dank, often unacceptable things that men feel required to do. 'All they talked about was football, nothing else,' Ian Ross recalled. 'You talked about anything else and they would shut you up.' No opening of hearts here. No sharing. And certainly no expression of one's most intimate feelings in an atmosphere of mutual trust and support.

Don Howe had been in the Army with Ronnie Moran. As manager of Arsenal and West Brom he sat in the bootroom many times. 'They liked to talk about the game,' he told me. 'You could have a beer or whatever you wanted. We all had a drink and laugh and they'd listen and learn things from you about how your club was doing things. It was a terrific group of men. Really terrific. What I would call real men.'

And perhaps this is what it was all about: men. Never mind the monkishness – and what is a monastery but a holy manhole? – the bootroom was a dark, sweaty, sock-stinking place of maleness. All men crave a garden shed, a place of cardigans and dusty boxes. The bootroom was football's great garden shed in the sky. Tommy Smith, a Liverpool captain, even called it 'The shed in the heart of Anfield'.

The pub parallel was also a big part of it. The fact is the bootroom only really came into existence because Fagan and Paisley needed somewhere to have a drink in private (Shankly was teetotal). Later Shankly himself, a regular but never a mainstay, would describe the bootroom as 'just like popping down to the local'. For years Fagan was given crates of Guinness Export, in return for training the Guinness works team. These were the drinks the bootroom boys would serve, charmingly domesticated like the wiseguys of *Goodfellas* camped out in their cell, slicing garlic with their cut-throat razors, making their perfect meat balls, smuggling in their black-market ciabatta.

Steve Heighway remembered the bootroom, fondly, as 'the tattiest, dirtiest, scruffiest little place you were ever likely to come across'. Phil Thompson, a European Cup-winning captain, spoke of 'metal shelves which would be full of rubbish'. This was not a place of women. But women were here, if only in trash pictorial form. The other big thing about the bootroom was the naked calendars on the wall. Thompson recalled: 'It was absolutely incredible. They'd come in and they'd have a good look at these before the chit-chat began. Around November/December time they'd start arriving and people knew the new calendars would go on the wall. Very popular with the apprentices who would sneak in for a look.'

While outside the Radical Feminist set about her guerrilla war against the layers of patriarchal iniquity, while a group called Angry Wimmin burned down sex shops and scrawled slogans, the manager sat on a beer crate in his bootroom surrounded by tits and drank warm Scotch. He did it with some gravitas too. He did it with the air of a holy man and a man of principle. This was the manager's last stand of the unacceptably one-eyed, his grand gesture in favour of the universal notion of being allowed to hide in the shed and read the paper.

Of course the bootroom couldn't last. In the end it was flushed away by the forces of modernism. It seems fitting that it should have been the strictures of staging Euro 96 that consigned the bootroom to history. A proper media lounge was required. The corridor needed widening. European regulation. Health and safety. The new world. The bootroom dissolved before all these and was demolished in 1993, on the orders of the club directors. Its holy rubbish was bagged up, the embers of its hearth stamped out, its sacred books crated or binned and perhaps a final discarded and musty cardigan flung in the contractor's skip.

Liverpool fans still mourn the bootroom, and not just because the club hasn't won the League since it was demolished. Even in its head-in-the-sand blokiness, it's impossible not to feel a little sad at its passing. All men carry within their hearts a tiny part of some bootroom or other, some shuttered, Heineken-guzzling Nintendo den. The manager has had his say. He gave us his bootroom, with all its secret, bestial peace.

CHAPTER 20

The Dawn of the Showmen

By the mid–1970s the manager would find he had plenty to feel satisfied about. Leaning back in his puffily upholstered leather armchair, chinking the ice cubes in his whisky tumbler, and scratching gently at the polyester chafe of his avocado-green roll-neck, he might even be forgiven a small surge of pride.

Since the end of the Second World War the ascent of the football manager had proceeded at giddy pace. Brandishing the Herbert Chapman blueprint, the manager had returned in his demob suit energised and spoiling for a fight. He was indisputably in charge now. More than this, he was famous. He'd had his hair done and his voice fixed. He spoke not just to the terraces but to the gossip pages and to the burgeoning academics of management theory. Life was good. The manager had, without doubt, made it.

Except that there was a problem. His stage had begun to look, if not exactly small, then at least as though it was fraying around the edges. Football in the mid–1970s wasn't in the same great shape. In fact the game in England was starting to look what it was, an industry in the middle of twenty years of sullen decline. The decay in football's infrastructure had become chronic. Ancient stadia groaned and leaked. Concrete terraces crumbled. Football smelled of mildew and wet rot. There was a leak in the roof and rats in the basement. At the same time the atmosphere around it had become hostile. Assorted firms and crews spent their Saturdays trashing the nation's railway carriages, terrorising the nation's bus-stops and dragging football in a jeering headlock through a succession of provincial town centres.

There was violence and there was also an imported dreariness. Its geographical proximity to the urban industrial centre had lent football a vibrant populism in the late Victorian era. As these industries declined, that same proximity gave football not just a front-row view but a starring role in the reverse syndrome, the deep-seated urban decay of the dispossessed and the abandoned.

Football had grown up around the bustle of mills and mines and factories. Now it was condemned to stand by while the corpses of its dead parent industries slowly rotted, a typhoid-ridden survivor rummaging through the mouldering wheelie bins. 'Has football a future?' Brian Glanville asked in the 1974 *Charles Buchan's Soccer Gift Book*. 'The public have been voting with their feet. Attendances in Britain have dropped alarmingly . . . Great changes of some sort are coming, but no one quite knows what they will be.'

Across this post-apocalyptic landscape, a single figure continued to stride, unbowed in beige-belted trench coat, jaw set against the drizzle. The emergent showman manager of the 1970s and 1980s was football's antidote to gloom and despair. These were the big men, the electrifying iconoclasts with their moon-age glamour and their operetta swagger. It was time for the manager to stand tall for everyone's sake. And for a while, Atlas-like, he carried football across the wilderness on his belted back.

This was a matter of economics as much as anything else. Appointing a manager was now a decision bound up with the need to 'sell' a football club. A figurehead was required, not simply to pick the team but to energise with his bluster. Back in the day the manager had been jostled to the front of things as a scapegoat, thrown to the crowds when things went wrong. Now football looked to him as a lure, a high-pressure salesman, all coiffured charisma and a single pink, signet-ringed hand wedged in the doorjamb.

At the same time TV was bringing football into people's homes as a form of light entertainment. *Match of the Day* began to pull in twelve million viewers. *The Big Match* on Sunday afternoon was getting ten million. The manager was more visible than ever. He was a piece of scenery and an essential dramatic close-up. Hot-housed beneath the televisual glare, he grew freakishly. As Tony Pawson wrote in 1973, 'One has seen the manager's job cocooned in mystique.'

No wonder the manager started to get some funny ideas about himself. For example, it was around this time the idea of a manager working 'without a contract' began to take hold, a strand of the manager's disdain for the workaday world, that sense of himself as standing aloof, a seeker and a visionary. As West Ham fans called for his sacking in 1971, Ron Greenwood was asked if his – self-imposed – lack of a contract bothered him. 'I would be worried if I had one,' was his brilliantly meaningless reply.

At Aston Villa Tommy Docherty offered to give up two years' salary as a gesture of superhuman faith in his own magic. Docherty was one of the founding showmen. On his arrival at Villa in 1968, *The Times* noted, 'He has the powers of an alchemist', and remarked on 'the refreshing new spurt of hope and support – clearly yearning to be awakened – that has been touched off at the club by Docherty's appearance on the scene . . . It is all wrapped up somewhere in the mysterious aura of personality.'

This was a trend that would continue right through into the manicured decay of the Thatcher era. Flat-packed door-to-door glamour was something you could do now. This was a career. And so the showman became football's Bowie-style glam rock androgyne, a luminous peacock in the dank, wet sludge of the macro-decline of the 1970s.

Malcolm Allison was the kingpin. And like Bowie there was much more to him than simply the trappings of his persona, the ludicrous Bugsy Malone-style fedora hat, the furred lapels and the easy access to the dolly bird and the discotheque. Also like Bowie, Big Mal attracted his fair share of imitators, his Adam Ants and Limahl-from-Kajagoogoos. But Allison was the real deal, both as an innovative coach and the epitome of the showman manager. This was a twin identity that would sit uneasily, offering a glimpse of the destructive power within the manager's own conflated persona, the black hole of his celebrity.

The essence of Big Mal was captured in the Granada documentary *City!*, shot behind the scenes at Manchester City in 1981 during the dog days of Allison's second spell there. Here he is sprinting out on the rutted and sludgy pitch ahead of his players, overcoat blown to the winds, greeted by huge roars from terraces warmed by the blowtorch of his star-proximity. And there he is again, shirtless in the dressing room, a love-handled warrior general, telling his players to go out there and 'play as if you're 1-0 down'.

Allison could often seem a bit silly. He had a restless intelligence that would occasionally spill over into wilful eccentricity. He'd started out as an angry young man kicking against the pricks. Allison had played under Jimmy Seed at Charlton. After questioning the club's training he was abruptly transferred to West Ham. He claimed to have shaken Seed's hand and said, 'I want to thank you for teaching me the art of communication, because you've just spoken to me for the third time in seven years.'

He played as a centre half at West Ham and became a member of the 'academy' of young players. These were football's own milk bar teenagers. They met regularly in Cassettari's café to hold noisy discussions about tactics. Allison was fully immersed in the 1950s notion of 'progress', itself an act of rebellion against a tired and leaden elite.

As Bobby Moore recalled, 'In the 1950s, he became a devotee of all that was Continental. He cut down his boots with a razor blade, shortened his shorts, turned in the collar of his football shirt.' Squeezing into his pencil-slim suit, polishing his Vespa, this is Big Mal as the street-smart Italian-inflected mod, a *Quadrophenia*-era Sting throwing managerial shapes on the Brighton dancefloor.

Allison retired as a player aged thirty-one after losing a lung during a bout of tuberculosis. Enthused by the teachings of Walter Winterbottom, he got his break as a manager at Bath City in 1963. In time he would become assistant to Joe Mercer at Manchester City between 1965 and 1973. Here he enjoyed perhaps his happiest times as City won the First Division, the FA Cup, League Cup and Cup Winners Cup.

Early symptoms of the Big Mal persona were harmless while City kept winning. In 1968 Allison announced that City 'would terrify Europe' (he also promised to 'take football to the moon'). They were knocked out in the first round of the European Cup by Fenerbahce. This is a great shame because the faintly European influence, that hankering after some distant sense of glamour, was a big part of Allison's aura. He twice claimed to have been approached by Juventus. At Manchester City he changed the away kit to a Milan-homage red and black.

In the end the closest Allison got to the soaring 1970s glamour of the global game was as a member of ITV's World Cup punditry panel in 1970. Put together by Jimmy Hill, then head of sport for the channel, the panel was the first of its kind. It was a loose conglomeration of woozy, kipper-tied, big swinging dicks of the soccer scene. Allison was joined by Bob McNab, Derek Dougan and Pat Crerand. Together they were encamped for the duration in a London hotel, where Allison managed to run up the biggest bar tab in the venue's history.

Allison was also the dominant personality on screen, smoking cigars on camera, talking tough and chafing against Hill's shrieking headmasterly presence. The panel were mobbed by female fans while out shopping in a London street. They were sent clothes to wear by would-be sponsors. There was theatre too: Alan Mullery, blamed by Allison for England's exit at the hands of West Germany, came into the studio and threw one of his international caps in Allison's face.

This was the manager's TV coronation, his emergence as a ratings-magnet and small-screen must-have. And with Allison now firmly ensconced in the popular consciousness as Big Mal, it seemed inevitable that he would fall out with the genial Mercer at City. Allison left to manage Crystal Palace. It was here among the pygmies of the Second Division that he emerged as the definitive showman, a manager whose 'presence' pretty much defined him. During Palace's run to an FA Cup semi-final in 1976 he was a constant on the TV screen, impossibly glamorous beneath his enormous hat, an extraterrestrial in South Norwood.

Big Mal provided a flash elder brother to a seam of ambitious imitators. These were the managers who, it was said, could 'lift' a club simply by walking through the door. John Bond had played alongside Allison at West Ham. As the *Guardian* noted of Bond during his time at Bournemouth, 'He is always immaculately dressed and groomed and he puffs cigars and dispenses "shorts" in Malcolm Allison's best showman style.' To *The Breedon Book of Managers* Bond was 'an outspoken character who brought glamour to ordinary clubs'. And what glamour it was. A grinning, bouffant, raincoated figure, Bond boasted equine good looks and an indefinable sense of being an operator and a face.

On first meeting him at Waterloo Station in 1970, his chairman at Bournemouth said he was gripped by the certainty they 'would go places together'. Bond talked the talk. 'We have got together a group of players who have a character,' he said of his Bees players. 'They are perhaps in the football sense, a wee bit conceited. But I like that.' Aping Big Mal, he too changed the Bournemouth kit to Milan-friendly red and black, bringing a touch of San Siro glamour to the Third Division.

Bond took the gathering storm of his big personality on to Norwich. Finally he got to replace Allison at City in 1981. This was his moment. Pressing the flesh, he strode into Maine Road as the daddy-elect. Things went well for a while. Bond's City reached an FA Cup final. Sadly he ended up resigning in 1983 over an extramarital affair.

For Bond there followed a disastrous spell at Burnley (in 1992 he was warned by police not to return to the club for fear of starting a riot) and a disastrous spell at Birmingham, where he was shabbily sacked in 1987. Throughout all this Big John Bond, acolyte of Big Mal, had his own mini-me in Not So Big John Benson, who would follow him from club to club and eventually take over at City. Benson was Bond's batman and chief wing-man. He once said of his friend, 'If Frank Sinatra were to come into a bar where he was drinking John Bond would not turn a hair.'

Others followed too. At Luton Harry Haslam, a natural comic and raconteur, enjoyed a period of Eric Morecambe-fanned celebrity. In 1983 David Pleat, not exactly a showman manager in his own right, would have his showman moment as he came veering across the Maine Road pitch on the final day of the season, beige suit flapping wildly, arms raised, even as in the opposite dugout John Benson thrashed about in his black raincoat and Manchester City were relegated.

I asked Pleat about that run, later a fixture on the *Match of the Day* credits. He didn't really want to talk about it. But he did, wearily. 'That week we'd lost two games,' he recalled. 'On that Saturday three other teams had won to put us in the shit. We were never in the shit before. But all of a sudden we were in the shit on the penultimate Saturday. The last game it was shit or bust at Man City. The pressure was on. We had a full house. We had great support. I remember all the cars with the supporters in going up honking their horns.

'I consulted a psychologist before that game. A guy called Fox from the Dunstable area. And I took them away to a health farm for a day where we had a yoga session. And I slated them for putting us in the shit. But I said, you can pull out of this, no one wants to see you go down.

'At the end I ran to the captain. I didn't know where I was running. I lost my head. It did become a defining moment and it's a shame because the previous season we won the Second Division title by a country mile playing proper football. But that was the moment.

'I always remember going into the treatment room after the game. John Bond was in there being consoled by Eddie Large. I felt terrible for him. I said, John, I'm so sorry. He got sacked straight afterwards of course.'

At times the showman phenomenon would become something of a problem for the manager. Egocentric, big-haired and prone to presidential pronouncements, it wouldn't be long before the showman lapsed into pastiche. The manager was about to become a bit of a joke. It's not hard to see why. Suddenly he was all things to all men: a ladies' man and fashion god, not to mention a wit and philosopher. While he was at Norwich John Bond once took his staff off on a management course called 'The systematic approach to getting things done and achieving objectives'.

It's from this period that all the most familiar jokes about the football manager originate. The comedian Peter Cook produced one of his genuinely funny moments with his depiction of 'the

most noticeable manager this country has ever produced', Alan
Latchley, on the chat show *Clive Anderson Talks Back*. The
Latchley character is a minutely observed compendium of tru-
isms from the showman era.

Anderson: 'So what can you bring to the team, Alan?'

Latchley: [Intense pause]. 'BELIEF . . .'

And there he is, pinned and wriggling on the wall, the
jewellery-draped beefcake, with his inspirational personality, his
bums-on-seats flair, his egomania. And before long the showman
would be sliding out of fashion. After his sacking at City Allison
was sacked at Middlesbrough. He launched an unfair dismissal
claim, in the course of which it turned out Allison had run up
a £3500 bill on champagne, brandy and cigars during a three-
month stay at a hotel owned by a club director. Inspired by a
spell coaching in America, he suggested the club dye its pitch
orange. And in the end it's for this kind of thing, the low
comedy, that Big Mal would be remembered.

This is a great shame as Allison was a pure coach at heart.
Beneath the sheepskin, there lay a deep thinker. That West Ham
academy group of the 1950s is often portrayed as something close
to an episode of *Minder*, a football version of the lads larking
about over a pint of Skol in Dave's club. In fact it was a bit more
scholarly. Noel Cantwell, Dave Sexton, Frank O'Farrell, Jimmy
Andrews, Malcolm Musgrave, Bond and Allison were nicknamed
'The Studious Seven'. All became managers, although Allison
was the one of whom great things were expected.

Somewhere along the way he just stopped being sufficiently
studious. There were glimpses. He wrote a book called *Soccer for
Thinkers*. At Bristol Rovers he introduced a tactical theory he
called 'the whirl', a lower league interpretation of total football.
Of his approach to coaching Allison told the 1974 *Charles
Buchan's Soccer Gift Book*, 'I've never met anyone who suffered
by going to school! Coaching is the schoolroom of soccer.
Everyone is born with a brain – and schooling, whether at

primary, secondary or university level, is designed to teach the individual to use his brain.'

This is as revolutionary as all the booze and birds and gold-braceleted self-empowerment. English managers just don't talk like that, even now. This concentrated approach was Allison's great strength during his first spell at City. After that it seemed he got a little distracted by things like having a really good time all the time – not to mention letting everybody know he was having a really good time all the time. The heavy gold medallion of the showman had turned out to be the millstone around Allison's neck that kept him earthbound.

It has been said that a more reserved Allison might have made a brilliant and innovative FA coaching director, the man to put right the malfeasance of successive regimes. Instead he chose to become Big Mal, the man who was ultimately dismissed from his job as a local radio pundit for saying 'oh fuck' on air as Middlesbrough conceded a goal.

There's a clip of Jimmy Hill interviewing Allison for *On the Ball*, just after Allison's appointment as Crystal Palace manager in 1972. In the interview he appears decked out in gingham blazer with check tie and shirt. Clearly disconcerted by the speed of events he starts to talk quite reflectively about his new job and his own exhaustion at home the night before. 'No champagne, even?' Hill interjects, pulling him up short.

Wearily, a smile creeps on to Allison's face. 'Well, I had a couple of bottles,' he lies, hastily erecting his TV facade for the benefit of a cackling Hill. This was his fate and his weakness too. For Big Mal there would be no escape from the showman.

Just as an addendum, it's worth noting that the rampant exhibitionism of the showman manager was in some ways going against historical type. As a showman the manager was on display, energetically revealing himself to the crowd. If it was practical, he might have attached a large arrow to his head or drawn attention to himself by wearing a high-visibility fluorescent vest. This was the whole point: to inspire by being seen.

Previously the manager had often played down his presence, perhaps by dressing in drab fashion or hiding himself in a small pitch-side shelter or beneath a tartan car blanket. A distinguished subset of managers had even chosen to go about in disguise, concealing their incendiary public presence, and entering a kind of managerial purdah.

The manager in disguise has a long history. Peter McWilliam, Spurs manager of the 1920s, once travelled to Mid Rhondda in order to scout the star player, Jimmy Seed. The club's fans were so upset about rumours of McWilliam's presence that they threatened to lynch him if he was found on the premises. McWilliam watched from the main stand wearing a false beard and spectacles. Unlynched, he signed Seed after the game.

Before taking over as manager at Coventry City Jimmy Hill went to watch them play with his collar turned up and what he describes as 'a trilby hat pulled own well over my forehead'. In spite of which, and to his bemusement, he still drew 'gasps of surprise' from the people around him. What on earth, you wonder, could it have been about the man with the huge, protruding chin and the trilby yanked down to his nose that caused such a stir?

More than thirty years later Kevin Keegan and Alan Shearer would meet in a pub to discuss Shearer signing for Newcastle. Both men avoided drawing attention to themselves by wearing large sunglasses and baseball caps pulled down over their eyes. Shearer then left to mull over the move at a Bryan Adams concert in Huddersfield, an even, that would, presumably, have allowed him to proceed without the need for a change of outfit.

This is now more the norm for the football manager, particularly as his fame is a barely controllable force of its own. The manager is a bushfire celebrity. He's ready to blow at any moment. He lurks behind tall gates and tinted windows. He creeps about his business in executive secrecy. Who knows how many times the beard may have been dusted down, the trilby dug out, to allow him to move unseen among us like Prince Hal on the night before battle? We'll never know of course. But it's still probably best not to stare too closely at that pair of mumbling men in the baseball caps in the corner of the Rat and Meathook.

CHAPTER 21

The Manager Hustles

In the 1950s Matt Busby had set the template for the football manager as workaholic one-job man, a lone figure building a new world order of titanic footballing city-states. Or, at the very least, not being constantly on the verge of giving it all up to become a newsagent. But sure enough, it wasn't long before things started to edge back the other way. In small but significant numbers the manager was about to start putting himself about again; to spread himself across the assorted neighbouring industries that had begun to bleed into his world.

This time it would be something grander than simply the odd BBC radio appearance or a turn on the music hall stage. This was the dawn of the pop hustler manager; the kind of manager for whom football was just one of many projects, one of many outlets for his talents. The pop hustler wasn't happy simply being the manager. He wanted to be the man.

Famously, this was also the era of the pop music impresario. Forged in the heady milieu of instant record labels, self-mythologising rock group managers and goateed venture capitalists, the music impresario was a force from the under-ground. The young Richard Branson would lurk by a phone box close to his Little Venice houseboat, pretending to be in an office whenever one of his clients rang. Elsewhere Tony Stratton-Smith, aka 'Mr Charisma', cruised the London club scene, a pudgy, long-haired man in a tight leather jacket with one foot in the world of football journalism and another in the fevered hubbub of the thriving independent record business.

By the end of the 1960s football was some way towards becoming an adjunct to this world, with the manager an eager exchange student. As Alec Stock remarked, 'This is a job for the man who likes to be in the public eye, a job for the man with a bit of an ego . . . I like people slapping me on the back, gently, and saying "Hello, Alec" when I am having a drink. I like the invitations that pour into my office . . . so many invitations that I cannot begin to cope.'

Stock, despite his taste for the cravat and the pencil-slim flan-nel, remained resolutely a football man. Others would be tempted further. In fact only two of them ever really made it. But what a pair, and what an assortment of side projects and noises off. To recap, then, those twin trivia-laden careers of Jimmy Hill and Terry Venables:

- Hill didn't win a League title or FA Cup during his six years as Coventry City manager. But he did write and record 'The Sky Blue Song', still played on match days and first sung at a press conference attended by Sid James and Frankie Howerd, who were appearing in panto at Coventry Theatre.
- Venables didn't win the League title with Spurs, Crystal Palace, QPR or Leeds. But he did once win a Butlins talent contest with his solo mime act – and got his first break in show business aged four in a dance troupe called the Happy Tappers.
- At Coventry Hill held hugely successful 'pop and crisp days' for local children. He was also the first manager to be interviewed by

TV cameras at half time (his comment: 'I'm only hoping that in the second half we shall be able to spread the game out a little more').

- Venables wrote three detective novels, based around the exploits of East End ex-cop and private dick James Hazell. He also invented a board game called The Manager.
- Hill wrote a book called *Striking for Soccer*, launched Radio Sky Blue, and once engaged a fireworks company with the idea of exploding a giant rocket over the ground whenever City scored. (He abandoned the idea of launching a mortar shell as it would have endangered players' lives.)
- As QPR manager Venables sang on the Russell Harty show, backed by a swaying first team, two of whom ended up having a fistfight during his performance. ('Ian Evans had taken the mickey out of Tony Hazell right in front of his wife,' Venables explained.)
- As head of LWT sport Hill single-handedly pioneered a four-hour Saturday-afternoon sports programme based around things like log-chopping and mountain biking. Later, as frontman for *Match of the Day*, he was flown around the country in a private plane and had mascara applied to his greying beard before going on camera. He also invented the slow-motion replay and the opinionated pundit.
- Venables wrote pop songs with Tony Hillier, the man responsible for 'Save All Your Kisses For Me'. He hung out with Adam Faith and the young Elton John. As Barcelona manager he sang 'My Way' on a Catalan radio station.
- Hill once spent a weekend escorting Raquel Welch around London: 'I said I'd pick her up between eleven and twelve o'clock at the Savoy.' He also turned down an offer to become her European agent.

Hill and Venables, it must be said, came at this from different angles. Where Hill was a natural born TV busybody who also became a football manager, Venables was a natural manager who got terribly bogged down in his own sense of himself as an entertainment product.

They can probably be joined by Kevin Keegan. Keegan did most of his crossover work while still a player, but retained an association with a certain strand of innocent, sexless early 1970s pop. A reader's letter to the *Daily Mirror* in October 1974 sheds some light on this: 'Unlike your readers who follow one pop star,' wrote Susan Pratley, twelve, of Weston-super-Mare, 'I have a lot of favourites. I have 10,539 pictures of the Osmonds, 8324 of David Cassidy, 5692 of the Sweet, 2468 of Mud, 598 of the Bay City Rollers and 229 of the Arrows. I'm also a fan of Kevin Keegan, the Liverpool footballer, and I've collected 695 pictures of him.'

Three times larger, in Susan Pratley's pop-world, than the Arrows: this was the star dust that would cling to Keegan. Hill, for his part, was known as 'the beatnik with a ball'. In 1973 Geoffrey Green wrote in *The Times* that he 'needs only a brass earring to play a part in the *Pirates of Penzance*'. This was Jimmy. He was edgy. He was beat. He was in fact a well-groomed, hard-nosed man with a taste for executive golf days in the company of Ronnie Corbett.

The son of a Balham milkman, Hill was a grammar school boy who played professionally for Fulham. There, as head of the players' union, he agitated successfully for the abolition of the maximum wage and immediately afterwards took over as manager of Coventry, a thoroughly modern man in a city thriving on the back of its own automobile-led consumer boom. He had some high times at Highfield Road, above all in transforming the club into a brilliantly branded popular success, adding twenty thousand supporters to the home gate over three years. But management couldn't hold Jimmy Hill. This was a man destined for something more.

Chin set like a jousting pole against the world, he did pretty much everything it was possible to do in football. Player, lines-man, activist, administrator, pundit, parliamentary official, pin-up, tearaway and grumpy old man, and either a considerable force, or a peculiarly irritating self-publicist, in all of these roles. It's still not quite clear which.

The real secret to Hill's sustained success – as manager, presen-ter, magnate and operator – is that he is essentially unembarrassable. By page two of his autobiography *The Jimmy Hill Story* he's already talking about the 'appetite in many men . . . to explore the delights of love and lust'. On page three he's telling us an anecdote about how his temporary colostomy bag once exploded on a flight back from a golf event in Kenya. One thing is for sure. When it came to ushering the humble football manager under the rope, up the main stairs and into the assorted VIP lounges of the televisual pop aristocracy, Hill was world-class.

Venables, in his flowery-shirted salad days, was sharper. What he brought was a sense of some effervescent personality overspill, and of cool, even, with his finely tailored, Andrew Loog Oldham-esque suit and that unwavering Dagenham stare. Taking over from Malcolm Allison at Palace, Venables became the epit-ome of the new breed of vigorous, tactically minded young managers, the public face of the tracksuit men. His Palace team was dubbed 'the team of the eighties' (but spent most of the decade in the Second Division). Venables was a coach of stature. He won the Spanish La Liga title with Barcelona, the high point of his achievements, and a moment when he looked poised to join the greats.

It didn't happen, though. An FA Cup followed at Spurs, as did assorted side projects, court cases and a general worrying away of his peak years. But, then, the pop hustler manager is associated with other things, beyond mere trophies and pots. Mainly he's associated with a particular gesture. It's the arms wide pose, with the head raised and the eyes bright, staring at some distant beau-tiful tomorrow. Jimmy Hill struck this pose for photographers inside Coventry's stadium in 1975. There he is, arms spread, a silhouette that seems to suggest the world is within his grasp, his to offer you.

Venables was pictured like this famously during his time at Spurs: cloaked in black, arms raised in a call for appeasement, for acclaim, for whatever. It was a gesture Kevin Keegan took to adopting as Newcastle manager. Arms aloft, face set, chin raised: it says, I am all you ever wanted of hope, happiness and inspiration. I am going to keep doing this while you clap for ages. And then do it some more. No. Not finished yet.

The gesture also says, I am about to burst into song, another common feature. Besides 'The Sky Blue Song', Hill also wrote Arsenal's 1971 Cup final anthem, sung to the tune of 'Rule, Britannia!' As a young man Venables sang with the Joe Loss band at the Hammersmith Palace, and has since 'cut' various discs. These include a 2002 England World Cup anthem called 'England Crazy' that reached number forty-six in the charts. Keegan, lest we forget, had a hit with 'Head Over Heels in Love' (B-side 'Move On Down'), which charted at number thirty-one.

Besides communicating via the mediums of gesture and song, the hustler manager also had a desire to transform himself into a corporate entity. Jimmy Hill became Jimmy Hill Limited in 1973, with the founding of his sports agent business. Through this Hill secured a lucrative promotional contract with Prince Faisal bin Fahad bin Abdul Aziz, a 'gentleman of considerable charm' and son of the Crown Prince of Saudi Arabia. Terry Venables Limited was formed a year after its chief executive made his Chelsea debut aged seventeen. The new company immediately launched a product called The Thingamawig, a hat with artificial hair inside it, intended for women who wanted to go outside with their curlers in. This was not a success.

There's a whiff here of the manager as proto-yuppie. Hill after all worked in the City for a while for a firm of stockbrokers called H. J. Garrett and Co. At Coventry he was known as 'JH', having 'eliminated the word boss'. He announced that he wanted his players to play 'like senior executives'. He later took up horse riding and hunting and by 1982 was living in a seventeenth-century Cotswold farmhouse with a thirty-acre paddock.

But, still, this is the manager we're talking about. And as ever something unfortunate has tended to lurk behind these ventures. There's an air of the Peckham-based market stall entrepreneur, of the manager as budding meeelionaire. While he was a player Hill formed a side business called the Immaculate Chimney Sweeping Company, his own duties bringing on 'uncontrollable bouts of sneezing' due to a terrible soot allergy. Venables' ventures have included a waste-paper business and a failed Soho tailoring firm (endorsed, counter-productively, by the ragged-trousered Norman Wisdom). In 1998 he was disqualified from acting as a company director for seven years over the mismanagement of four companies, including his own London nightclub, Scribes West.

Hill's own 1970s fortune was sunk into the Detroit Express and the Washington Diplomats of the North American Soccer League. In the last few years Keegan has ploughed much of his personal wealth into a company called Soccer Circus, a football theme park featuring attractions such as a 'hit the dummies' version of football ten-pin bowling. It might work out. But then of course it might not.

The motivation behind much of this is the old managerial urge to be the boss. This is just another expression of the same old will-to-power that brought the secretary rampaging out of his broom cupboard. Jimmy, not happy with merely being named Westclox Manager of Tomorrow in his promotion season, would become Coventry's managing director in 1975. Venables launched a doomed bid to take over Spurs in 1991, stating that his intention was 'to run my own football club from top to bottom'. Even Keegan has hinted he might return for his third incarnation as Newcastle manager if someone friendly buys the club.

This is what they want, really, these entertainers. They want to be in charge. They want the ultimate revenge. They want to drag the old directorial guard out on to the dancefloor, where life is fluid and the old order is reversed and the vigorously cha-chaing inspirational man is king. If only someone had said this was what it was all about. If only we'd known all along. For a start, we might have saved an awful lot of singing.

CHAPTER 22

In the Arms of the Tracksuit Men

Any history of activities involving British men in the 1970s and early 1980s – what you might call the Medallion Years – has a tendency to run along familiar lines. It's an era that has been repeatedly pillaged for its richly stocked pantry of the kitsch and the retro. The notion of bulky, side-burned men in tight brown flared slacks, men who weren't afraid to swear or to smoke incessantly and eat terrible food – all of this has been successfully repackaged via the period cop drama, the disco-era Hollywood film and the non-specific bloke-nostalgia of the lad's magazine.

Football has played its part in this. The notion of the sheep-skinned manager, with his squad of bearded alcoholic maverick geniuses, has been rehearsed so many times it's a mini-industry in itself. But beyond the headline posturing, something more lasting had begun to flower. This was also the era of the tracksuit men.

The tracksuit has a distinguished lineage in football management. Matt Busby wore one. Alf Ramsey had a powder-blue number. In the 1950s there were even tales of ageing managers keeping a tracksuit in their office in case a photographer dropped by, and of at least one dinosaur of the pre-war years causing his players to collapse into fits of giggles by appearing in front of them dressed in brand-new polyester (which was never seen again).

In the early 1970s this began to solidify into something else. There was a new-found cerebral intensity, a sense of intellectual confidence. The tracksuit man wasn't so much a reaction to the showman. He was more like his serious older brother. He was close to his players, ionically bonded through the deep ritual of the pack, the young soul rebels pumping iron and writing poetry and sharing their furrowed dreams.

The bastard manager had wanted you to be afraid of him. The tracksuit manager wanted you to trust him with your deeper feelings. As Freddie Goodwin, one of the original Busby Babes, remarked while he was Birmingham manager in the mid-1970s: 'I think all managers should deal in psychology. Getting the best out of a player is putting him in the right frame of mind . . . I don't think it costs anything to treat players right, to treat them in an honest way.'

This was the voice of the new breed, treating you right, earning your trust. But there was also a sense of menace here. The tracksuit manager was football's version of a new independent kind of 1970s man. No accurate figures have ever been compiled as to how many managers of the mid-1970s based their scowling, trench-coated, manfully groomed touchline presence on the wised-up geezer-cool of Jack Carter in 1971's *Get Carter*. But the answer appears to have been, quite a few.

The tracksuit manager was also the most obvious fruit of the coaching-badge culture instilled via the FA courses run by Walter Winterbottom. As David Pleat recalled: 'We all used to congregate at Lilleshall. There was a group who qualified reasonably young. The Taylors and the Wilkinsons and the Pleats and various others. And that was our annual pilgrimage.'

Graham Taylor also has fond memories of the Lilleshall years. 'It was very exciting going there and talking to other players and coaches,' Taylor told me. 'You'd meet people like Malcolm Allison and you'd talk about the game and they'd be willing to listen to your view on things, even as a young man. That was the atmosphere.'

The yearning for something more had always been there. At the start of the 1960s Millwall's manager Reg Smith had invented something called 'funnel football', which, according to *The Breedon Book of Managers*, 'made his team very hard to beat'. No details of 'funnel football' remain. Smith lasted two seasons before leaving to coach in South Africa.

The tracksuit itself attracted much attention over this period. This has been an issue throughout the manager's lifetime: what should he wear? Social ascent was signalled by the diamond tie-pin of the Major Buckley years. Matt Busby's Homburg indicated a new egalitarianism. The peacock sensibility of the newly mature manager was conveyed through his open-neck collar and – a new medium – his four-litre V6 limited-edition Jag.

The tracksuit granted membership to an exciting new club. 'When he reached Stamford Bridge he was ready to be out with his players – one of the breed of tracksuited managers,' the *Guardian* frothed over Tommy Docherty as early as 1967. When Busby retired in 1969 he remarked that maybe it was 'time for a younger tracksuited man to take over'. Two years later John Arlott wrote an article eulogising 'the track-suited managerial revolution', although for Arlott this was still a function of the Ramsey and Revie generation.

Four years later the sight of Middlesbrough manager Jack Charlton collecting his players' tracksuits before kick-off touched a chord. Tracksuit in hand, Charlton had the air of a mother hen and confidante. This closeness to his players was woven into the tracksuit man's rayon mix fibre. In 1973 Bob Stokoe, who twinned his tracksuit with a trilby hat, was described as 'a players' manager, putting their interests first. His close identification with them was neatly and publicly expressed when he led out his team at Wembley in the red track-suit of Sunderland, rather than the sober clothes of a manager'.

This is a development Pleat has mixed feelings about now. 'We were closer then to the players, but you still have to keep a distance,' he told me. 'As I always say, be careful when you become a manager, there are players that will take the milk out of your tea. The players are your friends but they're your foes as well. They'll get you the sack.'

The tracksuit man still faced the old familiar perils. In November 1978 the *Daily Mirror* carried the shocking headline 'Sacking of the Tracksuit Manager', above the story of Cardiff manager Jimmy Andrews being told he was losing his job 'as he stood in a tracksuit waiting to take his players out for training'. This seems indecent, like a sacrilege against the tracksuit itself. 'I am hurt,' Andrews said afterwards, unflinchingly honest to the last.

This new breed also shared a fascination with the razzmatazz-infused new world of the North American Soccer League. Ken Furphy became Workington player–manager aged just thirty-one. Furphy was sacked by Sheffield United in 1975 and left to find a new life in America, where he signed Pele for his Soccer Bowl-winning New York Cosmos.

Gordon Jago also made his name in the US, where he was briefly director of the US soccer federation, aged just thirty-seven, before returning to manage QPR. An air of new world can-do lingered around him. He even spoke with an American accent, startling his apprentices while coaching at Charlton with the exclamation 'Jeezy breeze, that was a little bit of magic'. He left Millwall in 1978 after things turned sour on the terraces, although, true to the deep emotional bonds of the new breed, he was at least replaced by 'a players' co-operative'.

Many aspects of the new breed were a throwback to the

player-manager of the pre-First World War era, the upwardly mobile shop-floor steward type. Jon Cameron was player-secretary-manager of Spurs between 1899 and 1907. He would later become a progressive thinker on training and preparation. He wrote a book called *Association Football* in which he advised players should eat 'a substantial meal' two hours before a match, to consist of steak, stale bread and vegetables (but not potatoes).

Incredibly, he was interned in the same First World War prison camp that would house Fred Pentland, later 'El Bombín' and the managerial father of Spanish football, and Steve Bloomer, who also managed successfully in Spain. Cameron, Pentland and Bloomer held coaching clinics and even wrote their own football manual. We can only guess what they were wearing all this time. But you can bet it was some kind of loose-fitting two-piece, perhaps made of cotton. The German word is *Trainingsanzug.*

Ultimately Ron Greenwood of West Ham and England would become the apogee of the tracksuit men. Greenwood was a close friend of Walter Winterbottom, a cornerstone of the academicians at West Ham, and helped develop England's World Cup-winning goal-scorers and captain, Geoff Hurst, Martin Peters and Bobby Moore. He was also mild-mannered, even ponderous.

Appointed West Ham manager in April 1961, he adopted a provocative kind of Puritanism, a throwback to the amateur spirit, infused with an allotment-shed hobbyist's notion of football for football's sake. Young players were sent on training courses dealing with 'the theory of the game', although Greenwood himself was an aesthete and a minimalist who made a big thing of not using a blackboard. Instead he illustrated his plans by walking them through on the training pitch over and over again. His obituary noted that he 'was so keen to educate that sometimes he had to be dragged off the field'.

Typically, however, elements of this would be bastardised by later breeds of tracksuit men, culminating in a distinctly 1980s type, the Manager as Maniac. This was the tracksuit man turned up to eleven. At Wimbledon Bobby Gould presided over the most cartoonish excesses of the Crazy Gang, an era in which the club defied its lowly means by remaining in the top division and even winning the FA Cup. Throughout this its chief weapon, at least to the public eye, was a sense of collective spirit, conveyed in the media as part riotous punk troupe and part prison gang. New players would routinely have their clothes burned and their car tyres let down. No club trip was complete without various hurlings into the swimming pool. Gould himself once cracked a rib during a training ground 'bundle' with his skipper Dennis Wise.

Don Howe coached Wimbledon during this period. 'You had to be on your toes,' he said. 'Somebody might have pinched your socks or tied your shoelaces together. But tactically they were very well organised. When people talk about the Crazy Gang it looks like they were playing for fun. But it was kidology. They knew exactly what they were doing.'

Later, as manager of Wales, Gould was at the centre of an incident involving the rock group the Manic Street Preachers. During a 1998 concert at Cardiff Castle in front of twenty thousand people the Manics sang a version of their song 'Everything Must Go', with the lyrics changed to 'Bobby Gould must go'. Gould hit back, accusing the group of not being 'good role models'. Who knows where it might have ended up if he hadn't left the job a few months later.

The later breed of tracksuit men stuck to a narrow but intense creed. Dave Bassett, Gould's predecessor with the Crazy Gang, had been an insurance broker. He brought his yuppified creed of ruthless shock motivation into football and back out again: at his high point with Wimbledon Bassett offered motivational management lectures to business. Presumably leaving out the bit about scrawling obscene graffiti all over your opponents' dressing room.

Vinnie Jones would write of Bassett in his autobiography, 'Dave Bassett has been a kind of God in my life. He created me.' Later Jones mentioned occasions where Bassett would come to him and say, 'He's getting out of his station, give him one in the changing rooms.'

Bassett found a kindred spirit in John Beck, a manager who once wrote in his programme notes that he had demanded his players 'flood the dark corners of fear and superstition with the bright light of reason and knowledge . . . dispersing hobgoblins of the imagination and revealing the truth that sets men free'. At the start of his second spell as Cambridge United manager in 2001 Beck pleaded, 'I want to portray myself as an intelligent, scientific manager', and he did complete a five-year practical philosophy course at university in Preston and also an introductory psychology course. He was successful too, taking Cambridge from the old Fourth Division to the play-offs for the Premier League.

In the midst of this he also provided the most eloquent expression of the manager as maniac, the tracksuit man's disturbed younger brother with his ruthlessly macho lateral thinking. Beck kept the grass deliberately long in the corners to suit his kick-and-rush style and soaked his opponents' kick-about balls in water.

He famously gave his players pre-match cold showers, although he later claimed 'that was after a long coach journey to wake them up'. He had a dressing-room fist-fight with his own player Steve Claridge. He worked in a burger van at one point after leaving Cambridge, but later returned fired up with ideas about creating a link with Cambridge University to 'market the club internationally'.

In the end it seems a little sad that the legacy of the tracksuit men – of their gloomy, muscular idealism – should be this kind of japery. The tracksuit gave a sense of purpose and drive. But it also opened the door to a misplaced sense of extreme bonding.

In 1991 the Millwall and England coach Steve Harrison, one of the brightest tracksuit men of his day, was sacked from both jobs for a stunt that culminated in him defecating into a plastic cup while perched on top of a piece of hotel furniture. In its own way the plop of Harrison's stool into its plastic receptacle provided an end note to the era of the new breed. That sense of freedom provided by shared goals, vigorous physical activity and loose nylon clothing – all of it flushed away along with the Harrison motion.

We still hear talk of the tracksuit. In 1997 the *Guardian* would note, cautiously, the prospect of English football 'moving towards the new breed of continental tracksuit manager'. And all managers will sport, at some point, at least one item of tracksuit apparel, even if it's simply an XXL club training top flatteringly embroidered with his initials by the club launderers (as though there were any danger of him being mixed up with the svelte left-sided midfielder).

This is the lasting gift of the tracksuit men; that lingering sense of the outdoors, the studious and the deep male bondings of the training pitch.

CHAPTER 23

The Manager as Successful 1980s Thatcherite Double-Glazing Magnate

The 1980s was a decade when people really started to talk about management. Not football management, but supply chain management, enterprise content management, asset convergence management and Total Quality Management. Fuelled by deregulation and given a new language by the industry theorists of Japan and the US, the new Thatcherite service economy seemed to overflow with a sense of its own theory-driven importance.

It's hardly surprising that some element of this should enter the parallel universe of the football manager. And so it did, most obviously in the posturings of Big Ron Atkinson of Manchester United, the most prominent manager of the decade. Atkinson can claim to have attracted the most active nicknames of any working manager in the history of English football. Flash Harry, Jack the Lad, Champagne Charlie, Big Ron, Romeo Ron, Goldfinger, Mr Bojangles. The names just kept piling up, jingle-jangling around his furred and suntanned wrists alongside the timpani of his celebrated jewellery.

Atkinson has also been called a showman, although this seems to miss the real point of him. Big Ron shared the volatility and the dandified charisma of the showmen. But really he was something else. As the most visible English football manager of the early 1980s he introduced a new character: the Manager as Aspirational Thatcherite Businessman.

Margaret Thatcher was a significant influence. Classically socialist and heavy industry-inflected, the manager had always been more or less a Labour man. But then along came Mrs Thatcher, and the notion of the self-made man, the argyle-sweatered, out-of-town villa-dwelling man of industry with his provincial haulage firm fortune or UPVC double-glazing powerbase.

And many people in football did love Mrs Thatcher, with her empowering talk of things like minimal top band income tax, conspicuous consumption and that sense of intoxicating ruthlessness. As Atkinson himself said in 1984, 'I've always liked the good things in life and believe in living life to the full . . . and I've always been prepared to graft hard for my luxuries.'

This could be the local Maggie-groupie bigwig at an Eastbourne Town Hall party fundraiser; or Kevin Keegan and Emlyn Hughes photographed planting a sycophantic kiss on each of the Iron Lady's cheeks during an England team visit to Downing Street in 1980.

Big Mal appeared to want you to know that he was having more sex than you, and more fun. Big Ron seemed simply to want to make it quite clear that he was richer than you, and drinking far more champagne. The champagne in particular became a recurrent shorthand. According to popular myth Atkinson practically bathed in the stuff, or at least rinsed his peculiar sticky comb-over rug with it.

The champagne would follow Big Ron into the big time. Just before the 1983 FA Cup final he appeared on *The Big Match* to add a touch of glitz and glamour to an end-of-season broadcast. Tanned and coiffed, there he is, looking every inch

Jimmy Hill finds common ground with Prince Faisal bin Fahad bin Abdul Aziz, a 'gentleman of considerable charm', in Riyadh, 1976. (PA Archive/Press Association)

On the touchline he seemed to ooze, not so much sex, as raw male strength. Ron Atkinson, April 1978. (Colorsport)

A typical scene from the bench. From left, Celtic's Joe Filippi, Bobby Lennox, trainer Neil Mochan, physio Bob Rooney, manager Billy McNeill, his assistant John Clark, and, far right, then Aberdeen manager Alex Ferguson, October 1978. (Peter Robinson/Empics Sport)

Ron Greenwood, the apogee of the tracksuit men, shares something vital with Kevin Keegan during England training in 1977. (Colorsport)

A bouffant, raincoated figure: John Bond at Manchester City in 1981. (Mark Leech/Offside)

A dark, sweaty, sock-stinking place: (from left) Joe Fagan, Roy Evans and Ronnie Moran with Bruce Grobbelaar in the Liverpool bootroom, 1982. (Bob Thomas/Getty Images)

Clough and Taylor at Forest in 1986: one of football's most tenderly guarded tales. (Topfoto)

Graeme Souness's surprise appearance (centre) at the 1992 FA Cup final just days after major heart surgery. (Mark Leech/Offside)

Graham Taylor: scrambled, incoherent and on TV, Rotterdam, 1993. (Mark Leech/Offside)

An irresistibly simple charisma: Jack Charlton on the touchline at USA 94. (Topfoto)

Kevin Keegan with Tony Blair at – for reasons that remain unclear – the 1995 Labour Party conference. (Topfoto)

Europe compacted into a single bald and courteous Swiss. Christian Gross shows the press his tube ticket in November 1997.
(Andrew Cowie/Colorsport)

Terry Venables 'staring at some distant beautiful tomorrow', Elland Road, July 2002.

Left: The first international superstar manager: Jose Mourinho.
(Mike Egerton/Empics/PA)

Below: Sven and Nancy take a break from inducing peace, Goodison Park, 2006. (Action Images/Carl Recine)

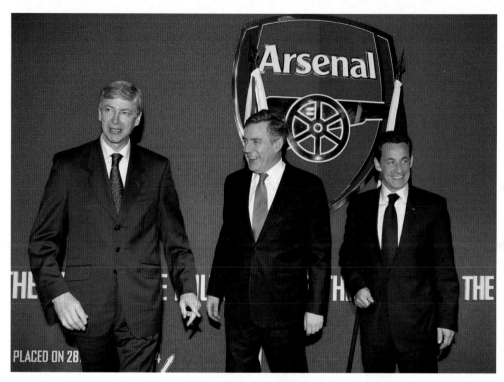

France's most influential man meets Gordon Brown and Nicolas Sarkozy, Emirates Stadium, March 2008. (Getty Images)

The complete modern manager: Sir Alex Ferguson, April 2004, with Gerard Houllier (right).

(Man Utd via Getty Images)

the good-time boy with his conscientious enjoyment of the Good Things In Life. Towards the end of the programme Atkinson produced and opened a bottle of champagne on camera, which he then proceeded to pour into flutes and hand to his fellow presenters. The credits rolled over a fast-edited montage of Big Ron quaffing, chuckling, mugging, raising an eyebrow, giving a thumbs-up and generally looking like he was Having a Really Good Time.

What was going on here? In retrospect, this was the start of football's long run-up to the billionaire-infused hyper-inflation of the Premier League. With Big Ron to the fore, it was year dot for football's distant commercial boom times, the first sense that some change might be in the air. The year 1983 was also the season that the principle of sharing gate receipts with the visiting team was abolished. This was a major change, and a thoroughly Thatcherite piece of anti-protectionist engineering. Manchester United's revenues would rise from close to £1m to £11.5m by 1990. The market was being ratcheted into place.

And in a sense Atkinson was simply the right kind of man in the right place at the right time: a man who liked a bit of flash. As a seventeen-year-old on the Aston Villa groundstaff he'd bought a Ford Anglia (cost: £34), in which he would ostentatiously pick up first-team players Jackie Sewell and Peter McParland when he saw them at the bus stop, warning them to 'mind the upholstery'.

He later spent much of his playing career at Oxford United. Pictures of the young Ron are illuminating. He doesn't really look like a footballer at all. He looks like a manager. It's all there: the middle-aged Teddy boy hair, the inflated head, the proprietorial air, and the huge but strangely unathletic legs. After stopping playing Atkinson accepted a job as a sales engineer with an Oxford firm of builders called GR Cooper. 'I learned many things during my association with that company which have proved invaluable in my management career,' he said later.

'I was taught business administration, office procedure, invoicing systems and general office organisation. Most important, I had to deal with people on a person-to-person level. Man-management.'

This is Ron as the self-made success story with his fully loaded walnut trim executive saloon and his Majorcan golfing villa. After GR Cooper he moved into coaching with Kettering in 1971. Here the pieces continued to fall into place. Ron had been head-hunted by the club chairman John Nash. 'I was immediately greatly impressed by the man himself . . . John Nash was the chairman of fifty-five companies, some of which were major concerns. He owned his own bank and was at one time the youngest ever Tory candidate for the town.'

Yes, he sounds dreadful. But Ron saw something of himself here. 'He believed that if he made eight out of ten correct decision in business, he would be successful. I am a bit like that with players.'

Instantly Kettering were energised: from mid-table they ended up winning the Southern League Second Division. 'I had made up my mind to try to run the place with a bit of style,' Atkinson recalled. 'My aim was to make the players feel important, superior to the opposition. They were all fitted out in club blazers and they had a luxury coach . . . We enjoyed pre-match meals both home and away.'

There's a great picture of Ron and his blazered boys fanning out in a perfect triangular phalanx in front of one of the goals, looking like a troupe of air stewards or a crack sales unit. Ron himself in those days was a *Sweeney* prototype. Mutton chops, too-tight brown slacks, leather Gestapo coat, horrible floral tie, brow creased in tough guy frown. On the touchline he seemed to ooze not so much sex as raw male strength.

Aged thirty-five Ron moved to Cambridge of the Fourth Division ('an ideal step-up'). Before long they were cooking too. 'I am a bouncy sort of person and I cannot bear to be surrounded by people with long, moping faces. Call it personality, if you like, or charisma.' This was Ron's way. And Cambridge of course won the Fourth Division title, clinching it at the Abbey Stadium where before long, according to the first of Ron's autobiographies, *United to Win*, it was 'carnival time'.

Ron performing the lambada, Ron – more likely – drinking a lot of champagne. Even at Cambridge an air of premier cru luxury living clung to him. In his last season Ron conducted a particularly bizarre transfer deal. Having just seen his team beat Bury to go top of Division Three, he organised a celebration dinner with John Bond and his family in the club lounge. His chairman later complained about the £50 bill for fine wines. Meanwhile Barry Fry was keen to sign the Cambridge full-back Billy Baldry. Ron had a solution.

'Ron phoned up on a Tuesday morning,' Fry told me thirty years later. 'He said, I've got no champagne left in my office. You can have Bill Baldry if you drive over with a case of Moët & Chandon. When I got there he took two bottles out and gave them back. He said, I've overcharged you.' Ron and his directors drank the rest after the following weekend's 5-0 defeat of Lincoln.

Still Ron continued to rise. On his first day as West Brom manager in the First Division the chairman presented him with a brand-new blue Jaguar XJ6. But there was a problem. Ron already had one. In white. And it was the four-litre, not the three. Before long he was telling the press, 'I have to be an egotist . . . I am a materialist. I don't deny it. I love the good things in life.' On the pitch he built a formidable team around the drive of Bryan Robson in midfield. Not to mention the diverse talents of a trio of young black players, Brendon Batson, Cyrille Regis and Laurie Cunningham, dubbed 'The Three Degrees' and, on at least one occasion, induced to pose listlessly in pimp-style fur coats with the all-black all-girl disco group of the same name.

In 1981 Ron moved on, triumphantly, to Manchester United, the biggest job in English football. He splashed huge amounts of cash on players, demanding an 'immediate injection of £3m' from his board just as the recession began to bite around football. 'At no time have I been overawed by the place,' he wrote in *United to Win*. A year and half later he led United out at Wembley for the first time. 'I was not overawed by the place,' he noted. This is Ron all over. Not overawed. No way.

Atkinson wasn't alone in all this. There were others, most notably Big Lawrie McMenemy, Big Ron's friend. McMenemy is described in the introduction to the diary of his 1978–9 season as Southampton manager as 'one of the best known men in Britain. His face is so familiar that he can't walk down a street without being stopped. He appears on TV more frequently than the Prime Minister.'

Extraordinary as this might seem, Big Mac did cut an imposing figure in the Ron-style mercurial business-manager template: more a troubleshooter, a roving John Harvey Jones-type, than a simple round-ball man. His diary notes: 'He is a managing director . . . he is running a business and can't afford to be sentimental'.

McMenemy once took his Grimsby players out on a fisherman's pontoon at the crack of dawn, in an *Apprentice*-style piece of workplace shock therapy. 'If there's a self-made manager, then it is McMenemy,' the *Daily Mirror* noted as he prepared to take his Southampton team to Wembley for the – victorious – 1976 FA Cup final. This was a reference to McMenemy's lack of Football League experience as a player and his history as a military guardsman. It also captured something of his bustle, his Ron-lite can-do.

A year before Atkinson was finally sacked at United, McMenemy was appointed both Sunderland manager and managing director. He 'strode into Roker Park through 300 back-slapping fans and wasted no time in punching home the

"I'm in charge" message' (according to the *Daily Mirror*). Never had the manager seen such business-savvy self-advancement.

And such bluster too. There is a false note in all of this. For all the talk of Big Ron and Big Lol as mandarins of the new corporate age, they were still essentially rough managerial stock. They still carried that transitory air inherited from the secretary, that sense of being indefinably doomed. They still worked to the Herbert Chapman big personality blueprint. They still wore the bastard cloak of a Harry Storer (at Southampton McMenemy famously had a fist-fight in the showers with centre half Mark Wright). They still talked with a Shankly inflection, built empires like Busby, dreamed themselves a Clough-style folk hero and swaggered about in Big Mal-derivative geezer-clobber.

What was Atkinson really like, anyway? We may never know. Even in the heights of his Old Trafford Big Ron bling he waged a constant campaign of teasing semi-denial. Of his bracelets, chains and rings he said, 'Everything I wore had been bought for me as presents.' His captain Bryan Robson commented, 'Ron's been depicted as a chap with a jeweller's shop on each hand, and the Crown Jewels on his wrists, who gets through a crate of champagne a day. But it's all part of a myth that he's happily let build up.'

In 1984 Ron himself would shrug, 'My favourite drink is tea, and there's more chance of me being regarded as a tea-aholic than an alcoholic' (in a confusing popular culture echo, this was the same year Boy George would inform Russell Harty he preferred 'a nice cup of tea' to sex). In fact there was much about Big Ron the successful Thatcherite businessman that was cartoonish and contrived.

At United tales circulated of him conducting negotiations over players' contracts while lying on the sunbed in his office dressed just in protective goggles and a skimpy thong. When he was sacked in 1986 he would joke that he'd had to swap his Mercedes for a BMW and was down to his last thirty-seven suits. Bluster, then: and also not a great deal of success. For all their high profile, neither Big Ron nor Bog Lol ever won a League title or a European trophy. For all the widescreen *amour propre*, real success happened elsewhere.

In many ways this seems even more fitting. Perhaps Big Ron is closer than we might think to capturing the essence of the times. Like Thatcher's Britain, with its chain-store glamour, its lurking shabbiness, Big Ron provided an illusion of success, a painted-on sense of prosperity. This wasn't the cathartic, energising glamour of a 1970s showman manager. This was simply a process of self-mythologising, a strictly personalised get-rich-quick scheme.

Big Ron may have made a lot of noise but he was essentially a sideshow. His achievement was to further the manager's own rise to popular prominence. The real action was going on elsewhere. For eight seasons leading up to the formation of the Premiership the League title would be divvied out between Kenny Dalglish, Howard Kendall, George Graham and Howard Wilkinson. Behind Ron's back, the dour men had taken the throne.

Taciturn and grim-faced, the dour men were closer to the reality of Big Ron's Britain, with its three million on the dole and weekly violence in the stands and city centres. This was a time when football came close to tipping point, to ceasing to exist as a workable spectacle. By the mid-1980s Britain was depressed, hung-over and parched. In English football the fizz was decisively gone, leaving just a frazzled and metallic aftertaste. With his Good Time shtick, Big Ron may have been a portent of what would come but at times he was also swimming against the tide. With the advent of the dour men the manager had a new public face. It wasn't suntanned. It didn't twinkle. It was pinched, careworn and unsmiling.

Dourness became an anti-fashion. Dalglish, by all accounts a charming man in private, developed an impenetrable matrix of facially immobile manager-speak, giving away nothing of himself even while winning the League title three times. Kendall, also a bon vivant among friends, presided over his Everton team's glories with little more than a twitch of the lip. And on the pitch the dour men produced dour teams playing dour football, a farrago of dourness that seemed to exist in another world to Big Ron's pantomime Good Times. In 1989 Wilkinson's Leeds played West Ham at Upton Park in the old Second Division (described by Steve Coppell at the time as 'a hell hole'). It was the kind of match – violent, cynical, stripped of beauty – that can define an era. David Lacey of the *Guardian* opened his match report with a kind of manifesto for the dour men of the 1980s: 'On Saturday the ground that came to represent much of what was good in the English game, an oasis of decency in a desert of cynical expediency, saw what remained of this ideal torn to shreds by two sets of pit bull terriers describing themselves as the Uniteds of West Ham and Leeds.'

Wilkinson would later justify his team's approach by pleading that he was 'in the front line with a platoon and needing to take a hill occasionally', adding, 'I either do it or I get shot.' There is a fascinating essay to be written on the manager's habitual confusion of the selection of a football team with various kinds of trench-based military manoeuvres. But this all sounded a lot more familiar, a lot more like the reality of the Bad Times.

In the middle of which, Big Ron, much like late-period Maggie, had started to look slightly ludicrous (by 1986, Thatcher herself was being described in the *Daily Mirror* as 'the Ron Atkinson of politics'). Atkinson continued to stalk the top tier of English football, by now a kind of in-joke, a walking piece of kitsch. Almost single-handedly he sustained the headline clichés of the showman manager, his accessories, his swagger and his egotism. Like a pearly king or an ironic post-punk punk posing for tourist photographs in Leicester Square with his pink

Mohican, at Coventry and Aston Villa Big Ron had the air of a heritage exhibit or a managerial tribute band.

Above all, rather than great teams or sustained success, he created a new brand of personalised manager speak, a mash-up of training-ground talk and his own stylised argot. In his final role as TV summariser he gave us 'Ronglish': early doors, the back stick, the spotters' badge and best of all 'He's in the wide-awake club', a middle-aged tipping of the hat to a short-lived Saturday-morning kids TV programme featuring Timmy Mallett.

Like many an ambitious early-1980s Thatcherite business-man, Big Ron had pretensions towards something lasting. In the end, true to the years of yuppies, nimbies, dinkies and people who said 'yah', his real gift to football was a few funny words.

Of course it's impossible to mention Ron Atkinson without touching on what happened after he'd stopped being a manager. In April 2004 Atkinson lost his job as an ITV pundit after racially abusing a Chelsea player on air during a transmission of a Champions League match. Atkinson thought his mic was off. It wasn't.

He resigned. He said it was a mistake and he didn't mean it, that he was 'an idiot but not a racist'. He was sacked from his national newspaper column. He was widely reviled, although certain black former players of his did stick up for him. And that was pretty much it for Big Ron, barring the odd ill-judged attempt at a comeback. This is an ugly subject but it's one it would be dishonest to ignore completely here. And what about Ron's own defence? It's true that he picked black players for his West Brom team in the late 1970s when this was still a rarity. In his first autobiography, written in 1984, Atkinson writes: 'My attitude has always been that it doesn't matter if a player is black, brown, yellow or purple.'

Which sounds reasonable enough. Except that a bit later on in his book he's still telling this joke: 'West Brom have had to cancel their Central League game?'

'Why's that?'

'Oh, the first team have eaten all the reserves.'

And then painting the following picture of racial harmony in the dressing room: 'The coloured lads took it all in their stride . . . Nothing was ever underhand. If the joke was to be told, it was not done behind the backs of the coloured boys.'

What a lovely place the dressing room sounds like. But a few pages later there he is again, unbidden, talking hopefully about his future dream of 'seven or eight coloured players at one time representing England'. And also praising the 'courage and dignity' of his own black players under terrible racial abuse from the crowds. The fact is, Ron was sixty-five years old when he resigned from ITV. This is a man who has spent fifty years around professional football, a game that has been both socially and geographically at the cutting edge of race tensions in this country. It's the frontline.

But there is good news too. Football is one of the places that black British people were first permitted to excel publicly. Essentially football is a very stark kind of meritocracy. If you're good enough, you'll play, and you'll also win. And in the end winning overrides everything else. So in 1982 John Motson on *Match of the Day* could marvel at Luton's 'colony of seven black players'. Their manager David Pleat's response was: 'They could be yellow-faced, all that matters is are they better players than what you've got.' This is oddly put, but it's also about as progressive a statement as you could hope to make at the time. The National Front was stalking the East End. There were race riots in south London. And a football manager, in a small way perhaps, was standing against it. This was something.

Black players are now thoroughly integrated into English football. Crowds are more mixed. And vocal racism is confined to the fringe lunatics or the unreconstructed minority bigot.

The new challenge is to engage black managers and to see them rise on their merits. Paul Ince has managed in the Premier League, and before him Jean Tigana and Ruud Gullit. More will surely follow. This has been the way of football: bumpy progress, but progress nonetheless. And football, often to its credit, does at least confront these issues. It has helped to progress the argument. Not least through its instant condemnation of – and occasional attempts to understand – the Big Ron of April 2004.

CHAPTER 24

The Manager Gets Hounded Out

By the early 1990s, football had begun to enter the dawn of another boom. A media-led, lad culture-infused revival was in train. Football was, cautiously, on its way to becoming a mainstream pursuit, a lifestyle choice in an era of aggressively marketed leisure. The manager was part of the wider scene now. There was no need for him to seek fame. It came looking for him. And in the process some peculiar things would start to happen.

Graham Taylor was England manager from 1990 to 1993. He took England to one tournament and narrowly missed out on another. Still, the defining images of his reign are all variations on the theme of excruciating failure. Taylor was not a showman, a big personality or a silk-hat impresario. Yet he remains one of the most famous of all England managers. Perhaps this is because his appearance coincided with the England manager, whoever the England manager might have been, becoming wider public property for the first time, in the same way the actor playing James Bond is, or the host of the Radio 1 breakfast show or the

Minister for Pensions. And make no mistake, Taylor was huge in his time.

There were practical reasons for this, not least the still hormonal and adolescent twenty-four-hour tabloid mass media. As Taylor himself told me, musing on the peculiar travails of his public life as England manager, 'My father was a journalist and I was always interested in the media empires, the Robert Maxwells and the Rupert Murdochs.

'Looking back I'm convinced there was a change going on in the media, with these two empires fighting a circulation war. For people in the public eye, like politicians and the England manager, so much depended on if they were on your side.'

For three years Taylor was daily fodder for the red-tops. He was also the first England football manager to feature regularly on *Spitting Image*, a weekly fixture of the slate-grey John Major years. Even this provided a flavour of Taylor's status as national whipping boy. His voice on the show was provided by Alistair McGowan, who would occasionally take the puppets out into the street to gauge public reaction. 'We'd taken Jean-Paul Gaultier out, and people had been very friendly,' McGowan recalled. 'But then we took Graham Taylor into the Coach and Horses in Soho. And this bloke said, "Oi, Taylor, come here: you are a disgrace. I don't know how you got the job. You should go now" . . . It was amazing, the vitriol I got on Graham's behalf. If that's what the puppet gets, what does Taylor get in person?'

Taylor in person was something we would become uncomfortably familiar with. You often hear people say there's no such thing as bad publicity. Graham Taylor got bad publicity. The documentary *An Impossible Job*, first screened on Channel 4 in 1994, was a career-defining moment. It started out as a fly-on-the-wall view of England's passage to the World Cup in America. Unfortunately for Taylor, his team performed poorly and were also luckless at key moments. Even more unfortunately, he turned out to be a brilliantly absorbing subject for a tragicomic documentary film.

The image of his face in extreme close-up, eyes wide, adrenalin-churned, scrambled and incoherent, is unbearably watchable and strangely poignant in ways that seem to go far beyond football. And like all great performances, it gives us great lines.

In Poland, as his team go 1-0 down, we get Taylor in extreme close-up: 'Ooooh . . . Fuck . . . Do I not like that . . . What a fuckin' . . . ball.'

In the crucial World Cup qualifier against Holland: 'David, no . . . Don't . . . Get round . . . *No Platty!*'

As David Platt is fouled by Ronald Koeman of Holland, who then wrongly stays on the field, Taylor accosts a pained-looking Uefa official: 'What have they been instructed? . . . You know the rules! . . . Linesman! *Linesman!* What sort of thing is happening here? You know it, don't you? You know.'

Then, as the linesman approaches. 'You know we've been cheated don't you? . . . You know.'

Leaning close Taylor becomes a bit more conciliatory. 'I know you can't say anything. I know you can't. You see, at the end of the day, I get the sack. I get the sack now.'

Before finally sneaking across to the linesman again, with a sting in his tail. 'I was just saying to your colleague, the referee's got me the sack. Thank him ever so much for that, won't you.'

And of course against Poland we get Taylor crying out in extreme close-up: 'We've done that . . . Fucking! . . . *Can we not knock it?*'

The answer to which appeared to be, no. We cannot knock it. England never made it to the World Cup. Taylor was half right: he wasn't sacked but he was forced to resign. And after his documentary no manager since Brian Clough had been so widely impersonated. Re-released by ITV in 2008, it remains a huge popular success. A twenty-second clip of Taylor shouting 'Go

Les! *Hit Les!!* Well . . . You tell 'em Les!' has to date been viewed over twenty-five thousand times on YouTube.

This was the comic post-mortem. In real time, the remarkable thing about Taylor's time with England was the level of scorn and personal abuse. For a while he seemed to be single-handedly carving an exciting new managerial niche: the manager as dork, loser and punch bag. 'We have to learn to laugh at ourselves a little bit,' he said on being given the job. But nobody in the press pack that followed Taylor about like an execution squad seemed to be laughing much.

'I'd been in management long enough to know you don't read every paper,' Taylor told me fifteen years after his resignation as England manager. 'But I was definitely aware of them. A small number of press people, I wouldn't want to describe them as evil, but they have agendas, and it suits their agendas sometimes if England lose.'

This may or may not be true. But it certainly seemed to loosen the creative juices. After defeat to Sweden at Euro 92, improvements in newspaper technology allowed the *Sun* to morph a cut-out of Taylor's head into a turnip, alongside the headline Swedes 2 Turnips 1. The spectre of Turniphead Taylor had been called forth. Just two years in, this was his tipping point.

Some years later Taylor would get a phone call from the *Sun*. The sub-editor responsible for Turniphead was retiring and in his honour the page had been framed for a farewell party. The newspaper wanted Taylor to present it to him. He refused. 'I thought it just a bit incredible that anyone at the *Sun* would have thought I would have wanted to have revisited that time in my life . . . What would I have said to the guy receiving the presentation? "Thank you for making me the laughing stock of the nation. Thank you for reducing my mother to tears."'

Because this was what Taylor got as England manager: ridicule, to a degree few, if any, public figures have ever been subjected to. Taylor told me about one incident during England's tour of the US in 1993, the high water mark of the fury that surrounded him, and something he had, until now, kept silent about. 'We had just lost 2-0 to the USA. That was when I got a phone call from my wife, who had been out shopping with her mother who was in a wheelchair at the time. She came back home and she couldn't get into the street let alone the house because there was a pack of media people waiting for her.

'She'd never done interviews. She was trying to get her groceries out, and she said, "Sorry, I don't do interviews." And the chap there from one of the tabloids said, "It's about time you fucking started then, love."

'So she phoned me in America. Luckily the FA security people gave me a number that went straight to the heart of the West Midlands police force. They came out and moved all the media people. And my wife kept that phone number with her the whole time we were away. That was the first time I thought, Is this job worth it?'

In the days before handing in his eventual resignation Taylor crept home via a back entrance and once again saw press in his front garden and cameras trained on his windows. The police told him not to go home. He spent the last few days of his time as England manager in hiding at his daughters' houses. This is an extraordinary thing to have happened, even for the manager, no stranger to highly personalised vilification. It was also a phenomenon that would be mirrored elsewhere. These were the John Major years, a uniquely twitchy and irate period in the public life of the nation.

It was a time of houndings-out, of grudges and grumbles and of recession-era knuckle-cracking. BBC Radio 5 launched in 1990, and the *6-0-6* phone-in a year later. Within a relatively short period of time the background music of daily life had been augmented by a kind of incessant aggrieved whine, a droning public lament against inadequacies, gaffes, blunders and neglected duties. An exciting new voice had emerged: the voice of a man stuck in roadworks in the rain on a shaky mobile phone connection talking in a wonderfully fluent monotone about the failings of some arm of government, some piece of infrastructure, some doomed sporting enterprise.

This was the new disappointment of the early 1990s: a sense of being thoroughly abandoned by leaders who weren't butch enough, or big enough. And Taylor was there right at the start. Grinning, intense and deeply wronged, he was kindling to this white-hot brazier of disaffection. It was all terribly undeserved. Taylor is an honourable man. And throughout all this he never lost his own essential niceness. During the early stages of his career he even wielded a low-level charisma. In 1980 *Shoot* magazine carried a picture spread of Taylor and his Watford chairman Elton John, in which Elton described Taylor as 'one of the most influential people I've ever met'.

Theirs was a touching relationship. Together they appeared on *The Big Match* in 1981, decked out in matching browns and beiges. Elton, lolling behind oversized shades, had 'just flown in from Paris' by private jet. 'I came to the match by bike,' Taylor quipped, looking vital and handsome, in a gentle, lunchtime TV drama kind of way, while beside him Elton collapsed in shrieks of laughter.

Taylor had started young, taking over at Lincoln after enforced retirement as a player aged twenty-eight. It was here he first caught Elton's eye, taking the club to the Fourth Division title. 'I thought it was the last thing I wanted,' he said later, 'an outrageous pop star messing around as chairman.' In 1977 Taylor finally gave in to Elton's sustained wooing and moved to Vicarage Road. Within five years Watford were in the First Division. In 1984 they would reach the FA Cup final, losing 2-0 to Everton, as a sequinned Elton wept in the stands.

Throughout all this Taylor set about zealously building links with the local community. Lewd chants were banned within the stadium. In 1983 Taylor ran the second London marathon and raised £34,000, on the back of which the club built a family terrace. Players were entered into a scheme whereby if Watford won by three goals or more, the next Thursday a group of them would come to your local pub and buy you a drink. Taylor recalled: 'Myself and my staff would take three players each and go round all these pubs. So you'd get John Barnes coming in and buying you a pint. You just couldn't do it now.'

For a while his players were also required to put on sketches and skits for supporters. They did a spoof Graham Taylor *This Is Your Life*, with Barnes dressed up as a pregnant woman pretending to be Taylor's long-lost lover. This, remember, is the man later to become the most vilified and – apparently – hated man in English football. It shouldn't have turned out like this. So where did it all go wrong? At which point bells chime, a whistling sound is heard and the screen begins slowly to dissolve as we head back in time. The date is now 25 November 1953. England are in the process of being beaten 6-3 by Hungary at Wembley, a shattering defeat that has become strangely pivotal to much that has followed.

In the stands at Wembley a dapper man of military bearing watches with a frown. In his hands are a pad and a pencil, with which he makes a series of notations. Not just when goals are scored or saves made but when a free kick is awarded, when a long pass is attempted, when one team loses the ball. This is Wing-Commander Charles Reep. And he's not going to take any of this lying down.

Thirty years later Reep would be described in *The Times* as 'the human computer of soccer's Fabled Fifties', testimony to his work with Stan Cullis. He is perhaps the most curious and unlikely figure to have played a part in the oscillating fates of English football. Reep was an ex-naval man, a number-cruncher and a geek. Two years previously he had begun to devise his own system of football 'match analysis', apparently the first person to come up with the idea of recording all that incidental data. He wasn't just a stat-freak. Reep was ambitious. He had ideas. More importantly he had a footballing theory called Random Chance. Through this Reep saw himself as a seeker after a kind of football Da Vinci code, a unified equation for success.

Reep was convinced that Hungary's overwhelming superiority at Wembley was 'a myth'. He later complained, 'Nearly everybody in English football believes that that defeat clearly demonstrated English football had fallen behind the Continentals.' This was a fallacy that could be exploded, he maintained, 'and I have all the relevant facts and figures necessary to do so'.

Essentially, Reep was an aggressive reductionist and a fanatical debunker of the artistic, the gilded and the foreign. His figures had but one purpose. Described as 'analysis' they were in fact the opposite: bald observations selected to an agenda. The most famous of Reep's maxims is the line: 'Between 70 and 80 per cent of goals in any match at any level of football come from three passes or fewer.' This is largely meaningless. It takes no account of the preceding conditions, of context, of pressure exerted, of momentum or rhythm within a game. Or of the skewing of the mean by one-pass set-piece goals. Or, more importantly, of the fact that Reep compiled his statistics by watching English teams playing variations on English kick and rush football.

In Reep's hands this 'fact' simply meant players should always attempt to play three passes or fewer. Hit and hope was their only hope. This was pure sun-goes-round-the-earth solipsism, a process of wilfully avoiding the evidence of your own eyes (your team has just been both thrashed and outclassed) in favour of the evidence of a notebook.

In the novel *Middlemarch* the impotent academic Casaubon pours his life's work into a study he calls 'The Key to All Mythologies'. This is an authorial joke at the expense of the over-literal academic mind. It's a contradiction in terms, the search for a nonexistent short-cut: mythology can have no key, just as the random artistry of top-level football can't be reduced to a series of stats. Match analysis was Reep's own fruitless and flawed Key to All Mythologies.

In spite of which, it seemed to hit the spot. Expert hobbyists, eloquent and persuasive nut-jobs: there have always been plenty of these about. All they need is an audience. And Reep found one in Cullis, who had also been disquieted by the triumph of the Hungarians. Fortunately help was on its way. Before long Reep would be presenting himself at Molineux, briefcase in hand. As he later recalled: 'I well remember Mr Cullis' great satisfaction at finding complete support for his own views on how football should be played, as established by my own research data, particularly regarding long ball play.'

Reep and Cullis worked together throughout the 1950s, with great success. Significantly, though, their long-ball tactics would come up short against foreign opposition who preferred to keep the ball when it was punted upfield towards them. In 1960 Wolves lost 9-2 on aggregate to Barcelona. Cullis considered it a blip and an injustice. Don Howe, who watched the game, remembers it slightly differently. 'Barcelona, tactically, were different class,' he told me over fifty years later. 'They had some brilliant, wonderful strikers. Some teams Wolves could overpower, but not them.'

This could have all passed off harmlessly enough, but the legacy of Cullis and Reep was tenacious. Having come up with a theory, a set of beliefs, some figures, even, English football stuck to it jealously. This was its first big idea and it wasn't going to let it go without a fight. In time the direct football mantra, and Reep's own garden-shed Eureka theorems, would be absorbed into the nerve centre of the Football Association itself under director of coaching Charles Hughes thirty years later.

Hughes is often portrayed as the great evil in English football's midst, its snickering bad guy. The influential journalist Brian Glanville described him as having 'poisoned the wells' of the English game. During his period as FA director of coaching between 1982 and 1997 Hughes consorted with the aged Reep and, as Glanville put it, gathered 'a little band of believers and acolytes' ready to enact his 'fanatical credo', his 'pseudo-religion'.

But Hughes was at least trying to do something. English football had no textbooks before him (after him it had two). Until then it had no science. Before the 1966 World Cup Brazil had spent £300,000 on 'scientific preparation', including a four-month training camp for players who were monitored by two hundred medical staff. What did England have? An inspirational egomaniac in a coat, some men with buckets and the ability to run around a lot.

There was much ground to make up. The long-ball game, or 'direct football', may be back-of-an-envelope, counter-intuitive stuff. It may even be a bit silly. But it evolved out of English football's only real concerted effort to theorise or think about the game. It did at least require coaching and discussion. Even if in the end what it produced was a kind of new brutalism, a style of football pared with Occam's razor to its idiot component parts.

This was a very English kind of bad science, one above all rooted in hierarchy and the looming silhouette of the manager. Under the Reep/Cullis/Hughes blueprint the players were simply objects to be manipulated. Don't think. Just get on with it. This style of football has been compared with the industrial 'de-skilling' of the 1970s, the corporate death of the machine-age employee. By way of a counterpoint, the beret-wearing football theorist would point to the highly successful methods at Ajax in Holland, where players were taught to think on their feet, to keep the manager off the pitch and safely in his dugout. These players were being empowered, or 'en-skilled' in the jargon of the day.

The 'en-skilling' process never quite reached the managerial door in England, which perhaps explains why it's not really a proper word. Still, this is where Graham Taylor suddenly re-enters the picture. Taylor, it turned out, was a Reep man and a vocal exponent of what he vigorously refused to call 'direct football'. As Watford made headlines Reep himself would refer to 'My system of play which took Watford to promotion and second place in the First Division'. Taylor would tell *Match of the Day* in 1982, 'I hate sophisticated football . . . The man on the terrace is not interested in seeing fifteen or sixteen consecutive passes in their own half of the field'. Sound familiar?

By 1990, with Bobby Robson on the way out, Taylor was the obvious choice to replace him as England manager. With Taylor and Hughes together in harness, and Reep the absent spectre, the England team was ready, finally, to put into action a set of beliefs that had percolated around for fifty years. And so they did. Even in grey and freezing Katowice, the day before the vital drawn World Cup qualifier, Taylor could be glimpsed preaching theory to his players while they huddled inside a small concrete dugout, his talk all of 'variety of restarts . . . Until they change the rules restarts will always win or lose games'.

Of course it was all a bit of a disaster. Wedded to a system, and racked by injuries, Taylor seemed overwhelmed by the wealth of resources at his disposal. Over three and a half years he called up seventy-eight different players, but not Chris Waddle, then playing brilliantly in France, or the sublimely skilled Peter Beardsley.

England failed to qualify for the World Cup, but this time they failed to qualify while trumpeting a self-important little-England style methodology. The public is no fool. We got this stuff. As early as 1981 Taylor had been the subject of an *Alas Smith and Jones* monologue on BBC2: Mel: 'Graham Taylor is a svengali of football. He likes getting his players into the box and concentrating on them long balls.'

Griff: 'Of course . . . that's why he needs them long baggy shorts below the knee . . .'

Cue gales of mocking laughter. Oh yes, we knew what Taylor and his men were up to. And so we watched on anxiously as English football's big short-cut, its quick-fix scheme for a century of neglected basic coaching, unravelled before us. None of this was entirely Taylor's fault. Unwilling to take the traditional route of trusting in his own cunning, his own chest-thumping persona, he took what he could find with the only coherent theory handed down to him. Tasked with reviving the hopes of a nation in apparently terminal decay, he presented us with our own brown paper and string solution that, inevitably, came to pieces in his hands.

Which brings us back to the scorn. And the loathing. And the sheer sense of Taylor-engendered embarrassment. This was all-too familiar. As a nation in apparently terminal decay on all sorts of fronts, we knew all about brown paper and string solutions. So Taylor's England took its place in the stocks. This was the manager's contribution to a particularly English acme of awfulness.

And for the time being Taylor's England gave us football's fungi-ridden 1960s housing estate. This was its gridlocked M25, spam, ready meals and the pile 'em high supermarket. This was the Little Chef, Milton Keynes and British Rail, football management's addition to every under-funded, backyard attempt to solve a world-class problem. In a sense Taylor took the rap for something else, and at a particularly virulent time for handing out the rap.

It seems doubly unfortunate that his tenure as England manager should coincide with Major's term as Prime Minister. Nasal and suburban, for a while the Major persona seemed to bleed into Taylor's own. Both appeared to embody some sense of ineradicable top-tier mediocrity. Major had come to power in 1992. His time in office would be marked by howls of discontent from the sidelines and by its own array of public sackings. David Mellor had departed amid invented tabloid tales of extramarital adventures in a Chelsea shirt. Just a few months before Taylor resigned, the chancellor Norman Lamont got it.

As Taylor himself recalled (albeit, it has to be said, surprised to be asked about all this): 'You couldn't say any of this at the time. But the fact is the Conservative government was coming to an end. We'd had the Poll Tax. There were all those things people had to moan about. There was a recession going on. Generally my relationship with the media has been very good. But that twelve-month period was just so intense. Non-qualification for the World Cup definitely did not help the national mood.'

This was the tide that Taylor surfed. He may not have devised the policy. But he implemented it, he stood by it, and he bore the brunt of our squealed anguish when the whole thing went wrong. The shame, the horror, the public ousting. This was a coronation of sorts for the manager. Welcome to the big stage. Welcome to the brilliantly unpleasant tomorrow.

There is an interesting postscript to Graham Taylor's story. While he was in charge of England, Ireland were managed by Jack Charlton, or Big Jack as it became briefly compulsory to call him. Charlton had managed Middlesbrough and Newcastle before becoming Ireland manager in 1986. He had great success with a group of players culled from far afield under the 'one Irish grandparent' rule. As Taylor prepared to take the England job in the summer of 1990, the cult of Jack's Lads, Jack's Boys, Jack's Army and Jack's Improbable And Unstoppable Rise To Popular Fame was fully in train.

Ireland reached the quarter-finals of Italia 90 where they lost to the hosts. This was a match watched by 90 per cent of the Republic's population. As the *Guardian* noted: 'For Ireland this has been a period of delirium which very few people, even as they dance with total strangers in O'Connell Street, claim fully to understand.'

Jack's Lads had a visceral appeal. Everything they touched

turned to chocolate. Factory owners appeared on TV to announce they would be closing for the day so that workers could watch the games. Banks announced that extra credit would be extended to fans who found themselves stranded in Italy. The crime rate dropped sharply.

And all the while the Cult of Big Jack deepened and spread. Four years later, with Taylor's England failing to make it to USA 94, Big Jack and Big Jack's Boys had become an unignorable presence. Shortly before the tournament Big Jack himself was voted Ireland's most popular man, polling 38 per cent of an Irish Press Group survey. In turn Ireland were adopted by the BBC and ITV World Cup coverage as the home-team-by-proxy and Big Jack and his men projected in a blizzard of Brand Ireland clichés: cheeky, passionate, feisty, eternally underdog, doomed to failure, up for the craic, wonky and drunk.

For the 1-0 defeat of Italy, Giants Stadium was transformed into what the *New York Times* called 'the world's largest Irish pub'. And for a heady couple of weeks, Big Jack became an international superstar. Having conquered the UK, he broke America, always a sucker for sentimental headline Irishness. The *Orlando Tribune* noted that 'Jack and the boys are truly the lovable misfits of the 1994 World Cup', advising that 'Big Jack would fit in comfortably in your living room. Just pop open a cold one (Guinness, if you please), offer him a smoke, and listen closely.'

Charlton went down a storm in the States, presenting his uniquely unpretentious ordinary Jack shtick to a captive and adoring audience. He drank with fans in hotel bars. He played billiards. He joined a wedding party he'd bumped into on the way to the bathroom, eating chicken wings and chatting with the bride and groom.

On the face of it, the similarities with Taylor and his intense – and ultimately failed – England regime are pretty thin on the ground. And Big Jack's own strolling, straight-backed charisma was a perfect ballast for the England-shaped hole in the TV and publicity schedules ahead of football's biggest month-long beano. But if Charlton benefited from Taylor's failure, in the process adding his own weather-beaten, romantic outsider strand to the cult of the managerial personality, he was also quite similar to Taylor in some ways.

After stopping playing Charlton had turned to coaching with some zeal, gaining his full FA badge at Lilleshall. Like Taylor he was influenced by Charles Hughes the FA's coaching director. His teams played an even more basic variation of long-ball, direct football. At Middlesbrough he had employed a tall, strong striker called Alan Foggon to sprint on to diagonal passes lumped forward by his full-backs. With Ireland Charlton succeeded using the same methods that brought Taylor such vilification.

For this Big Jack was hugely fêted, albeit by his public rather than his more purist critics. Charlton was even familiar with the works of Wing-Commander Charles Reep, who would himself outlive his nadir as an associate partner in the Taylor England regime, by resurfacing in the Premier League in 2000 – at the age of ninety-five – as an adviser to the Wimbledon manager Egil Olsen.

Which just goes to show how fine are the margins for the manager. Taylor espoused a controversial brand of long-ball football, failed, and was reviled as few public figures of the modern age. Charlton did the same, succeeded, and became unconditionally adored, a swoonworthy housewives' favourite, the dream drinking partner, a nation's favoured wise uncle. Largely this was circumstance. Taylor was working with England, where a craven inferiority complex goes hand in hand with unflinching assumptions of a divine right to success. All England managers are reviled in time. This is their function.

Charlton was in charge of Ireland, a nation unaccustomed to success, and giddy with whatever it could get, by any means necessary. But more than this, Charlton had the personality to take flight with his success. Where Taylor seemed troublingly old-fashioned, Charlton was thrillingly old-fashioned and brilliantly rustic. Before playing for Leeds United he had worked for a single day in a coal mine and then toyed with joining the police. Eventually he played in England's World Cup-winning team in England in 1966. His post-match celebrations ended up with him sleeping on the sofa of a complete stranger in a house in Dagenham. Shuffling outside in the morning for a turn round the complete stranger's garden he looked over the fence and by chance came face to face with an old friend from the north-east.

This was the kind of thing that just happened to Big Jack. He was rough and gregarious and open to possibility, infused with a bracing sense of the practical and the outdoors. For a while he had his own TV programme about field sports. And in his hands football, and indeed life itself, seemed no more than an extension of rambling, fishing and field sports, a matter of colour in your cheeks, a good long walk and maybe a fresh trout down the front of your trousers.

Charlton made you feel vaguely proud of his abrasive, rousing, semi-Gaelic football, carried along by the underdog's broad-shouldered optimism. He was perhaps always more likely to make this kind of game work than Taylor, with his air of the hopeful geography teacher. And once he did, Big Jack had all the Big Man personality you needed, an irresistibly simple charisma.

Taylor would find himself reinterpreted as a rather vicious root vegetable-based newspaper caricature. Charlton, for his part, remains canonised, garlanded, and preserved in the form of a vaguely grotesque bronze statue at Cork airport, which depicts him fondly cradling a huge fish.

CHAPTER 25

The Shock of the Foreign

It was in the summer of 1994 that the *Sun* newspaper first broke the story of the EU campaign against the bent banana, devoting its front page to news that 'Brussels bureaucrats proved yesterday what a barmy bunch they are – by outlawing curved bananas'. This story would come to define the floating notion of some vast EU-dalek-conspiracy. It was a call-to-arms, a rallying cry against an insurgent army of humourless Benelux-loyalists bent on sodomising the pound, downgrading the Queen, burning the complete works of Anthony Trollope and generally emasculating the Great British Way of Life.

As the years passed the *Sun* would stick doggedly to its line of inquiry. Other crackpot laws exposed have included: the move towards square strawberries, decibel limiters for bagpipes, a ban on barmaids wearing low-cut tops, and the ongoing and malicious campaign to abolish the pint of lager. Perhaps the most interesting thing about all of these headline disasters is that, as it turns out, life has carried on largely uninterrupted. Bananas remain bananas. Cleavage-flashing barmaids still serve pints of lager. Fishermen don't wear hairnets. Butchers are still allowed to give bones to dogs.

Only the suspicion remains, and the fear of the unsmiling European with his briefcase full of vindictive reform. The UK had entered the European Union proper in 1992. As the *Sun's* bananas testify, this was a time of gathering millennial anxiety all round, of a sense of identity slippage and sovereignty erosion, of great sweeping covert changes being winched into place.

That same year, 1992, the Premiership was launched, a break-away league formed by the top twenty clubs, who had decided to split from the traditional collective Football League TV deal and take up an offer from the new satellite force, BSkyB. The Premier League, football's plastic new dawn, had always been a pan-European idea, aimed at the global TV markets of the new satellite world. At the same time there was much talk of a federal monster-super league being set up. Silvio Berlusconi, president of AC Milan and later Italy, announced, 'There will be a league formed outside of Uefa with a team from each country, spon- sored by that country's biggest company.'

Europe was coming. It was all terribly exciting – and trou- bling too. English football was in the process of being filleted and prised open. And as ever, the hot-dog seller in the background of history, the manager would find himself caught up in all this, not least as an unlikely lightning rod for that sense of lurking straight-banana anxiety.

Foreign-inflected managers were not an entirely new thing. Sammy Chung, whose father was Chinese and mother English, had managed Watford, Ipswich and Wolves in the 1960s. Eddie Firmani was a South African who later played for Italy and man- aged Charlton. But it would take the appointment of Josef Venglos at Aston Villa in 1990 to focus the mind properly on the terrible shock of the foreign. Venglos was the first born and bred foreign national to manage a First Division club. He was a peculiar choice too: a softly spoken, white-haired Slovakian doctor of philosophy. Villa were almost relegated during his single season in charge. He left bewildered, among many other things, by the Anglo-Saxon sportsman's capacity for lager, of which he commented, thoughtfully, 'I never dreamed human beings could drink so much.'

Graham Taylor still occasionally sees Venglos, now a Uefa delegate. 'Venglos is a very nice man,' he says. 'But the players just weren't ready for him. And he had massive problems understanding what Second, Third and Fourth Division football was about. When he went to watch a game, that type of football was so foreign to him he didn't know who or what he was watching.'

David Pleat, coach of Luton during the Venglos interlude, agreed. 'He was a nice man but he couldn't cope with the intricacies of how the game was run behind the scenes here. He could coach, but the rest of it was just too much.'

But what was the rest of it? 'He wouldn't let them have cups of tea,' Taylor recalled. 'So all of a sudden at half time there wasn't a cuppa for you. He also introduced his training sessions, where they'd have to go and drink water at set times and so on. The problem was, if you're not winning games you're going to be in trouble and it doesn't matter if you're drinking water, tea or beer.'

As Paul McGrath, a player under Venglos, later remarked, 'He was too quiet. We just didn't agree with Dr Jo's training methods.' Chiefly, these 'methods' involved an aversion to shouting that seemed genuinely to spook his charges. Where were his foghorn denunciations? Where was the sense of some terrible and unanswerable wrong? Where were the wild eyes and pinched mouth?

Villa lost 2–1 to Spurs in one of his first League matches. The manager's bewilderingly amiable verdict: 'A good entertaining game of football. All are happy, one with the win, one with the performance.' No choked and tearful rebuke. No fist-fight. This was kinky. This was weird. It also couldn't be allowed to go on. Two days before he left in 1991, he told his chairman: 'Whatever is best for Aston Villa, you must do. Don't worry about me, I will be OK. You must do what is right for the club.'

Venglos seemed like an oddity and a diversion, but Ossie Ardiles would bring the notion of the bungling and fundamentally destructive foreigner into sharper managerial focus. Despite being Argentinian, as a manager Ardiles seemed marked in the popular press by the notion of the scuttling and weak-chinned Spanish waiter, vulnerable, quivering and put-upon. A former Spurs player, he was appointed at his old club in 1993, the first foreign manager of the Premiership era. Ardiles was an educated man, from a family of lawyers. He immediately caused consternation by announcing that football was 'an art and a beautiful one'. 'As a manager I am a little bit lyrical,' he proclaimed. 'Maybe I dream too much. I go for beauty.'

Oh dear. Here was foreign weirdness made flesh in the form of the manager. Ardiles obliged by bringing his 'Samba style' football – previously honed at Swindon – to bear on producing a terribly unbalanced team that was heading for a farcical all-guns-blazing relegation when he was sacked. As one broadsheet concluded, in a powerful echo of the Eurocrat-vandal, 'Had Ardiles been an Egyptian king, he'd have ordered that his pyramid be built peak downwards.'

It was open season now. Most famously on Christian Gross, who would follow Ardiles to White Hart Lane three years later. Gross launched his single season in excruciating fashion, having travelled from Heathrow by tube for his unveiling. Brandishing his travelcard for the photographers he announced, 'Listen here. I'll show you my ticket – and hopefully it'll be the ticket of my dreams.'

Flourishing its manifold jewels, thrumming the engines of its fleet of executive supercars, English football goggled in dismay.

And with Gross the backlash began straight away. In fact this wasn't strictly a backlash. This was simply a lash. Here was the European, the eccentric and the easily mocked, compacted into a single bald Swiss.

Pleat, who worked with Gross at Spurs, still regrets his ousting. 'Christian Gross was a nice, hard-working guy,' he sighed. 'But he was defeated by hard-nosed professionals who wouldn't have him. There was an inbuilt hostility. We just weren't ready for it. The media murdered him.'

Not that Gross didn't give them plenty of chance, gaily handing round the candlestick, the lead pipe and the revolver. His first home game saw Spurs lose 6-1 to Chelsea. He introduced training on Sundays. He took a public stand against binge drinking. A section of the squad were infuriated when he asked them to wear flip-flops at the training ground. Others were enraged by hearing him speak to David Ginola, a Frenchman, in French. Within a month the *Sun* would be jeering 'Tottenham need a Herr transplant', focusing above all on the fact that Gross spoke only 'sketchy English', sneering at his comment that 'We have to work on the training pitch to bring the luck on our side', and noting his calls for 'changements'.

This sense of the non-native manager being essentially powerless, a linguistic eunuch, is still with us. In October 2008 another Spurs manager, the Spaniard Juande Ramos, was described in the *Daily Telegraph* as 'a man in a vortex of escalating doom . . . trapped in his Spanish silence . . . a man without a voice'. Like Ardiles and Gross, Ramos lasted a year. Interestingly, he was also perhaps the most foreign-looking of all foreign managers to have entered English football. He spoke impenetrably Spanish Spanish. He looked incredibly Spanish (also like one of those portraits of a handsome well-groomed stern man in the window of a 1970s barber shop). In March of the year he was appointed at Spurs, while managing Seville, Ramos had been knocked unconscious by a bottle thrown from the crowd during a derby with Real Betis. This lingering air of wonky Euro-misfortune never quite left him in England.

In fact Ramos almost seemed like a throwback to a decade earlier, a time when it seemed somehow acceptable – and in truth unavoidable – that Jan Sorensen, a Dane, should be appointed Walsall manager despite being out of the game for eight years, most recently working as a time-share salesman. Colourful, outspoken and fat, Sorensen lasted the standard season of eccentrically yo-yoing results. Still this sense of impermanence, of some inevitable but bitterly wrong-headed affliction from afar, lingered around the foreign manager. As late as March 1998 Crystal Palace would be taking the bizarre decision to appoint Italian international Attilio Lombardo as manager, with the Swede Tomas Brolin as his assistant, despite neither man having any coaching experience.

Steve Coppell, Palace's director of football, conceded, 'It is a bold, massive step and some people will look on it as foolish.' These included Lombardo himself, who said he felt 'as though I had been run over by a lorry'. Palace had just ten games to escape relegation. They lost six of them. Lombardo, who spoke almost no English and looked genuinely stricken by the experience, was allowed to step down.

This was the tail-end of a period where the appointment of a foreign manager seemed an act of self-immolation, a might-as-well-get-on-with-it running jump into the icy waters of some inevitable Euro-future. You can fight it, football seemed to be saying, but you'll only be fighting it. Pretty much the end of the line for all this was Egil Olsen, manager of Wimbledon for a single season at the turn of the century. Olsen was all the foreign gimmick merchant you could ever need. A bespectacled Norwegian, he was a member of the Communist Party. He wore wellies. He collected data and styled himself as 'a professor of football'. A keen geographer, he knew the height of every mountain in Europe. On one occasion he asked a visiting

German journalist to name five European countries larger than his homeland. 'Russia, Ukraine, France, Spain and Sweden,' Olsen informed him, deadpan. This was almost too much.

And in fact, even before the low comedy of the Olsen era, it had become apparent that England, incredibly, was a little out of step on this one. In many ways there was something almost sentimental about the lingering distrust of the EU cyberman with his bonkers process of federal homogenisation, his bananas bananas. This is an imagined world, born of curdled nostalgia. And in the Premier league, where the bottom line has always been the bottom line, it wasn't going to wash for long.

The manager – and more importantly the club director – knew this couldn't last, that the bogeyman wasn't real, and that perhaps, conceivably, it was we who were out of step. Josef Venglos had walked away from his purgatory at Villa into a lucrative job at Fenerbahce. Life was proceeding apace elsewhere. It was time to adapt. Fortunately, in August 1996 Arsène Wenger had arrived at Arsenal. Not before time, the dawning of the age of modernity was at hand. The thin white duke was stalking the land, furrowed with his own intense reforming will.

And from here on in the overseas manager would find himself increasingly divorced from that imaginary Euro-realm where mushy peas are about to be banned, Brandy butter renamed 'brandy spreadable fat' and B&B's forced to close because they have a dog. The *Sunday Mirror* greeted Wenger's arrival in standard fashion, commenting that Arsenal vice-chairman David Dein hoped 'to persuade us that the lanky M'sieu Wenger, despite sounding like Rory Bremner auditioning for 'Allo, 'Allo, is, 'ow you say, fantastique!'

But it was off-message on this one. To those who were there, Wenger's first press conference as Arsenal manager seems to have acted as a kind of hallelujah, a moment of evangelical conversion. English football was ready for this. Swollen with a new-found sense of its own importance, it had money and it had exposure. What it needed was vindication, and above all some class. As ever, it would look to the manager.

Myles Palmer's Wenger biography *The Professor* recalls his first sight of the man himself on that fateful day: 'A tall slim, Frenchman walks in and steps up on to the dais. Arsène Wenger is, we quickly realise, a completely different animal . . . He has an ambassadorial presence. He is firm, calm, diplomatic and very articulate . . . Everything he says makes sense.'

This was the new world and it felt good. 'Wenger came across as a serious technocrat who knew he was accepting a serious responsibility. He was everything we wanted him to be and more than we expected.' Football was in the mood to swank and to strut and it found it liked the look of this new, reassuringly restrained, and wonderfully attentive new presence. Mark Hateley, who played under Wenger at Monaco, described the new man as 'the most intense coach I've known . . . a football alcoholic'. Two years after his appointment the *Mirror* would be noting that 'King Arsène' was 'ready to take his place in history'.

And almost a decade on from the barmy banana days of Ossie Ardiles, the foreign manager was now credible and thoroughly integrated. 'Island mentalities are historically mistrustful of foreign influences,' Arsenal's new manager had noted shortly after his arrival. Wenger himself has done more than most to prove otherwise.

CHAPTER 26

The Scoundrel

In October 1990, as a rather desperate and Pritt-Sticked together publicity stunt, Rupert Murdoch, one of the world's least gregarious self-made billionaires, made a personal appearance on the doorstep of the millionth UK subscriber to his struggling satellite company Sky TV. Awkwardly posed in inch-thick specs and beige raincoat, Murdoch forced himself to grin for the cameras alongside a bemused-looking family dragged away from their expensively acquired TV hardware in order to shake hands with a creepy-looking Australian senior citizen.

This is a measure of how bad things had got. Murdoch was losing £10m a week on Sky. He'd staked the future of News International on the improbable future popularity of the gigantic bronze-age satellite dishes, of the type he could be seen cradling gingerly beneath one arm as he posed with his new friends. We know what happened next. Football intervened. In 1992 Murdoch struck the decisive deal with the Football Association and Premier League that would transform not just his company but the sport itself and a great deal besides. And over the next decade his dishes would sprout like urban fungi on the sides of tower blocks, and appear like great inverted bird baths on the side of the pebble-dashed semis of soccer-hungry suburbia.

By 1997 the space age was in full swing. That summer the entire country was plastered with billboards proclaiming Sky Sports' Maoist maxims: 'Football is our life,' enthused one. 'Football is our religion,' intoned another. For so long television had been kept at arm's length by the upturned nose and scented handkerchief – not to mention the essentially retrograde business plan – of the Football Association. Less inclined to pursue the old tactic of knocking politely every few months with his pamphlets and his hopeful smile, Murdoch had instead come cartwheeling in through the living-room window twirling an enormous, putty-coloured dish about his head like a scimitar.

Football had become drama, light entertainment, tragedy and farce. It was constantly exciting. It was brought to you by urgent, forceful men in mustard-coloured blazers. It was a fast-edit, rap-music-montage-friendly piece of family fun. Above all it was fizzy and flashy and increasingly contorted by the spectacle of its own preening self-regard. In the middle of this the manager would of course emerge as a central actor. Television demands a recognisable face. The chorus, the cut-away reaction shot, the interpreter and expert analyst: overnight the manager would become an almost embarrassingly central presence in the small-screen universe. And in time he would start to behave differently too. If it's true that you change something simply by observing it, perhaps it's not surprising that when you point twelve TV cameras at someone, backed up by a dedicated global media machine, they start to get a few funny ideas.

Giddy with his own subscription-era celebrity, the manager developed a range of new gestures. He had his teeth done. He adopted the quasi-military costume of the US sports coach, the executive shellsuit and advanced communication earpiece. And he stood up. Lured from the dugout by the glare of his new stage, the manager – for so long a hunched and furtive creature – took to his hind legs and walked.

And so a new set of behavioural conventions emerged. These were the made-for-TV tics that told us a manager was doing his job, literally 'managing' before our very eyes. Stalking the touch-line. Wrestling the fourth official. Adopting the arms-wide bemused appeal of the profoundly wronged. And perfecting the twinkly, tracksuited chin-stroke, a pose reminiscent of Christian youth group leader or energetic inner city geography teacher, albeit accompanied by motivational phrases like 'Nigel! Sustain!' or 'Maximise the opportunity!'

Football was famous now. And the manager – once again uncannily well-placed to take centre stage – was hot. With TV on board you no longer had to be a famous manager to be a famous manager. You simply had to be a manager. The manager was fresh product. He had what his agent might have called 'great exposure'. He had buzz.

Unfortunately he also had his deep and dirty managerial past. Let's not forget who we're dealing with here. You can plaster the TV slap over those open pores in his nose, you can pluck his mono-brow, you can arrange favourably his remaining lank strands of hair across his flaking scalp. Give him a nice coat. But the managerial gene runs deep. Underneath it all this was still the bastard, the showman, the gimmick-merchant, the pressed-man and the fall-guy. It was also, as it turned out, the scoundrel.

The emergence of the scoundrel manager was one of the first major developments of the Premiership years. This might have come as something of a surprise. But with hindsight it seems a natural process of purging and refining, of becoming, as a species, camera-ready. For over a hundred years the manager had manoeuvred furtively from within his musty bachelor pad. He'd blown his nose on the tea-towels, left the washing up, reheated last night's Chinese and generally snuffled and rooted and pursued his own treacle-dark practices. Sure, he'd had his moments. But always he had his retreat, that shuttered and insular private world where manager spake only unto manager, with perhaps a little help from certain interested parties able to facilitate a mutually beneficial business arrangement. This was the manager's lost world of out-of-town hotel complexes, motorway service stations and horrible shiny city centre wine bars. It was a realm of secrecy, the comforting managerial gloom of the inner office behind the inner door.

This had to go. All of it. And sharpish. Or at least it had to relocate, to diversify and to retreat. Never really a businessman, schooled only in the strictures of deal-doing and back-scratching, the manager had nevertheless somehow managed to conduct transactions and to maintain a robust series of Chinese walls between private and corporate gain, ever since the days when men first started selling men to other men. Now the operation had got too big. It was all too public. The old-style managerial business apparatus, the wonky abacus and broken biro, the tattered accounts book, this simply wouldn't do any more.

It wasn't so much the being watched constantly, although it was also that. It was more the sheer money-rush, the purging effect of all that cash foaming its way around football's interminable U-bends. The Premier League was founded on money, with money and for the propagation of more money. Club directors had never been particularly nice, and never concerned with much more than self-aggrandisement. But they'd also never really made money from the game, try as they might. This was about to change dramatically.

Under the terms of the first TV rights deal in 1992, twenty-two top tier clubs would share £305m. Five years later they got £670m. In the language of the times supporters were now deemed 'a captive market'. And they were duly milked. Newcastle owner Sir John Hall would eventually make £100m out of floating Newcastle on the stock exchange. Martin

Edwards, Manchester United director and son of Louis – who had previously sacked Tommy Docherty for falling in love – made £33m from the sale of shares in Manchester United (he bought them for £600,000 in 1978).

Highly visible fortunes were swooshing through the game's rapidly expanding infrastructure. For the manager there was temptation. And there was also scrutiny. For the first time there was the hard-core, digging-through-the-bins attention of the tabloid scandal-squad. Something had to give. And so it did. In 1993 the High Court battle between Tottenham chairman Alan Sugar and his former manager Terry Venables would introduce the word 'bung' for the first time. Sugar told the court Spurs had paid Forest £50,000 to speed the £2.1m transfer of Teddy Sheringham on the grounds that Brian Clough 'liked a bung'.

Clough denied it, calling Sugar 'just a spiv and a barrow boy'. But there it was out in the open. The bung had arrived. Within six months the *Daily Mirror* would be asking its readers, 'Don't we all pick up the papers or switch on these days wondering: Who's next? Who's run amok in a pizza parlour, flogged match tickets, fiddled a transfer or taken a bung?'

In fact George Graham was next. Already a double-title-winning manager with Arsenal, Graham was banned from football for a year in 1995 after receiving £425,000 in connection with two transfer deals (although on being discovered he returned the money, as he thought it was just 'a present'). Graham would later find himself accused of receiving a further £30,000 in the toilet of a swanky London nightclub. 'I gave Graham the money in a toilet at an exclusive men's club in London. Graham started to count the money over the toilet seat and the deal was OK,' the agent Lars Peterson, whose clients include the former Arsenal player Stefan Schwarz, told a Swedish newspaper. Graham denied it.

But really, what did we expect? Throughout his history the manager has found himself in a terribly difficult position. Nose pressed up against the glass, panting hoarsely, he has watched from the fringes as fortunes have sailed past, as the vagaries of player recruitment or a scrambled end of season point divided triumph and catastrophe. Tortured by possibility, empowered but helpless, it's little wonder the manager should have such a long and richly embroidered rap sheet.

Early football was dogged by murkiness. The most famous scoundrel manager of the times was Arthur Maley of Manchester City, who was banned from football for life in 1905 for overseeing the payment of wages in excess of the £4 maximum. George Jobey, celebrated manager of Derby County during the 1930s, was banned from the game in 1946 after it emerged he'd spent at least fourteen years offering backhanders to players he wanted to sign. This was the tone of the early managerial scandal, a matter of small sums passed furtively, of pathetically titchy bribes regretted at leisure.

The exception, and the great early proto-managerial rogue, was William Sudell of Preston North End. Fine-featured and ferret-like, Sudell can be seen peering out of the languidly posed Preston North End team photos of the 1880s, a face in the gloom behind a double-tier of flannelled moustaches. In his time he was a figure of some weight: first treasurer of the Football League (he also came up with its name); the man who led the drive for professional football; and the figure who comes closest to providing a template for the modern football manager.

Sudell is also curiously absent from the front rank of football's official history. This is a function of the other side of his story: a fall from grace that ended in a criminal trial, prison and exile. Some or all of which might, for close students of the manager, possibly start to ring a bell or two. Born in Preston in 1851, Sudell was an all-round local big nob: a major in the Volunteer Force, vice-president of the Preston Bicycle Club and manager of a prosperous cotton mill. In 1874 he became chairman of the football club and imported an influential captain in Nick Ross. Together they brought a blackboard into the dressing room and demonstrated prehistoric tactical moves using chess players on a billiard table. Presumably this went something like: queen hoofs heavy leather ball towards corner pocket, pawns all charge after it, rook dies of scurvy. But you see what he was getting at.

Other innovations involved hiring a professional distance runner from Widnes called Jack Concannon, who put the players though a high-end boxing-style training regime, and engaging a cobbler to travel with the players to adapt their boots according to the state of the grass. The results were a revelation. Over three seasons Preston won the League three times and the Cup twice. In 1887 they beat Hyde FC 26-0. The good times were rolling in unstoppable fashion. What could possibly go wrong?

Something quite major, as it turned out. In April 1895 *The Times* carried an article in its court pages under the headline, 'Embezzlement by a Preston Mill Manager', which told the story of Sudell's conviction for pinching up to £6000. At his trial he was described as 'more or less . . . the founder of Association football in England'. He pleaded guilty to funnelling cash from the mill into Preston's coffers, money which, according to the judge, Sudell 'spent freely upon those directly or indirectly associated with the game. He had lavishly entertained visiting clubs to Preston, and in consequence was a very popular man.'

This is a brilliantly typical feat of self-destruction. The manager has always been a roaring good-time Charlie and a natural spendthrift. High-denomination notes cascade from his turn-ups. A crocodile of maxed-out credit cards flutters from his inside pocket. In success he gargles on champagne, in failure he remortgages catastrophically. The manager makes no kind of financial sense at all. In fact he's exactly the kind of person who robs a cotton mill in order to take visiting club directors out for a jug of porter and a platter of Whitby oysters.

Sudell served three years. Released in 1898, he emigrated to South Africa and became a newspaper reporter. His death in 1913 was greeted with a grudging hundred-word obituary in *The Times* that revealed 'Mr W. Sudell . . . well known in the north of England . . . died of heart failure while at work on returning from a football match'.

All in all it seems fitting that the closest thing we have to the first proper football manager, the prototype for over a century of fevered ascent, wasn't a manager at all but a chairman. Not to mention a morally compromised, overly ambitious egomaniac who ended up fading away into tragic semi-obscurity. So clearly quite different in many ways, then.

This is the manager's historical position on these matters. It's a family history of scoundrelism that still colours his celebrity present. Although there was little follow-up to the early Premiership rush of scoundrel-mongering, the manager remains a target and a suspect at all times. Attempting to catch some car-coated, beady-eyed type passing a crumpled brown envelope (what football usually calls 'a drink' rather than 'a bung') under the table of a South Wales branch of the Little Chef has become an industry in itself. Every few years some heavyweight current affairs TV programme will bring us a series of grainy hidden camera exchanges purporting to be the definitive exposé on managerial corruption.

Nothing ever sticks, though. No one is going down. Nothing has been proved. In fact the whole thing has become occasionally farcical. In 2008 Hampshire police, accompanied by a photographer from the *Sun*, called at Portsmouth manager Harry Redknapp's house at 6 a.m. in connection with a corruption inquiry. As a Bournemouth player in the 1960s Redknapp was known as a tricky winger with only one trick: toe-poking the ball past his opponent and sprinting after it, then stopping and doing exactly the same thing again. It is tempting to imagine a similarly frenetic Benny Hill-style police chase though his luxurious Poole residence, the dressing-gowned gaffer dropping his shoulder, pausing momentarily and then scooting off into the conservatory.

Except, as it emerged, Redknapp wasn't actually in. And he later successfully sued them for harassment. There's a message there. Don't mess with the manager. He's been playing this game a long time. And he's wised up now. He knows his rights. He knows your rights too. And he's whiter than white and clean as a whistle. All right?

CHAPTER 27

The Messiah

Of course there was another side to all this. The manager had been flushed decisively into the forefront of things. Backlit, soft-focused and vigorously fluffed, he came curtsying into centre-stage. This was his moment, his perfect moment. So why not revel in it?

Just as he had been as a player, Kevin Keegan was a break-through artist here. During his time at Hamburg in the late 1970s Keegan had turned himself into a strangely anodyne pop football celebrity. He had the first 'face deal' with his club giving him a degree of image rights control. He put his name to everything from the freshly launched and moribund Patrick boots, to a frightening and didactic TV road safety campaign. In the fresh dawn of the manager's early Premiership celebrity ascent, Keegan would again rise to the moment. This time he wasn't simply a bubble-permed, stack-heeled teen idol. Now he was something else. Now he was the messiah.

In fact Keegan had always been messianic, even during the white heat of his mid-1970s German period. In January 1978 the *Daily Express* produced a colour-spread interview detailing his millionaire's exile: 'He arrived last summer as a messiah – the man who destroyed Germany's most resilient defender, Berti Vogts, in a European Cup Final.' Which is of course what messiahs always do.

By the time the Premier League launched, Keegan had last been seen being helicoptered dramatically from the pitch at St James' Park at the final whistle of his final game for Newcastle United in 1984. For many this was a deeply silly gesture that may or may not have been intended to generate a kind of aspirational, can-do action Thatcherite tableau. Instead it seemed to implant irreversibly the notion of Keegan visibly ascending. This is a man who in some fundamental fashion levitates.

So it would prove to be on his return to the top level of English football as manager of Newcastle United in 1992, year dot for the new TV soccer world. Keegan was perfect for the Premier League. He was energetic, studio-ready, and prone to an expressive range of capering on-screen theatrics. The new channel had a product. It had stars. All it needed now was a storyline. It needed a real zinger. And in Keegan it got not just any old story. It got the greatest story ever told.

The fact is, the messiah, the redeemer and the extended godhead had been knocking around football for some time. Religion, and religious imagery, are deeply intertwined in the game. Many clubs were originally formed out of either the church or the temperance movement. Everton have a church, St Luke's, entwined within Goodison Park. In the 1950s Celtic had a separate turnstile purely for Catholic priests, who would be allowed in free, in part because they might then recommend some promising young parishioner. Supporters without a ticket for a big game would often arrive in a dog collar and announce themselves as Father someone or other.

And as Tommy Docherty once said: 'To me football has always been more than a game. It is akin to religion, the player as its disciples, the supporters its congregation.' And what, exactly, would that make the manager? Priest? Or something a little more special, a little more upstairs? Bill Shankly was God, or at least a god. 'Shankly is our god,' was a common chant among Liverpool fans in the 1960s and 1970s. He once gave a team talk that consisted simply of talking about the Red Sea for half an hour ('Amazing how it opened up'). Bob Greaves, a Granada TV reporter, remembered Shankly going to watch matches after his retirement: 'He would always leave his seat in the directors box or the guest spot in the stand about four minutes before the end . . . When the crowd of directors, pressmen and honoured guests came out they would always find Bill at the top of some chairs. He would just stand there like the Pope, and many people on Merseyside did consider him to be a Pope-like person. He would stand there with his arms outstretched.'

And while this was going on Bob Paisley, Joe Fagan and the bootroom monks lived exemplary lives in their dubbin-stinking shrine. Brian Clough walked on water. Sir Alf Ramsey sacrificed himself so that others might enjoy winning the World Cup. And Sunderland manager Bob Stokoe seemed to spend a career waving, double-fisted, to what the *Daily Mirror* described as 'the enormous crowd his Messianic presence has lured back to support the side'.

In 1978 even Don Revie, upcoming managerial super-villain, was being pushed in the *Daily Express* as 'the Messiah delegated to restore English Soccer to the peak it reached 10 years ago'. This is how Messiah-hungry the game is, how messiah-dependent we remain. And this is after all a popular kind of chap to have about the place. Turn around too quickly and you're always likely to bump into a messiah or two. Bruce Wayne, Obi-Wan Kenobi, Keanu Reeves in a leather coat. ET the extraterrestrial. The messiah is still our number-one narrative archetype.

Little wonder, then, that in October 1993 King Kev of the Geordie Nation should find himself already being described in a national newspaper as 'bubbly Kevin Keegan, the undoubted Messiah of Newcastle'. Hungry for a big, swaggering plotline, the Premiership went for the big one right from the off, as Keegan found himself repeatedly enshrined as a Geordie messiah, a black-and-white-striped divinity incarnate. This was his tagline and his brand.

And you have to hand it to him. He got right in there. Football's thirst for the gaffer-messiah may be historic and apparently unshakeable. But while many come, few are chosen. The messiah remains an elusive calling. This is not an easy business. So pay attention. A Keegan-based five-point guide to becoming a messiah might look a bit like this.

1. Perform miracles

This is essential. Before his return to Newcastle Keegan had pretty much slipped off the radar, enduring a quasi-biblical eight years of golfing purgatory in Spain. But then something happened. 'One day at Las Brisas, when I was standing ready to play a shot at the par-five twelfth over water, it suddenly hit me that golf was not the be-all and end-all. As I waited for the group in front to clear the green I asked myself what the hell I was doing.'

For Keegan this, perhaps rather underwhelming, revelation was the turning point. He took the Newcastle job in February 1992. Immediately, he saved them from relegation to the old Third Division. The next year he steered them to a triumphant promotion. They were third in their first season back in the top division. Ultimately, they blew a twelve-point lead to finish runners-up to Manchester United in 1996. These were Keegan's miracles. And they're not bad actually.

2. Develop an intoxicating personality

Keegan was always there on this one. As a manager he retained an air of big-time demagoguery, of some deeply felt and unavoidable urge to wave and clap and gambol in front of vast teeming banks of scarf-waving supplicants. He has a highly visible emotional energy. Like a character in a French farce, he projects an intense, single-note fix of the more pungent emotions through a limited range of gestures, hitting the big notes, always turning it up to eleven.

3. Have a touch of the divine lineage about you

Keegan knew what he was doing. He knew all about the managerial messiah-complex. This was a man who had played under Shankly and Revie, and often quoted the former. But let's face it, we were all complicit in this. The Keegan-as-messiah episode was another case of the corporate recycling of the classic managerial persona, of the co-opting of something that was once pure and genuine but has since been done to death. The 1960s are still football's 1960s: its era of authenticity.

The connection between the supporter and his manager has never been so intense or so evocative of a kind of geographical and social community. The televised messiah-capering of the early Premier League Keegan era was perhaps affected by this. Sky and the Premier League were rebooting football, writing a new sporting history that began in 1992. They needed a passionately enacted original myth, a new-age legend. Luckily one presented itself. Goaded, milked and expertly wrung out, Keegan-as-messiah was a necessary episode, a media-led furore, and perhaps even at heart something rather cynical and spoon-fed.

4. Find a troubled people in search of a promised land

This might have been a difficult one. But step forward Sir John Hall, Newcastle's arch-capitalist chairman and owner. Hall was a retail magnate and all-round can-do guy, the force behind Newcastle's Arndale shopping centre. And in the figures of Hall and Keegan the manager would come up against a broader managerial type of the recent present, the Thatcherite rainmaker and self-made tycoon. Hall rebranded Newcastle for his own ends, parroting regularly the notion of the Geordie Nation. In the Geordie Nation Hall conjured an instant sense of brand awareness, plus a consumer fanbase of cut-me-and-I-bleed shirt collectors perpetually in search of footballing salvation, or at least some kind of long overdue challenge for a major trophy. This was, in some ways, a trick of the light, an Arndale centre own-brand regionalism. But the notion of the Geordie Nation would fuel decisively the messiah complex. Keegan was rocking.

5. Be horribly betrayed

By May 1996, as Newcastle fell agonisingly short of what would have been a brilliantly swashbuckling League title, Keegan was being described in the *Daily Mirror* not as the messiah but as 'the God on the Tyne'. This was the high water mark of his ascension. Within eight months he would be gone, forced out in confusing circumstances, leaving Newcastle 'a town in mourning'.

Keegan was no more. The messiah had been slain. All we needed now was a Judas. In his autobiography Keegan fingered the club itself and the strictures of its imminent flotation on the stock exchange. As a messiah-betrayal this was only so-so. But fortunately something much better was just around the corner. In March 1999 the *Daily Mirror* would be able to trumpet,

'They're a pair of Judases' above the story of Newcastle directors Freddie Shepherd and Douglas Hall's revelatory drunken night in Marbella. Shepherd and Hall, the men who effectively dispensed with Keegan's services, had been taped by an undercover reporter. This would provide the perfect denouement. In between describing Newcastle fans as drunken troublemakers and laughing about selling replica kits for £50 when they cost just £5 to make, the two men made the ultimate mistake of sticking the ceremonial knife, the stigmata nail, into Kev himself. 'We used to call him Shirley Temple,' Shepherd was quoted as saying (oddly he also called Alan Shearer 'Mary Poppins'). The messiah paradigm was now triumphantly complete. As the secretary of the Independent Newcastle United Supporters' Association duly raged: 'This is a betrayal. Shepherd and Hall are Judases. They have to go.' They did go too, both men resigning shortly afterwards.

Keegan, however, would be back at Newcastle. His second managerial coming arrived a full ten years later, and a short-lived affair it was too. By now there was definitely something knowing about the way all this was conducted. The freshness of Keegan's initial messiah-hood had been dulled. The Premier League felt like a worldly and weathered kind of place. By now we knew the score: an unveiling, some double-fisted waving, a few hugs. Something about the club – or better, the entire Geordie Nation – being like a rubber dinghy of battered dreams set adrift on the choppy tides of the footballing Cape Horn. Cue energetically enacted descent into wildly listing schooner of unrealistic expectation, a plummet through the frothing white waters of footballing reality. Cut to TV close-up of an angelic child in a replica shirt about to cry.

Keegan left Newcastle, again, a year into his second stint, complaining, again, about a lack of boardroom support. There was disbelief and much public mourning, again. Beleaguered Newcastle fans would congregate at the club gates. And all that remains now of the first great modern football managerial messiah is the memories, the YouTube clips, the indelible televised post-match rant.

Still, it's tempting to believe that somewhere out there, Keegan is still fighting for that 1995–6 season Premier League title. And that he will still love it, love it, if he beats them. Never one to renege on a promise, perhaps he is still chasing the dream. Still glimpsed occasionally giving feisty post-match interviews on the town's buses and trams. Perhaps we can still believe. Or at least watch the whole thing again, on a nostalgia-based TV clip show.

Which isn't to say that the messianic strand in football management has been completely devalued. The yearning is still there. This is still a heady notion, and football is still the kind of environment in which it flourishes. In November 2007 thousands of Liverpool fans staged a ritualistic 'march of support' through the streets of the city, as a way of backing the manager Rafa Benitez in his contract wrangles with the club's board. Like supplicants on some headline Catholic saint's day parade, the marchers carried flags and banners and solemnly chanted the manager's name. A gold-framed portrait was hoisted aloft at the head of the procession, its caption dubbing Benitez 'The Rafatollah'. Other banners read, 'Rafa Benitez, God's gift to Liverpool' and 'In Rafa We Trust'. This was worship, after a fashion, or at least an unconditional and oddly fevered celebration. Benitez, a priestly, astute, gnomic figure, does seem to fit an Anfield definition of the divine: a bootroom messiah, less twitchy, entirely serious and associated above all with quiet and unarguable success. This kind of thing, you sense, will carry on for as long as there are football clubs and football supporters. Not to mention a conviction – perhaps even something close to desperation – that one man with the right patter, the right body language and the right egomaniacal vision, might just solve and settle and put everything in order finally. Or in other words, for as long as there are football managers.

CHAPTER 28

The Manager Disappears

As has already been noted, something strange began to happen to football managers during the early Premier League years of the mid-1990s. Mainly, they started to become incredibly and irreversibly famous – and famous in a way that didn't include you. This is new. Even during the great rush of the manager's early fame, his rock and roll years of the 1960s, there was still a sense that he was comfortably in touch with his public. Jock Stein still picked up the phone occasionally at Celtic. Bill Shankly could be reached without much trouble by any junior reporter with a plausible pitch.

The world has of course moved on. The full-time occupation of being famous is now an industry in itself. The manager is famous now too, and accordingly he has people to keep the people away. In many ways he's even more valuable and therefore more unattainable than his players, who can generally be flattered into emerging from behind their astral gates. As a result of which, trying to engage with a Premier League manager is now a labyrinthine business. First there are people. Then behind the people are other people. And somewhere at the centre of this dizzying whirlpool of people lies the manager on his velveteen chaise longue.

Also, the people are suspicious, neurotically difficult, tearfully hostile. The suspicion is that you don't simply want to talk to the manager. What you want to do is judo-throw the manager, burgle him, rub baked beans on his new chinos and generally diminish him in some fundamental way. Like all cranks and nut-jobs, you must be kept away. This is the fiercely held conviction of the people.

In fact this isn't really fair on the manager's people. They're just dealing with people of their own, wave after wave of media people with unceasing and unanswerable demands. If the manager had no protective ring of people he would no longer be a manager. He would instead be someone who gives interviews all the time, to Belgian cable TV, Gulf State Radio and SoccerNob.com.

This is an issue I had to rub up against at some point writing this book. Ex-managers, resting managers, people who used to play for famous managers: there are plenty of these around and they have interesting stories to tell. But spending some quality time with a serving Premier League manager would be something else. How better to observe him than from inside the bubble, shoulder to shoulder against the magnesium flash of the papps? Except serving Premier League managers don't want to be observed like this. They basically don't give interviews any more, not unless there's some quantifiable personal agenda involved, some mind-game potential or profile maintenance.

Still, I had to try, even if only because – like any other grail quest – the journey towards an impossible goal is often far more interesting than the goal itself. I work on the sports desk of a national newspaper. I might have tried to infiltrate the manager's world from this direction. Through the fraudulent pretend-newspaper approach. The trench warfare of the club media department. Or perhaps just the simple post-match press conference mugging.

Instead of doing this – and largely, I told myself, because this is a book about what the manager looks like from a distance, rather than specifically his thoughts about zonal marking or his own terrible childhood – I decided to do it another way. Instead I wrote a personal letter to every Premier League manager on my own low-grade notepaper asking to spend a morning with them, no strings attached. Not only did this bypass the people arranged in concentric club-blazered circles around the manager's personage. It was also interesting to imagine what, if any replies, I might get. It felt like a public experiment.

Best of all would perhaps be none at all, a total blank. Actually, that's rubbish. Best of all would be a personal invitation to spend the weekend hiking around the Western Isles and sharing a two-man tent with Alex Ferguson.

In fact neither of these happened. I received several polite and guarded replies. Paul Ince of Blackburn responded almost immediately, regretfully explaining that 'the Training Centre is kept private'. I instantly felt cheap and voyeuristic. He was sacked two weeks later, which helped a little. Phil Brown was characteristically upbeat and enthusiastic, thanking me 'for my interest in Hull City AFC', and promising, tantalisingly, that 'if we can arrange anything in the new year, we will be in touch'. I felt more hopeful. The new year came and went.

Everton's David Moyes claimed to receive 'many requests of this nature', which immediately made me feel anxious about all those other people out there currently writing an occasionally tangential book about the history of the modern superstar football managers. He did say 'good luck with your research', though, which seemed like some kind of distant managerial blessing. Maybe we can put it on the front cover. Mark Hughes of Manchester City was more encouraging, even while explaining that 'due to confidentiality' it was impossible to let me stare at Darius Vassell doing laps of the pitch for half an hour (again a creeping sense of shame at my own pushiness). Hughes was also worried about 'setting a precedent', which would 'leave the door open for others'. God forbid, eh? But he did wish me all the best 'for the future', which was oddly calming.

Best of all – wouldn't you know it? – was Arsène Wenger, who wrote a long and courteous reply, in which he seemed genuinely interested in the book ('I do appreciate your interest in writing') and also wishing me 'every success'. This was more like it. I felt keen-eyed and rubber-limbed like some Wenger prodigy being given the official thumbs-up. For at least three or four minutes I'd say.

I'd had hopes of Wenger. He always seems unusually friendly. I've sat in his press conferences before. And I once bumped into him in slightly unusual circumstances. It was in Vienna during Euro 2008. I was walking down a long elevated walkway that led to the press room. In the distance I could see a tall, slender figure in a brown suit approaching. As the figure got larger I realised it was him. We clattered towards each other for what seemed like a long time, alone on our sun-bleached gantry. He really is very tall. Eventually we met at a door in the wall. I said, 'Hello'. He said, 'Hi' in his Arsène Wenger voice. We spent a few moments trying to open the door (it was jammed). He seemed annoyed. And then we had a really long and involved discussion about his hopes, his dreams and the real shocking reason he never put himself forward for the England job.

Actually that's not true. I asked him which players he was there to watch. He said he was doing TV commentary. And then we went inside. The next couple of times I saw him he nodded at me. The third time, he didn't.

And that was about it for the letters. To date Rafa Benitez, Harry Redknapp, Sir Alex Ferguson, Tony Mowbray, Steve Bruce, Gianfranco Zola, Tony Pulis, Gary Megson, Martin O'Neill and Roy Hodgson are still ransacking their diaries and frantically rescheduling appointments in the hope of being able to send a positive reply. Roy Keane, Juande Ramos, Big Phil Scolari and Tony Adams have either been sacked or moved on, so I'm letting them off.

This was all pretty much what you'd expect of course. I'd wanted a glimpse through the manager's window, some sense of his peculiarly rarefied world. And that was what I got. Premier League managers are too famous. Too neurotically cautious. Too besieged by billions of other hopefuls with their uncompleted Ph.D.s in Stochastic Dynamics of Football Management. Too already spoken for. Too global for this kind of thing. The velvet rope has been lowered, for now at least. That's the news from the manager.

CHAPTER 29

The International Statesman and Playboy

Certain things have tended to stick to the football manager throughout his many incarnations. He has a particular smell, a heady cocktail of liniment, cough sweets, stale sweat and the damp sod of a churned and boggy February touchline. If he's known for a particular sound, it's the clatter of studs on corridor floor, the eavesdropped dressing-room bellowings, the whisper of motorway traffic.

These things are always subject to change of course. If anything characterises the appearance of a new type of manager – as the Premier League completed its first decade of hot-housed expansion – it is perhaps these sensory factors. The new type of manager smelled different. He smelled of homogenised international luxury: factory-fresh leather upholstery, executive grooming, private beach and high-end gastronomy. His soundtrack was the delicate tinklings of some sky-high Dubai piano bar, the discreet tap-tap of room service, the grunted assurances of the A-list security team.

The elevation of Ruud Gullit to player-coach at Chelsea in

1995 brought the new breed of super-rich superstar player into management in the Premier League for the first time. With his Ruud Wear clothing line, his occasional reggae band Revelation Time – with whom he once performed in front of three thousand people in Milan – and his early adoption of the uniform of elegantly cut black Italian formal wear, Gullit blazed a trail. This was the beginning of the era of the international statesman manager, and his cousin the Eurotrash playboy.

It brought a fundamental change in the manager's environment, its surfaces and its styling. The world had come calling at the manager's door. Giddy with the scent of global overclass, the 'thunk' of executive limousine, the gentle hypnosis of the private jet and the duplex suite, he packed just a few things in a small bag and was off. This was all terribly modern and, it has to be said, at times a little silly. In 2003 the England manager Sven-Goran Eriksson and his girlfriend Nancy Del' Ollio appeared in a VH1 TV programme called *All We Are Saying . . . A Peace Documentary*. Designed to publicise their new charity, Truce International, the programme cast Sven and Nancy as a kind of footballing John and Yoko, reaching a manicured hand out to the world from inside their ostrich-skin Prada sleeping bag.

As Sven himself explained: 'The vision is to try to help the peace in the world, and the world you see around you today. You really need that, absolutely.' Stirring sentiments indeed, echoed on VH1 by none other than David Beckham: 'I think my advice to any children out there looking for world peace is you've got to enjoy life, be happy, and if football or sport is going to make that difference then, you know, go for it.'

And go for it Truce International did. Amid great solemnity Sven was pictured handing a football (thereafter known as the Peace Ball) to UN ambassador Dr Jane Goodall. Who was then charged not with doing twenty keep-ups and catching it on the back of her neck but with delivering it to UN secretary-general Kofi Annan. The idea was that the Peace Ball would be taken by

Annan on a triumphant tour of wartorn countries, with world leaders encouraged to kick it to promote peace. It's not clear if this actually happened. But you'd like to think it did, even just once or twice.

The central plank of Eriksson's vast dream is still the Kick-a-Ball for Peace day, also known as 'The Day Football Stops War'. Reading the extremely long press release explaining what this is all about has a strangely soothing effect. After a while its hyperbole seems to slide off into some other realm, a parallel world of limitless possibility. There's talk of 'a global telethon and humanitarian broadcast . . . on the scale of Live Aid . . . 3 billion people from over 150 countries . . . 90% of the televisions on the planet . . . over a billion radio listeners, with more than a billion internet hits . . . to reach every human being on the planet . . . live shots from outer space, five minute shorts from world famous directors and interviews with world personalities . . . the biggest single event . . . in the history of the planet'.

Which is, undeniably, a big event. All underpinned by a simple managerial message. Not 'work the channels' or 'deliver quality ball'. But Sven's 'We can play football for peace.' And this is no mere one-manager enterprise. Alongside Eriksson on the peace plinth are fellow patrons and ex-England coaches Sir Bobby Robson, Glenn Hoddle and Graham Taylor. We may not have been able to bring you the World Cup, they seem to be saying. But here's the next best thing: world peace.

Much as it might sound like an elaborate pastiche, this all really happened. Truce International, the first-ever football manager-based global humanitarian crusade, is still with us now. In the interests of journalistic rigour I phoned them up to try and find out what on earth was going on. 'We were founded by Nancy and Sven,' Truce's PR officer admits, although I get the sense things haven't so far worked out quite as planned.

'When the war in Iraq and Afghanistan broke out, everyone back-pedalled a bit on the idea of peace. To be perfectly honest all the celebrities who had got involved up until then got a little bit left out in the cold.' Our sympathies remain of course with these celebrities – including Sven himself – inconvenienced by the war. But there are green shoots of a recovery at Truce. The borough of Rochdale has been mooted as 'a strategic partner', with some hopeful talk of a day of peace in the town. But no confirmation yet of whether we might see any shots of Rochdale from the moon, or Rochdale celebrities making international Rochdale short films.

It's easy to snigger. It might also be easy to point out that while little has been heard of Truce since its bravura opening, Sven and Nancy have, at least, been on telly quite a lot, and – who knows? – might be on telly a lot in the future too.

The fact remains that this kind of thing is a recurrent theme in the brief history of the international statesman/playboy. For the first time we find the manager going the whole hog and attempting to save the world (although Willie Bell, former Birmingham and Lincoln manager, did resign in 1978 in order to run a Christian ministry in the US).

While he was at Chelsea Jose Mourinho dabbled with bringing peace to the Middle East. At the request of a humanitarian charity Mourinho staged a rapturously received kickabout with Shimon Perez, lectured local children, and did lots of striding around looking stern and purposeful. Even Gullit, a Mourinho predecessor at Chelsea, ended his autobiography with a message of hope for the world: 'I've a strong feeling there will be some breakthrough in discovering sources of energy within ourselves. Isn't it amazing that sometimes when you think of a person, at that precise moment the phone rings and they are there? . . . There are so many things I would like to change, perhaps too many even to discuss . . . Surely it's impossible that we are the only intelligent beings in the whole vast galaxy?'

These are interesting questions, deserving of thorough and carefully reasoned answers. Unfortunately that's where Gullit's book ends, so we may never get to find out the truth. Another interesting question is: how did this all happen? In a certain light the international statesman manager looks the logical final stage in the evolution from pale, half-glimpsed intruder at the back of the team photo to global celebrity, philosopher and philanthropist. Perhaps these kind of overblown pronouncements are a standard response to any process of fast-track personal empowerment. This is the jeering triumphalism of the formerly thwarted. The manager is big time, baby. And he's going to make sure everybody knows about it.

Perhaps it's even simpler than this. Like most new things in football, the appearance of the uber-manager was about money and power. Following the Bosman ruling in 1995, a cycle of player-salary hyperinflation had been set in train. The modern footballer was rich, independent and mobile. He could come. He could go. He could buy lots of cars and houses while he was doing it. Faced with a wildly over-remunerated generation of itinerant left-backs and wandering gadfly centre forwards, the manager was required to come up with a response. Already there were dark mutterings of 'player power', of barrack-room mutiny, of the disempowering of the ringmaster and zoo keeper.

And so at the highest level successive managers would attempt to out-flash, out-fame and out-swank their cosseted charges. Mourinho remains the most striking example. The first real superstar manager, at Chelsea he looked and dressed like his players' more intelligent, better-looking older brother. He drove a cooler car. He dressed more stylishly. He was more famous. He even earned more, with a salary said to be at least £5.2m.

The magazine interviews, the tabloid front pages, the theatrical appearances pitch-side: Mourinho claimed he kept such a high profile to deflect attention, and therefore pressure, from his players. This might have been the case. But he also appeared to be enjoying himself a great deal.

Eriksson, who as England manager between 2001 and 2006 was paid a salary forty-five times that of the Prime Minister, was instrumental in creating this template. His was very much a style-setting administration, although in many ways it was the manner of his departure – clogged by successively more bizarre tabloid scandals – that defined his time in charge. This is the way of England managers, a process of trial by public humiliation. Usually some terminal weakness is identified in mid-term, a murder weapon that will wax in importance as the manager squirms and retreats. Taylor failed to qualify for the World Cup. Terry Venables had a cloud of unfathomable behind-the-scenes chicanery following him around. Hoddle became odd and quackish.

With Sven it was personal. Or at least, uncomfortably inti-mate. Cursed not just with untameable priapic middle age, but also with a mercurial Delilah in Nancy, Eriksson would spend the final three years of his reign not simply saving the world but pressing himself up against its leg, dry-humping its knee and thrusting his leopard-print posing thong in its general direction.

Many blamed Nancy for all of this. But then the English were never going to like, or get, Nancy, with her perma-tanned stylings, her boisterousness and her naked ambition. In Italy things had been so different. When Sven and Nancy fell in love 'at first sight' in 1998, he was Lazio's new coach and she was already spoken for as the wife of Giancarlo Mazza, a major share-holder in the team. Sensationally, they shacked up. Sven took Mazza out to lunch to break the news as Nancy announced, 'My Sven is anything but a Swede. He seems a Sicilian. He's mega-jealous.' Public reaction was warm. He was curiously bland. She was spirited, beautiful and loud. Lazio won the Serie A title with Nancy a visible presence at every match. The fans nick-named her 'La Dama Nera', the black woman, which was a complement and not a reference to overly heavy use of mascara.

And so with Sven appointed England manager in 2001,

Nancy made the scene, striding through customs at Heathrow in skin-tight scarlet catsuit and pixie boots; pouting on some Mediterranean beach in diamante bikini and satin pumps; and ultimately appearing with a wearying regularity to denounce publicly the latest round of sex-claim shock-phone hotel-love rendezvous allegations. This is how things would go. After it emerged he had had an affair with an FA secretary, Faria Alam, Eriksson became embroiled in the most intense managerial sex scandal of all time. Much has been made of the fact that this was two unmarried work colleagues having a brief fling. But Eriksson himself had set the stakes so high, with his adoption of the uniform and the mannerisms of the global celebrity, that a media furore was inevitable.

Newspaper back- and front-page headlines from this period included: 'Nancy . . . 1 Faria . . . 0 Sven's Lover Joy as Rival Says: I'll Flee UK'; 'What a Hoop-La!' (Sven and Nancy meet in a hotel under the amusing alias of Mr and Mrs Eric Jones); 'Carmen Down Dear' (Sven and Nancy listen to some music); 'Going Faria Away' (more holiday stuff); 'Svendetta' (Sven wises up: 'Someone is trying to make life difficult for me'). 'Nancy: It's Lies', and 'Nancy: It's Rubbish'.

As England suffered a traumatic 1-0 defeat in Northern Ireland, the mood was perhaps best summed up by a message in the *Star*'s 'Text Maniacs' column: 'Sven's good at da booty thing – not so good at da footy thing.' But really Eriksson's problem was the emerging impossibility of taking him seriously. Stroking his chin pensively in the dugout, we saw him checking into the 'superior mansion king room' at Watford's Grove hotel, or alone in his Regent's Park terrace thumbing his wrinkled black book. We noticed his consistency. This is a man who knows what he likes: 4-4-2, tall centre forwards and bosomy brunettes of a certain age.

Later we learned that among Eriksson's effects as he moved out of his Bayswater home was a glass toilet, which sounds like one of those famously useless things, like a chocolate teapot or a lead zeppelin. His period in charge had started out with such optimism: England were sped on their way to the World Cup by the famous 5-1 defeat of Germany in Munich. A quarter-final defeat by Brazil had fired hopes that his team might do a little better at Euro 2004. It wasn't to be. Vividly inventive in the baroque details of his boudoir, Eriksson would ultimately prove a rather dour and one-dimensional international manager; if not quite a glass toilet, then at least a disappointment.

Mourinho remains the real deal, the reigning champion in this peculiar modern managerial subset. English football has yet to produce its own domestic international statesman manager. Perhaps this is because it takes just the right combination of European imagination, mixed with the overblown wealth and opportunity of the English League, and infused with the uniquely English personality cult of the manager. Whatever the reason, England took Mourinho to its heart.

Our first real sight of him came at Old Trafford in 2004, as his Porto team scored a late equaliser that eliminated Manchester united from the Champions League. And suddenly there was Mourinho – or at least, there was an alarmingly youthful man in overcoat, gloves and scarf, sprinting along the touchline punching the air wildly. This was an inflammatory celebration that Mourinho would later make his own – memorably sliding on the knees of his Hugo Boss suit past the Barcelona bench in the Camp Nou – only occasionally alternating it with his impression of a man very deliberately and repeatedly puncturing an imaginary waterbed with a butter knife.

After Old Trafford Porto went on to win the Champions League and Mourinho arrived at Chelsea in the summer, the level of compensation paid making this effectively the first genuine transfer involving a manager. After which, for the next three years, the public fascination with Chelsea's manager took in pretty much every emotional response it's possible to have to a haughty, infuriatingly handsome man in a well-cut dark suit.

This sense of style received a hysterically favourable press, although in truth the black overcoat, symbol of Mourinho the cosmopolitan and the urbane, is only remarkable for one thing: it's not a tracksuit. This, however, seemed to be enough. In May of his first season that 'lucky' black overcoat fetched £22,000 at a charity auction in aid of the Pacific Tsunami relief fund.

In November the previous year he had been voted best-dressed football manager of all time in a nationwide survey. Other public votes placed him as: the world's sixth sexiest man (with Claudia Schiffer and Elton John on the judging panel); and Britain's second best-dressed man according to style magazine *GQ* (after Clive Owen), the editorial musing on how 'he makes minimalism work in the everyday, and by doing so makes it modern'.

Mourinho was also the *New Statesman*'s man of the year for 2005, reward for 'his swagger, his sense of melodrama . . . his polyglot sophistication'. Qualities no doubt captured by the Mourinho waxwork unveiled at Madame Tussaud's two months later, and perhaps still to come in the rumoured film of his life, with George Clooney (seriously) pencilled in for the lead role. All of this, however, was less surprising than Mourinho's progress towards the impossible feat of transforming Roman Abramovich's monstrously constructed Chelsea empire into something almost likeable. Mourinho arrived a season after the Russian oligarch bought the club and began spending wildly. Abramovich remained a mute celebrity-billionaire chairman throughout this process, offering no mission statement, no smiling public face and no point to the whole gargantuan enterprise. So Mourinho came to fill the void, offering a wry, diverting and always entertaining public face.

In the flesh he has a rock star-ish magnetism. Shortly after his arrival at Chelsea I got to watch him closely from the touchline during a Premier League match as part of a feature for the magazine *When Saturday Comes*. He certainly knew how to make an entrance. Poised at the mouth of the tunnel, Mourinho spent at least thirty seconds enduring with a practised show of nonchalance the applause of a suddenly very excited crowd. Shortly after kick-off he strode suddenly right to the edge of the pitch and there was a communal sucking in of breath, as though something incredibly important was about to happen (Mourinho pointed at Frank Lampard and said something).

At the press conference after the match the place fell silent as finally Jose wandered in. Close up he seemed almost embarrassingly in control of things, batting away questions with phrases such as 'it doesn't matter' and 'why?' 'The position and mobility of the triangle was very good,' he drawled, and a room full of hardened, fag-stinking, sherry-stained football reporters swooned. Which is particularly interesting, because outside of these magnetic personal qualities, Mourinho didn't bring any great technical innovation to his job. He liked PowerPoint presentations instead of the chalkboard, and would send his players inspirational emails and text messages. He had a certain bookish thoroughness and liked to delegate, peopling his backroom staff with experts on fitness, physiology and statistics.

But there were no revolutionary tactics or Arsène Wenger-style dietary control freakery. There was simply Mourinho himself and his vertiginous profile, a willing lightning rod for his players and the burden – a burden, with a sigh and a shrug, he condescended to share – of being a global football celebrity. Plus there were the incidents. Mourinho was the first manager to engage the media in a deliberate and ultimately exhausting dialogue of intrigue. In January of his first season there was that first devastating checkmate in English football's much-trumpeted 'mind games'. Mourinho shook hands with each Manchester United player as they ran out on to the pitch for a Carling Cup quarter-final – and Mourinho has a wonderful handshake, a pioneering mixture of neck-cuffs, cheek-pinches and high-fives – as though conferring some lofty honour. United looked bemused. Chelsea won 2-1.

Then there was the time he was banned from the touchline for a Champions League tie against Bayern Munich, but still managed to give his team talk through the extraordinary chutzpah – or so it was later reported – of having himself wheeled in and out of the dressing room inside a laundry basket. This was perhaps the height of Mourinho fever. In time the bust-ups, the pronouncements and the continual aggravation would become slightly wearing. Perhaps the intensive Mourinho-style statesman manager was only ever going to have a limited shelf-life.

Eventually he left Chelsea, toyed with the notion of taking the England job in succession to Steve McClaren, and ended up going to Internazionale in Italy. From there tales emerged of a summer spent conducting the Italian media like a maestro. On his first day in the job he addressed the press in flawless Italian, introduced a bizarre and draconian system of fines and banned the public from training sessions after inventing a self-mythologising 'spying' scandal.

But it has still been a rougher ride in Italy. Perhaps the white heat of early Premier League Mourinho could never really be repeated. Those were his golden years, when the manager burned as brightly as he ever has in the celebrity-media nexus. Or perhaps they just dress better in Italy. Either way Milanese designers bemoaned his penchant for loosely knotted ties. His tracksuit bottoms were said to be too tight. 'He may have been a fashion icon in England but this is Milan,' one fashionista was quoted as saying.

Still, Mourinho is a thoroughbred manager and not the mere show-off he may have occasionally been painted. 'I know football very well,' he once said. 'I was nine when my father was sacked on Christmas Day. He was a manager, but he lost a game on December 22 or 23. On Christmas Day, the telephone rang and he was sacked in the middle of lunch.' This is old school manager talk, an unexpected homage to the likes of Johnny Carey, sacked as Everton manager in a London taxi, and Haydn Green, Swansea manager of the 1940s, who famously gave up his own Christmas day to sign future star centre forward Trevor Ford.

And by the end of his first season as Inter manager Mourinho was no longer the handsome misfit or the vigorously youthful Hollywood gangster. Four years on from the Old Trafford touchline dash, he looked heart-rendingly tired. His eyes were deep set. His silky hair had atrophied into a greying bouffant. Basically, he looked like a football manager. And with the Premier League too showing signs of age, of recession and retreat, the thought occurred that perhaps we'll not see the like of those golden Mourinho years again. In many ways it already seems like a terribly long time ago. In 2006 Mourinho won his second Premier League winners' medal and immediately threw it into the Stamford Bridge crowd, a gesture that seemed to combine arrogance, iconoclasm and reckless generosity.

That year the UK economy was still growing, unemployment was flat-lining, house prices were increasing by £45 a day. Gordon Brown said, 'No return to boom and bust'. Mourinho, still vital and fresh-faced, was in the middle of spending £160m on players over his first two years. Eriksson was quietly and methodically saving the world.

There seemed no reason to think this shouldn't all go on for ever. That the bubble wouldn't ever burst. That Jose would always be handsome. That the Peace Ball could heal the Gaza strip. And that the international statesman manager was in fact the template for the future. Rather than, as might well turn out to be the case, just another peculiar lacuna in an ongoing, fast-paced and always thrillingly current managerial evolution.

CHAPTER 30

The Enlightenment

This is a history that, by now, has almost caught up with itself. We're nearly right back where we started. And in the distance, down that clanking gantry, a figure in a chocolate-brown suit is approaching once more. He has a familiar loping walk. He's still surprisingly tall. He still speaks with a French accent. He's still, at the time of writing, manager of Arsenal, and one half of a senior managerial pairing that has dominated English football in the first decade of the twenty-first century.

In a way this book is all about Arsène Wenger and Alex Ferguson. Never mind that it hasn't got around to talking about them until the penultimate chapter. Wenger and Ferguson are what it has all been building up to. And here they are, fully formed, hyper-evolved, every patch of their magnificent coats of many colours infused with a little bit of what has come before. This has been their extended back story.

Wenger is no longer as disconcertingly advanced as he seemed when he first appeared in England in 1996. He's now thoroughly embedded and acclimatised, a man who will leave an indelible mark not just on football but on the circles of hoopla that surround it. Wenger is lots of other things too. He's been a guest speaker to the Wellcome Trust. According to the lead singer of the Sex Pistols, he's 'the best manager in the Premier League'. Kevin Costner, no less, has advanced the view that his team play 'stylish football . . . and that is down to the manager Arsène Wenger'.

Like Herbert Chapman before him – and like Major Buckley, Stan Cullis and Bill Shankly – Wenger isn't just a very good manager, he's a famous one too, a crossover star, and a figure of some political complexity. He's also, of course, the professor: in his first twelve years in English football he was called 'the professor' 703 times in the UK press. This is Wenger's default setting, the super-brain. In August 2008 he was being described in the *Daily Mail* as 'the wise professor'. By February 2009 this had become 'the nutty professor'. When he says things like 'If I know that the passing ability of a player is averaging 3.2 seconds to receive the ball and pass it, and suddenly he goes up to 4.5, I can say to him, "Listen, you keep the ball too much, we need you to pass it quicker." If he says, "No", I can say, "Look at the last three games – 2.9 seconds, 3.1, 3.2, 4.5",' then that's just fine. This is what we expect.

In fact Wenger's most high-profile innovation has been to do with bodily intake rather than the high-end maths of the instant lay-off. Landing in north London during a diet-obsessed decade, Arsenal's new manager would mine a fruitful seam of retarded nutrition and its accompanying neuroses. And pre-Wenger English football really did have its funny ways in the kitchen. For many years the pre-match meal, object of generations of managerial fascination, was all about meat. In his autobiography Jimmy Greaves describes 'heading off to Moody's cafe in Canning Town where we would order our pre-match meal of roast beef and Yorkshire with all the trimmings or pie and mash followed by blackcurrant crumble and custard'.

Greaves also writes of Gordon Banks tucking into 'a large steak with peas and both boiled and roast potatoes, followed by a large bowl of rice pudding'. Which at least makes Banks's sudden food poisoning at the 1970 World Cup less of an enduring mystery. Incidentally I later challenged Banks about his preference for both boiled and roast potatoes. He denied it. But, then, post–Wenger he would, wouldn't he?

Bill Shankly was one of the first to eschew meat, even going so far as to send 'spies' on train journeys to monitor his players' ham roll consumption. Don Howe confirmed that Bertie Mee of Arsenal shared Shankly's aversion. 'In those days we were eating a fillet steak with a fried egg on top,' Howe recalled. 'But Bertie changed all that. He had them eating cornflakes.'

Bread was an enduring bugbear. One Division One manager became so determined that his players eat no more than a single roll at pre-game lunches that he would count up the rolls before and after a meal and demand to know who had eaten any missing ones. At Highbury Wenger is said to have introduced grilled broccoli to the training-ground canteen like a conjuror producing a beautiful white dove from a homburg hat. Chips, sensationally, were out. Pasta was in. Sauces were served on the side. A single glass of red wine was grandly admitted. In hindsight this might all sound like simple common sense. But at the time football reeled, blinded by the brilliant white light of Wenger's uber-science.

The most notable gains were made in the battle with the bottle. This was Wenger's other great early triumph, persuading his players that regularly drinking fourteen pints of lager and dancing around in a circle might not be a very good idea. As Graham Taylor told me: 'Where Wenger was very very fortunate, he inherited a captain in Tony Adams who was a recovering alcoholic. I'd been the England manager when Tony came out of prison for his drink-driving. And everybody wanted Tony to recover, so the dressing room was onside with Wenger in getting rid of heavy drinking.'

And so English football began its decade-long dry-out. Since its Victorian infancy the professional game, and the figure of the manager himself, had been inescapably entwined with the consumption of alcohol. In his 1973 book *The Football Managers* Tony Pawson remembered his own debut as a player at Charlton: 'There was no word about our tactics or about Tottenham's. The club doctor prescribed a tot of whisky to calm the nerves . . . After twenty minutes I had run myself breathless.'

During the early 1960s the England manager Walter Winterbottom still felt the need to rail against booze. 'The "nip" of whisky, the glass of champagne before a match,' Winterbottom sighed. 'These are considered the thing to make fighting furies of footballers. There is no scientific basis for claiming they are effective.'

Perhaps not. But the manager has rarely followed a strictly empirical formula. His approach is more that of the guru and the holistic hunch-merchant. Twenty years later one of the mottos of the all-conquering Liverpool team of the 1980s would be 'the team that drinks together sticks together', a philosophy vigorously enacted by its own Scotch-soaked bootroom.

Not binging wildly on junk food, staying off the cooking sherry: it's hardly surprising these innovations should have some effect, one that perhaps leant additional credence to some of Wenger's more witch doctor-ish early masterstrokes. Players were sent to the dentist regularly (to improve their 'healing times'). The manager turned up the temperature on the team bus to keep their muscles supple. He encouraged a period of silence at half time. Before his first match in charge he asked the players to practise muscle-honing poses in a hotel ballroom. At the club's £12 million state-of-the-art complex he placed a waterfall in the eyeline of players working out in the gym.

At which point it's hard not to chuckle a little on Major Buckley's behalf, to offer Wenger a respectful Buckley nod at the updating of his diathermy-machine kidology, his monkey-gland mystique. Here we had the modern myth-maker putting about his white-coated voodoo, freaking out the natives with his iron horse, his eating properly and his gentle warm-down exercises.

'I think in England you eat too much sugar and meat and not enough vegetables,' Wenger would later muse, and accordingly we swooned. And in fact there was a great deal of swooning all round as a minor cult of the professorial personality emerged. Wenger would duly be absorbed and consumed, imitated even, but strangely at first. This was the era of the New Managerial Bullshit. As it had been in Herbert Chapman's time, it became necessary not simply to ape Wenger's common-sense methods but to recreate his instant shock value. What was needed was a comparable gimmick. So Southampton chairman Rupert Lowe could announce, in all seriousness, 'I am very much into and do believe in alternative medicine such as Zen therapy and reflexology.'

And for a while in the fevered mind of the manager this was definitely the way to go. So the world would come to know of Glenn Hoddle's reliance on the faith healer Eileen Drewery. Later Hoddle, a close friend of Wenger from their time at Monaco, would reveal in his 1998 World Cup England manager's diary that he believed not just in faith healing, but in astrology, the importance of 'vibrations' and the predictive power of dreams. Plus, apparently, the importance of playing M People records on the team bus and telling his players he was cutting them from the squad to the soothing sax sounds of Kenny G.

If Hoddle erred towards the speculative and the oddball, Sam Allardyce would find himself hoist as a homegrown totem of some new strain of post-Wenger science. This was paradoxical, as Allardyce's appliance of statistics, advanced training methods and clunky black plastic earpieces seemed ideologically at odds with the old-school direct football practised by his team. He seemed both a footballing scientist and a footballing caveman, or perhaps a particularly English hybrid: a scientific caveman.

Allardyce would later import his team of experts wholesale into Newcastle United, where he talked about creating a more positive atmosphere with 'a new mirror there, a window here and a picture over there'. It didn't work. Newcastle weren't ready for his mirrors. He lasted just eight months. Still the Wenger-inspired new quackery flourished elsewhere. Tony Adams, another Wenger disciple from his playing days, managed Portsmouth for sixteen League games (winning just two of them), during which he projected at all times a sense of tortuously melancholic self-analysis. 'We are living in a society of "now"', he announced. 'I'm a loner and if I had my way I'd just walk my dogs every day, never talk to anyone and then die,' he added, later, by way of clarification.

And for a while the Premier League had its own brooding, cobwebbed managerial ogre, a parody of Wenger's hawk-like, tortured touchline prowl. He smelled of straw. He slept in a puddle. He breakfasted off thistles.

This is all something of a diversion, a smokescreen for the real Wenger. With the benefit of hindsight it turns out the most interesting thing about the most innovative and influential manager in English football since Herbert Chapman is something other than the sensible diet or the stretching. It's worth noting at this point that Wenger isn't really a professor. He does, though, have a master's degree in economics. This is his real gimmick. Wenger is an aggressive global free-marketeer and a perfect fit for the new Arsenal, with its north London new internationalism.

Housed in their great glass and steel inverted spaceship stadium, Wenger's Arsenal have come to represent some fluid, unfenced vision of the future. Nobody has spoken out more eloquently against Fifa plans to limit the number of overseas players in the Premier League. 'I have always felt that sport rewards quality and does not hide behind artificial rules,' Wenger once mused, as though reading from a textbook on the new hypermobile European workforce. 'In Europe we are very rigid and difficult to move forward because we are all countries and a bit conservative.'

One of Wenger's finds, the young midfielder Amaury Bischoff, embodies this European futurism better than most. Born in Alsace, of German descent with a Portuguese mother, Bischoff played under-18 football for France, then in 2005 moved to Germany to play for Werder Bremen, the same year he switched international allegiance to Portugal, before moving to north London, where he could eventually qualify to play for England. It doesn't really seem to matter where Bischoff comes from. He is the acme of the Wenger ethos. He jinks, he glides, he vaults arbitrary historical borders.

'We represent a football club which is about values and not passports,' Wenger has said and he means it too. The Arsenal team that won the League title in 1989 was made up of players from Manchester, Coventry, Stoke, Lewisham and Birmingham. In 2005 Wenger's title-winners were from Londi Kribi, Abidjan, Dakar, São Paolo, Amsterdam, Geneva, Pamplona and Paris. Widely harvested but homogenously skilled, this is the Wenger vision of Euro-ball, a game refined and smoothed by the economist's grand dream of the endless market. Not least in his team's uniquely frictionless style of play, a fluid and inter-changeable skating across the surface of things, rooted in nothing more than a sense of its own portable excellence.

This is the future of international Wenger-ism, a beautiful dissolution into a sinuous global meritocracy. With broccoli. And maybe just one glass of wine with dinner. And that vague sense of having been led slightly closer to the end of something.

CHAPTER 31

The Dawning of the Old

If Arsène Wenger points us forward, into some gleaming new future football-world, then Alex Ferguson leads us backwards. It's taken a while to get to him but Ferguson is the real colossus here. Nobody can match his achievements at Manchester United, where he has won the League title ten times and the Champions League twice. The modern era is the Ferguson era, which is odd in a way because if anything he more than anyone else seems to stand as an emblem of things past, of old virtues rather than new.

As long ago as May 1999 Ferguson was being described in the *Daily Mirror* as 'the last of his buccaneering line'. And while he may be unique in many ways, he's above all a deeply familiar figure. We know exactly what Ferguson is about, with his authentic and fully loaded managerial repertoire and his umbilical link to the deep managerial past. For a start Ferguson is unusually old for a modern manager. He was born in December 1941, just as America made its decisive entry into the Second World War – his fawning authorised biography appears, rather weirdly, to link the two events, the Ferguson nativity and the ultimate defeat of fascism in Europe.

And even now perhaps the most interesting thing about Ferguson is the way he resolutely refuses to become any more interesting, even after twenty-three years as Manchester United manager. It's not that he doesn't have great presence; it's just that he has a relentlessly concentrated presence, a single, indelible point rather than a kaleidoscope of many moods. He has an insoluble intensity, based around one thing: being intense.

He has only two public moods: cross or pleased. There are shades, particularly in his anger. Sometimes he's very cross. Occasionally he's just mildly irritated. Now and then he makes jokes, although generally only as a means of expressing vehemence. But really his public persona remains a brilliant and indelible cartoon, instantly recognisable, complete and fully realised in its unshaded ferocity.

This is Ferguson's great strength, an undiluted sense of galvanising adversity. His successful thirty-five-year career as manager is founded in this ingrained ancestral pique, the inherited slights, the furtive manoeuvrings, the constant brinkmanship of his trade. He has the obligatory hard-boiled industrial youth to draw on. His teenage years were spent working as an apprentice tool-maker in the Clyde shipyards while making his way as a player with the amateurs of Queen's Park. His playing peak involved a famously embattled and unsatisfactory stint at Rangers. After which for a while he ran a pub called Fergie's.

But this was all just a prelude to the real stuff. He was appointed manager of East Stirlingshire aged thirty-two and immediately gained a reputation as an unforgiving disciplinarian. One of his players, Bobby McCulley, later commented, 'I've never been afraid of anyone before but Ferguson was a frightening bastard from the start.' He was only there for three months. Momentum established, he left to join St Mirren. It's here that the Ferguson legend began to foment: both in terms of the inevitable upturn in club fortunes and the concomitant, and always vaguely embarrassing, skirmishes. In three years he transformed the team from Second Division drifters to First Division champions.

Amazingly, he was then sacked. He took the club to an industrial tribunal and saw his case rather shamingly dismissed. The panel found St Mirren were justified in sacking Ferguson because of 'the arrogant and overbearing way he tried to run the club', in particular his behaviour towards his office secretary after a minor skirmish over players' expenses: Ferguson didn't speak to her for six weeks, confiscated her keys and communicated only through a seventeen-year-old assistant.

Barely missing a step, he took up the reins at Aberdeen. Success came quickly, as did confirmation of the force of Ferguson's talent, and its peculiarly inflammatory texture. The Aberdeen years remain perhaps his most remarkable spell of success. Certainly there is a small-town romance there that the headline glories at Old Trafford could never quite assume. Geographically Aberdeen was a perfect fit. Braced against the North Sea, the city occasionally feels its cultural isolation from the urban centres of Glasgow and Edinburgh. Fuelling a sense that his players were overlooked and disregarded by the metropolitan football media, Ferguson drove an already successful team to unexpected heights. Before long the players had nicknamed him 'Furious Fergie'. Famously, he fined one of them for overtaking him on a public road. Equally famously, a tea urn – classical, old school – was hoofed across the dressing room after a poor first-half performance.

In 1983 Ferguson led Aberdeen to the European Cup Winners' Cup, beating Real Madrid in the final. A year later they won the League for the first time since 1955. The following season they won it again. Pictures of him during this period have a retrospective stamp of destiny about them: encased in shiny nylon sports coat, hair parted, eyes bright, Ferguson looks strangely luminous, a tableau of vengeful intelligence and uncontainable ambition.

The success at Aberdeen was followed by a move south in 1986 to Manchester United. Here Ferguson would explore the limits of his unyielding appetite for adversity. United didn't win a trophy in his first five years. Twice he came close to being sacked. Finally, in 1992, the almost incidental signing of Eric Cantona would prove the decisive catalyst. United won the League that season, ending a twenty-six-year wait for a first title since the Busby days.

The extended success that followed has been founded in part on a continual vampiric recycling of his playing personnel. The star names come and go. Only Ferguson remains constant. The so-called Fergie Fledglings appeared in 1995, a crop of young players that included David Beckham and would prove the armature of the great success of the late 1990s, culminating in a first European Cup since 1968 in 1999.

And still that sense of constantly renewed adversity, of perpetual-motion ire, has kept Ferguson cooking. The arrival of Arsène Wenger at Arsenal, initially an irritant, later a respected adversary, provided impetus. As did the increasingly spiky relationships with Jose Mourinho and Rafa Benitez. Ferguson is pure managerial stock: he feeds on this stuff, hoovering up the black eyes, the rivalries, the short-lived triumphs and turning it all into gold. And really, for all his outward landscaping, the New Labour stylings, the statesmanship, the media manner, Ferguson still seems like an elemental creature. You can do a kind of dot-to-dot thing with his career that takes you right back to the beginning. In the mid-1980s he was assistant Scotland manager to Jock Stein, who was from the same mining region as Bill Shankly, who was succeeded by Bob Paisley, who played at Liverpool under George Kay, who was managed at West Ham by Syd King, who as long ago as 1904 was featured on the back of a team postcard with the words 'When training, Oxo is the only beverage used by our team and all speak of the supreme strength and power of endurance which they have derived from its use. – E. S. King, Secretary, West Ham United F.C.'

Or how about Ferguson took over from Ron Atkinson, who was coached by Jimmy Hogan, who taught Hungary how to beat England at Wembley in 1953, a match brooded over by Stan Cullis, who was succeeded by Major Buckley, who along with Herbert Chapman formed the original Ferguson-Wenger-style double act of the 1920s.

As time has passed Ferguson has come to resemble some National Trust tribute exhibit, or a glittering managerial theme park. Postmodern rather than old-fashioned, he has a little bit of everything. There's that potent sense of deep Glaswegian managerial authenticity. He can summon the salty phrasemaking of a descendant of Shankly and the bastard appeal of a Cullis. He's even worn a splendid array of managerial coats, my own favourite that slick and rain-sodden quilted ski-jacket of the Aberdeen years.

At Manchester United he brought us the patriarchal team-building of a Busby, the media-mastery of a Buckley and the magnetic and overbearing personality of a Chapman, not to mention a classically devoted old-school managerial wife in the exemplary Cathy. At times it's simply his presence and his mannerisms. Just looking at him, ancient and embattled on the touchline, we feel a deep emotional connection to the secretary, with his watch-chain and his rising sense of panic and futility. Ferguson has the lot. He's encyclopedic. Right now he is every manager, it's all in him, everything from A–Z.

This is a feat of total management that will never be repeated. Mainly because other things have begun to happen. There is the future to consider. Even now the touchline is dissolving and the dugout being re-upholstered and rejigged. The ground has begun to shift beneath Ferguson's feet. And the manager as we know him is in the process of being recast. This story is in many ways circular. Gathering strength from his bronze-age dawn as a pre-mechanical administrative serf, the manager has so far enjoyed a hundred years of strident advance. How strange, then, that overlapping with his most comprehensive incarnation, the Ferguson years, he should start to feel himself threatened from a familiar quarter, his authority undermined by a new breed of global super-capitalist club owner.

Graham Taylor is well qualified to describe this process. 'There is no doubt that Alex Ferguson is the last of the old breed,' he told me. 'For at least 85 per cent of top-level football managers, the best description for them is "head coach", because they are no longer managers. They manage the first team as head coach and that's it.'

Why should this be? Because of money of course. And the ineffable creep of the global and the macro-economic, the dissolution of the paltry domestic stage into something more vast in its horizons. Taylor blames the businessmen, the billionaires and – in a gesture of ancestral solidarity – the directors. 'What we've got now are owners who are expecting to make money out of football. These wealthy men are used to running organisations, to having the last word in everything. And the manager's role is undermined. He simply doesn't have the same power to shape a club.'

Taylor is referring to the new billionairism, a cult, if not of personality, then of the wallet of a breed of super-rich investor-owners. At the time of writing Manchester United, Liverpool, Chelsea, Aston Villa, Manchester City, West Ham, Fulham, Sunderland, Portsmouth and Tottenham are all owned by overseas rich folk. This is a process that perhaps began in the 1970s with the emergence of a new breed of publicity-hungry club chairman. The first of the breed, 'Deadly' Doug Ellis, enjoyed a twenty-year stint of tabloid notoriety grounded in his own high-profile yen for sacking managers. Ken Bates found fame as a 'colourful' boardroom presence at Chelsea. Even Brentford have one: Andy Scott's ultimate boss is the former BBC director general Greg Dyke.

Ellis and Bates were both subsumed by this rising tide of global leisure capitalism. Ellis, aged eighty-three, finally sold Aston Villa to the US entrepreneur Randy Lerner. Bates sold a debt-ridden Chelsea to the Siberian oligarch Roman Abramovich. The change of tone was stark. At Chelsea the real transformational power lay with the boundless finance of the new Pygmalion-owner. Not only were the manager's old spell books, his personality-driven reforms, overshadowed by the new money. But in the personage of Abramovich himself the manager found a peculiar new adversary.

Here we had the chairman as denim-clad player, moneyed celeb aristocracy. For three years, before his own discreet lowering of profile, Abramovich would appear in the paparazzi shot and the money-porn tabloid splash as frequently as his new superstar manager, Jose Mourinho. His divorce, and shacking up with the model Daria Zhukova, was played out in public. Abramovich, mute behind his interview embargo, became something new: the chairman as heart-throb and yacht-lounging playboy. More recently, the Premier League has seen the arrival of Abu Dhabi royal Sheikh Mansour bin Zayed Al Nahyan, whose purchase of Manchester City was fronted up by Sulaiman Al Fahim, a thirty-one-year-old trillionaire who hangs out with Leonardo DiCaprio and Pamela Anderson.

These are people unschooled in the cult of the football manager. These are also people who perhaps see the loopiness of the traditional managerial range of powers, his overreaching influence, his financial clout, his needless prominence. As Taylor recalled: 'When I first went to Watford in 1977 my title was manager of the club. I could dismiss pretty much anybody there. That's a very strange kind of power. Alex Ferguson has something similar, but it's not going to last past him.'

And so, emasculated, the manager has already begun to rage

against the dying of his powers. Resistance to the 'Continental-style' director of football is widespread and has been effective so far. Still, power has already shifted decisively. In a few short years the dawning of the age of the billionaire has brought with it an unanswerably modern off-the-peg plc business model, a hierarchy of finance directors and chief executives. All of which leaves little room for English football's traditional – and frankly bonkers – ad hoc twentieth-century reimagining of the mill or the jam factory, with the manager as stovepipe-hatted shop-floor inspirationalist.

And suddenly, in a certain light, the manager looks old. This latest threat to his pre-eminence may seem to have come from the murky depths and steepling rip tides of international finance, but in fact this is simply the re-awakening of the first great enemy. At which point things start to sound oddly, even comfortingly, familiar. Battered by the wind and stalked by the crowd. Shovelled up by his bosses. Visibility without power. A patsy and a fall-guy. This is the old familiar territory of the first men, the moustachioed and wing-collared men.

Should we be alarmed by this? The manager knows what it is to be squeezed out, to be diminished, put upon and terribly worried about the future. Ferguson and Wenger, both in their sixties as of this year, will soon, amid much ceremony, begin to shrink from view. But no matter. The back-office room is still snug. The one-bar fire has been left on. The sherry bottle is only half drunk. And from somewhere, there's already a gentle clink of watch-chain in the corridor, and – could it be? – a looming, straw-boatered shadow against the wall.

Here he comes, the secretary, eyes lolling in his parched and yellowing skull, the heavy tweed thick with coal dust. So let's settle down and light the paraffin lamp. At the manager's back he can already hear the chill, hacking breaths. On his shoulder he feels the skeletal hand. He's been away for so long. But he's back now. And he wants to hear all about it.

Acknowledgements

Thanks to the British Library and also to Alvering Library. Thanks to *When Saturday Comes*. Thanks to Sean Ingle. Thanks to Adam Strange and Iain Hunt. Thanks again to Paul Moreton. Thanks to Andy Ronay for some very good advice.

In researching this book these books were particularly illuminating: *The Football Manager* by Neil Carter, *The Football Managers* by Tony Pawson and *The Breedon Book of Football Managers*.

Index

Index